TO DEBBY—
YOU'RE ONE OF
MY WRITING GURUS!
MAHALO,
Barb

Super Simple Guide to Creating Hawaiian Gardens

For Kama`aina and Malihini

by
Barbara Fahs

Illustrations by Terry Lee

authorHOUSE™

1663 LIBERTY DRIVE, SUITE 200
BLOOMINGTON, INDIANA 47403
(800) 839-8640
WWW.AUTHORHOUSE.COM

First published by AuthorHouse 3/1/2006

ISBN: 1-4208-8700-9 (e)
ISBN: 1-4208-8699-1 (sc)

Printed in the United States of America
Bloomington, Indiana

This book is printed on acid-free paper.

Acknowledgments

I would like to thank all of the following people for the help and support they have given me in life and especially in the preparation of this book:

Betty-Mom for teaching me her love of language
René Siracusa, dedicated founder of Malama O Puna
Patrick Conant, entomologist extraordinaire
Peter Van Dyke and Momi Subiono, gentle shepherds of the Amy B.H.
Greenwell Ethnobotanical Garden
David Orr, stupendous man of the Waimea Valley Audubon Center
Piper Selden, diva of worms
Tommy Blair, bulldozin' cousin
Big Island Invasive Species Committee
Kaua`i Invasive Species Committee
Maui Invasive Species Committee
Moloka`i Subcommittee of the Maui Invasive Species Committee
O`ahu Invasive Species Committee
Ano Tarletz and Mercedes Kirkel of GaiaYoga Gardens
Manis Martin, Ella Pickens and everyone at Pangaia Permaculture farm

Table of Contents

Table of Illustrations

Preface

Whether you're dreaming of owning a home in Hawai`i or you already do, this book will help you get through a number of decisions you need to make about many aspects of developing your property, from clearing the land to planting trees, shrubs, vegetables and fruit trees. In it, I will present ideas for growing easy-care native Hawaiian plants as ornamentals.

Whether you have already purchased your home or land in Hawai`i or are still wishing, hoping and dreaming about it, congratulations! It's a big step to make the decision to buy real estate in Hawai`i. Parts of this state are among the fastest-growing places in the United States--and for good reason: the weather is warm year-round, the pace of life is slower and more relaxed than on the mainland, prices are still affordable in many areas, and the spirit of aloha abounds. But building a home and developing your property can be very different experiences than in other places, even if you have done it before on the mainland. And if you have never done it before, watch out! Even if you're a kama`aina, it can be a much more complicated process than you could ever imagine.

This book is for you if:
- ✓ You are considering buying a home or property in Hawai`i.
- ✓ You already own a home or property in Hawai`i.
- ✓ You're new to gardening and have a backyard you'd like to landscape with easy to care for, attractive plants.
- ✓ You are an experienced gardener who is interested in learning super simple new techniques for creating garden spaces, both large and small.
- ✓ You want to know how to control common weedy and invasive plants by natural methods.
- ✓ You would rather learn to live with insect pests than to kill them.
- ✓ You want to help the environment by cutting down on your use of pesticides and herbicides.
- ✓ You're interested in utilizing easy to grow native Hawaiian plants in your yard.

What You Will Learn From This Guide

Chapter 1 discusses the joys and pitfalls of developing and landscaping your property, whether it's a house lot in a suburban area or undeveloped acreage in a remote part of the state. You will learn about hiring a contractor and an arborist, how to talk to a bulldozer operator, different ways of clearing your property and other things to consider before you begin.

Chapter 2 talks about undesirable plants that you should know about because some of the plants that have been introduced to Hawai`i can cause a lifetime of troublesome weediness. We'll talk about what are referred to as "weed trees," and suggest that sometimes the worst weeds can have redeeming value as compost or mulch. Then we'll describe some trees and other plants that are undesirable because of their invasiveness, and suggest ways to control them or eliminate them by natural methods.

Chapter 3 gives suggestions about how you can control weedy plants without using chemical herbicides. We include a few basic principles of permaculture and sustainability--techniques such as using cardboard and other forms of mulch to suffocate weeds. We'll also describe several of the most common small weeds, such as spurge and introduced grasses.

Chapter 4 tells everything you'll need to know about building a simple raised bed garden for flowers, trees, vegetables and herbs. We'll discuss different types of soil mixes, the benefits of NOT using topsoil at all, whether you need to build rock walls, and step-by-step directions for a super simple raised bed garden.

Chapter 5 gives practical directions for fertilizing your new garden without chemical fertilizers. We'll tell you how to build a simple compost pile that can significantly reduce your reliance on chemical fertilizers. And for fun, we'll give instructions for composting with red wiggler worms.

In Chapter 6 you will learn about insects--which ones are our friends and which are our foes. Then, you'll learn how to control the foes without poisons. We'll also mention one special insect that you should *not* kill--the endangered Blackburn's Sphinx moth that starts its life as an ugly hornworm.

Chapter 7 contains information about a number of "wonderful weeds"--plants that are likely to appear on your property whether you want them or not. Many plants that can pop up as weeds are great additions to a natural-looking garden and can provide food, medicine, shade and beauty. You will learn all about bamboo orchids, Hawaiian prickly poppies, guava, passionfruit, papayas and more.

Chapter 8 is all about our wonderful Hawaiian native plants and others that were introduced to the islands in ancient times. We include growing instructions for 21 easy to grow native Hawaiian plants or canoe plants.

The bibliography lists useful books and articles that are mentioned in this Guide.

The Appendixes contain helpful resources you might need when you search for plants, seeds, tools and other information and they provide quick reference to information contained in the various chapters.

And finally, an index wraps up this Guide. It will help you to find information quickly and serves as a guide to the common and botanical names of the plants included in this book.

The Story of My Garden

I fell in love with the windward side of the Big Island during my first visit in 1981. What turned out to be a fortuitous broken arm sent me here because I was given seven weeks of paid medical leave from my job at the University of California, Santa Cruz library. After the doctor surgically installed pins in my left elbow, I left the hospital five days later feeling quite well, thank you, and couldn't imagine spending the next six weeks languishing in the cold damp of a Santa Cruz February. So I tracked down an old high school friend whom I heard was living here, and headed over as soon as I was able.

I "felt something" when I first arrived on the Big Island--I've heard it happens to a certain percentage of people who visit. I knew then that someday I would call the Big Island home. Whatever the draw--whether it's Madame Pele (the volcano goddess), the slower, more casual pace of life, or the soft, warm air scented with tropical flowers--it's a very real attraction for many people. At any rate, I was hooked and spent a blissful four weeks relaxing and recuperating from my injury. But I had recently started working on a Master's degree program in education at San Jose State University and had no idea that it would be 1998 before I would finally be able to make the big move. The delay happened because I wanted to achieve my goal of working in the high tech industry as a software technical writer and corporate trainer.

I came back to this amazing place almost every year after that initial visit, then in 1992 was fortunate enough to spend over seven weeks living here during my sabbatical from Tandem Computers. It was an idyllic time, living next to Kapoho Bay, with wonderful warm water to snorkel in a few steps from my back yard, parties with my friends who live here, and lots of time to read and relax. It was truly rejuvenating, but that made going home to my "real life" all the more difficult.

One of the books I read during that peaceful time was called *Myths and Legends of Hawai`i*, by William D. Westervelt. I was particularly enchanted by the story of the Pele family, and first learned about Hi`iaka, the youngest sister of the infamous volcano goddess, in this book. Hi`iaka was a gardener who lovingly tended an `ohi`a forest and made leis of the `ohi`a lehua, the beautiful red, yellow or orange blossoms of our native myrtle family tree. She was also an herbalist: she grew and collected many medicinal plants, which she ground up and prepared as medicine for her friends and family. And that makes her a healer, which definitely attracted me: I have been interested in medicinal plants and healing since 1972 when I took my first "edible plant walk" in the Santa Cruz mountains.

One of the most famous stories about Hi`iaka's healing prowess comes from the time that she traveled to Kaua`i to fetch Pele's lover, Lohiau. During a battle, however, Lohiau was killed. Distraught for that reason alone, and terrified of what her big sister might do in retribution, Hi`iaka began praying with all her might until, miraculously, Lohiau was restored to life. There are other tales in the mythology that credit Hi`iaka with similar "revivification rituals" on other occasions. No wonder she was considered supernatural and came to be known as a goddess!

After that magical seven weeks in 1992, I began plotting my getaway. I never lost sight of the knowledge I had gained about Hi`iaka and her colorful and inspirational legend. In time, I decided to create an educational botanical garden, which would be a sanctuary for medicinal plants, and call it Hi`iaka's Healing Herb Garden, in honor of the goddess with whom I felt an affinity. I completed the training to become a California Master Gardener in 1994, and that was more incentive for moving to a place where I could truly put my skills, knowledge and interests into practice. So, finally, in November of 1998 I packed up my household, including two dogs and two cats, and moved here to the home and property that would soon become Hi`iaka's Garden.

Allow Yourself to Dream

In order to make a move of this kind, you must be focused. I feel extremely fortunate because I've learned that not all people have a "calling," and I most definitely do have a calling to work with nature and educate people about it.

Before my big move to Hawai`i, I allowed myself to have lots of fantasies, thereby "writing" or "inventing" the new lifestyle that I knew I wanted. Many of those fantasies, as I read through them now, seem silly and are not the way I've actually created my new life, but they are all part of an evolutionary process that I went through in order to get where I am.

I created what I called my "Hawai'i Dream Book." It took two forms: an actual "book," which is a 3-ring binder where I put articles that I clipped, writings I did, and information that I gathered; the other form is an on-line version where I keep my computer files, web pages of interest, etc. I have kept both of these and frequently refer to one or the other when I need information today.

You need to be a bit of a designer: you can and should design the new life that you want. I participated in a number of exercises during career assessment classes and workshops I took in the past, and I think they are valuable: one I remember was to write about your "ideal day." I found the printout of it recently and it was amazing how close to the life I have now that it was! It must be 20 years old and I had forgotten about it. OK, so I haven't yet roasted my own Kona coffee like I wrote about, but the basics are much the same... living in Hawai'i, having animals and growing my own food, etc. Here again, ALLOW YOURSELF TO DREAM. Only then do you know what dreams you have and that you can work to turn them into reality.

The bottom line here is DO NOT BE AFRAID to let your mind go where it will. If you're familiar with the exercise called brainstorming, all participants of the brainstorming group are allowed and encouraged to toss out the wackiest ideas they can dream up, even if they're totally illogical and impractical. Then a leader writes them down and the group discusses and refines them later. That's what I allowed myself to do. It's only human nature to start making judgments on preliminary ideas right away instead of allowing them to have an evolution, to allow them to grow, change and become what might turn into reality later on. Dare to dream! I like to live my life based on possibilities and always try not to limit my thinking with negative thoughts about what I cannot do. Where there's a will, there's a way!

I feel that I should add a bit of personal information. At this writing in 2005, I am 58 years old. In 2000, I had total hip replacement surgery done on my right hip, which made me able to walk through my property without pain and changed my life 100% for the better. But I do have a few physical limitations because of it and cannot do all of the heavy gardening work that I did when I was younger and stronger. I feel that this knowledge is important for my readers to know because it means that if I can do it, so can you!

I've had many wonderful helpers along the way: when I use the word "we" in this book, I'm thinking of everyone who has ever pulled a weed, pushed a wheelbarrow, swung a hammer, or operated a bulldozer to create the garden that exists today.

The Mechanics of Creating the Garden

On March 22, 2000, the garden began her existence when a small bulldozer cleared the lower half of my one-acre property. The goal was to remove the invasive, non-native, weedy plants that had grown since the last major lava flow covered this part of the Puna coast about 350 years ago. I told the bulldozer operator to spare the native `ohi`a trees, because they were sacred to Hi`iaka and I wanted to create, or rather RE-create, a garden space that held as many of the plants that Hi`iaka used as possible.

It didn't take very long to create the garden: within the first year, I built the major garden beds by purchasing large truckloads of black cinder, macadamia nut compost, and sometimes topsoil. With the help of many intrepid workers--some volunteer and some paid--the garden took shape.

In the chapters that you'll be reading, I'll go into the details about how to clear your land, what kind of soil to use, how to create your garden space and a lot more.

Today, I continually search for new species of native Hawaiian plants that are suited to the garden's low coastal elevation, meaning it is warmer and drier here than in nearby Hilo, the "rainiest city in America." I have had many successes and probably an equal number of failures in establishing the plants that reside in the garden. We learn through our mistakes and failures, and I hope to pass along my knowledge to you in the pages of this book. Many of the traditional western medicinal plants that I wanted to grow have not taken to this microclimate: lemon balm, valerian, feverfew, echinacea, and even a few of the mint family plants have not survived the drenching rains or searing droughts that sometimes last for a month or more. Although I am always sadly disappointed when any plant fails, I realize now that this garden was always intended to be *Hi`iaka's* garden, in the truest sense of the word. When I ask myself, "would Hi`iaka have grown feverfew?" the answer is always a comforting and resounding "no." So as time goes by, the number of traditional western plants that live here continues to decline, while the number of native Hawaiian plants continues to increase. This comforts me, because I realize that's the way it is supposed to be, and that's what I came here to accomplish. The forces of nature are seeing to it that my vision is carried out, and I have no doubt that my beloved goddess Hi`iaka is close by, guiding and watching over the lives of these rare and miraculous plants.

Chapter 1
Transforming Your Property

Whether you're a backyard gardener in a residential area of Oʻahu or a pioneer on the Big Island who wants to tame a larger piece of property, this chapter is for you. If you are thinking about purchasing an empty lot or multiple acres, we'll guide you in making many of the decisions you'll need to make. It will also prepare you for some issues that you might not have considered.

Because reasonable prices are still available in parts of Hawaiʻi, buying a piece of undeveloped property might look attractive at the outset. In addition to the great bargain you might be getting, undeveloped property allows you the opportunity to make your garden truly reflect your tastes and lifestyle. In addition to warning you about the amount of work involved in clearing and preparing your property before you lay a foundation for your dream house, we will also emphasize how satisfying it can be to create an environment that is uniquely "you" and that treats the environment as an ally and not an enemy.

Basic Things You'll Need To Do First

Before you buy any home or property, visit it in person. It's tempting and exciting to daydream about living in Hawaiʻi and building a wonderful little house while you're snowbound in Minnesota, but the first rule of this book has got to be this: if you're not already living in Hawaiʻi, *invest in a trip to the islands.* Talk to a reputable realtor. Ask lots of questions about the property, such as:

✓ If you have children, how are the schools in the area you're interested in living?
✓ How far is it to the nearest stores and other services such as hospitals?
✓ If you plan to work, what is the job market for your chosen profession?
✓ How much does it rain at your elevation and side of the island?
✓ Who are the neighbors? Are there roosters or barking dogs in the neighborhood?
✓ What are the existing trees and plants on the property?
✓ Will you have access to telephone lines and electricity?

1

- ✓ Does the property have water lines or will you need to provide your own source of water through a catchment system or a well?
- ✓ How much will it cost to bring in electrical lines, install a water system or dig a well?
- ✓ Will you need to dig a septic tank and how much will that cost?

Permits are important

Although this book is not about how to build a house, here are several guidelines that will help you get started in the process of planning for construction.

- ✓ First of all, be sure everything you build complies with your county's building code and other legal requirements. You will save yourself a lot of headaches and very possibly expense if you follow the rules from the beginning. Permits are essential for any kind of building project: be sure you thoroughly research what your county requires and learn the important details. You may need separate permits for digging a septic tank, installing your dishwasher, and many other things. Your county's Department of Public Works or Planning can be a great resource in answering your questions and helping you to stay safely within the law. Lots of information and even application forms are available on the Internet: you can fill out and submit many applications online. Search for your county and building permits. For example, Maui county building permits are located at www.co.maui. hi.us/departments/Planning (be sure to capitalize "Planning"). This site also includes the building code, plumbing and electrical codes, and much more. A little searching can provide you with a lot of information in the comfort of your home.
- ✓ Secondly, use and trust professionals, from the architect who designs your house to the contractor who builds it, to the plumber and electrician who finish it. These are people who know their business and are experts in the job that they do.

Hiring a contractor

You can save yourself a lot of time and headaches if you let a qualified, experienced contractor take charge of the job of clearing your land and building your house. Don't worry--you will often be involved in every small detail of the process, on a daily basis!

Talk to several contractors before you make your decision: your contractor can be much more than a project overseer and can become a counselor, materials expert and cost-control coordinator, according to the article "Ask Contractors The Right Questions" by David Bradley. (Refer to the Bibliography for the Internet address.) I used a contractor to build my 1/2 acre garden, and his longtime Hawai`i residency proved valuable in making many decisions that I simply would not have considered. For example, he suggested pressure washing certain areas of the lava rock after it was cleared to remove the remnants of dirt that could provide a breeding ground for weeds. If you are new to Hawai`i, it's even more important to rely on an experienced professional.

Get referrals for contractors from your realtor and neighbors who have built homes recently. And then conduct in-depth interviews of your prospective contractors. This article wisely advises that when homeowners are too soft on contractors or skip the hard questions, this can lead to miscommunication, cost overruns, and finger pointing. You have no doubt heard nightmare stories about contractors from friends and family members who have built a home or undertaken a remodeling project, but many problems can be avoided if you ask these questions:

✓ What is your job experience? (Be sure to ask for the contractor's license.)
✓ How long have you worked in Hawai`i? This is important because an experienced contractor will know the particulars about building here, such as the fact that if your property is on the windward side of an island, your house will need wide eaves to protect it from the prevailing trade winds and rain that can damage your house.
✓ What is the scope of your work? In other words, what kinds of houses or other buildings have you constructed?
✓ What will be the budget and materials involved?
✓ Do you have any history of liens?

Finally, ask yourself if it is easy to communicate with the contractor. Does he listen to you and understand your needs without trying to convince you of things you don't necessarily want?

The article concludes by advising that you should not assume anything and that it's better to ask early than be surprised later on. A good contractor will welcome your questions because the interview process helps weed out contractors who may skirt answers or pursue jobs based on price alone.

To Bulldoze Or Not To Bulldoze: In Favor of Natural Landscaping

"You have such beautiful pahoehoe!" This is a compliment I often receive from visitors to my garden when they first enter and observe the swirling configurations of lava rock and the dramatic backdrops it forms to showcase different garden beds. I used to laugh--what humorous praise, I thought. But now I find it oddly sad because so few homeowners keep their terrain in its natural state. It's not that my pahoehoe (pronounced PA-hoy-hoy) is more attractive than other pahoehoe--the reason my visitors admire it is because they simply don't see much undisturbed lava unless they travel to a wilderness area, or watch the new landscape being formed by active lava flows on the Big Island.

Ripping up the land

When I first began building my garden in 2000, I had a difficult time finding a bulldozer operator who didn't want to totally destroy my beautiful pahoehoe lava. The practice of "ripping" breaks up all the rock and creates a level area. It is the most common method of clearing land that consists of rocky lava flow and weedy bushes. Ripping might be necessary or appropriate in order to create a level area where your house will stand, but I recommend that you do not rip areas that will be gardens. If your property contains `ohi`a trees or other indigenous plants, please consider working around them and keeping them as a focal point of your landscaping.

Hawai`i's native forests are disappearing rapidly and the numbers of native plants are dwindling on a daily basis. You have no doubt heard that Hawai`i has the dubious distinction of being called the "endangered species capital of the world." If you can help to save even one `ohi`a tree or other indigenous plant, you are contributing to the conservation of a species that exists nowhere else on earth. And that's pretty wonderful in my book!

Know your dozers

The bulldozer called the Caterpillar D-11 is the biggest, meanest dozer in existence. They are not commonly found in Hawai`i, but smaller models called the D-10 and D-9 are often used to rip through solid rock lava flows to flatten them and make them level.

Other smaller bulldozer models include:

- D-8: almost as big as the D-9 or D-10. All three of these models are preferred for clearing and ripping.
- D-7: smaller than D-8s and D-9s, these are not very common in Hawai`i.
- D-6: this is the smallest dozer you should use for ripping, as it isn't heavy enough for the kind of lava we typically have.
- D-4 or D-3: one of these smaller models is what I used to simply clear the weedy plants from my lava flow.
- Bobcat: a small front-end loader that can have attachments (such as a backhoe) for digging fairly small trenches, sprinkler lines, and so forth. Bobcats are convenient for scooping dirt or other material and moving it to where you want it. Bobcats are especially useful after your bulldozing is finished, when you want the mountain of topsoil you just had delivered spread around your garden.

How to speak bulldozer-eze: words of wisdom from Tommy Blair of the Big Island

Tommy worked as an operating engineer for 35 years in California and Hawai`i and is familiar with all aspects of heavy equipment and dirt moving. Here's what he told me:

When you first start calling bulldozer operators or companies, ask what size dozers they have. Does it come with a ripper? If you don't want to rip, ask if they use D-3's or D-4's to clear the "overburden" (surface dirt and vegetation). Most companies have either the very large D-9's or the smaller models, so you might need to call several companies to find what you need. These guys are busy: tell them specifically what you need when you leave a message (for example, "I want to build a home"). Don't talk price until they call you back and you talk about the details. Make sure to ask them to visit your site and look at what they'll be dealing with. Then they will be able to figure out how big the job will be and at that time they should be able to give you an estimate of cost. Get at least three estimates from different companies. And this is very important: make sure you get a written price quote. You might be charged a "move in charge" which is a one-time charge for bringing the dozer to your property on a lowbed truck. This should cost no more than $250 (at this time). If they are already working in your neighborhood, you might save a little. If you have any kind of problem with a bulldozer company, you can report it to your island's Department of Commerce and Consumers Affairs, which has a State of Hawai`i Regulated Industries Complaints Office.

Another thing you should ask the bulldozer people to do before they bring their equipment to your property is to clean the dozer so it doesn't accidentally bring in the seeds of any invasive plant, or other undesirable things such as the very noisy foreign coqui frog. Bulldozers can and should be pressure washed to prevent introducing a lot of undesirable plants and animals.

It took some time, but through my contractor I finally found a fellow with a smaller bulldozer who agreed to "gently" bulldoze the unwanted plants from my property and leave the `ohi`as and pahoehoe intact.

After my land was cleared, I could finally see the lava formations, the little hills and valleys, even a couple of vortexes.

Illustration 1.1: My first walk on the lower half of my property that soon became Hi`iaka's Garden (accompanied by Rhiannon the cat)

From that point on, a garden can design itself, which makes it easier for you because you don't need to figure out where a path should go or where a bed should be built. Of all the gardens I have designed and built in California, this is the first one where I have not been "in charge." Instead of sitting indoors with a pencil and a piece of graph paper, carefully mapping out garden beds, boundaries, areas for sitting and so forth, this garden directed its own design through the rock that is its very sturdy foundation. I've found that if I do not try to control nature so much and work with what it provides, life is much easier. I have also gained a more relaxed attitude about my garden by letting the garden tell me what to do, both in terms of its design as well as the types of plants that are best suited to growing in it. That's why I favor the native Hawaiian plants: many of them are extremely hardy and carefree, whereas plants from other parts of the world are simply less well adapted to the conditions here.

Developing a Project Plan

Before I hired my contractor, I forced myself to sit down and write a project plan for the clearing of the land and basic construction of the garden. I recommend that you do something similar, even if it's simply a few notes scribbled on a notepad. It helps you to clarify what you truly want, and it is an invaluable tool toward opening communication with your contractor and other workers. Your plan doesn't need to be as detailed, but mine serves an example of the thinking that went into it. My plan described the following topics:

✓ Vision and goals for the garden
✓ Component parts of the garden
✓ People required to complete this project
✓ Rough first draft sketch of the completed Garden

In their book, *The Herbalist's Garden*, Shatoiya and Richard de la Tour offer this sage advice about creating gardens:

Spend some time just experiencing your space or garden. Don't rush headlong into your garden projects before making sure that you have the time and energy to care for them. Before you put a great investment of time and money into planning and building your garden, really get to know the rhythms of your land. Spending some time simply observing the land will save you a lot of mistakes. Watch for the details. During the wet season, is there always a swampy part of your yard? Are there areas that seem drier? To really get to know your garden, use it as a meditation space. Just sit in the garden quietly, breathing slowly and listening to every little sound.

In my project plan, I figured out what I wanted and described the preliminary component parts of my vision for the Garden, such as:

✓ An access road. Vehicles will need access to the bottom of the Garden to deliver soil, plants, lumber and other supplies. I also want the Garden to be somewhat handicap accessible, so this will provide a means for transporting people to the bottom of the Garden.

✓ A water catchment tank. Size and type to be determined. Rainfall from the house's lanai roof can easily be diverted to this tank.

✓ A pond below the new catchment tank. Type and size to be determined. This pond can serve as emergency water for irrigation when necessary.

Questions that must be discussed are:

What are the options for the pond? That is, will it have a liner bottom or perhaps gunnite?

Will it need a pump to circulate water to keep it from going stagnant and breeding mosquitoes and other undesirable insects and creatures?

✓ Plumbing for irrigation system. I envision that a straight pipe will go down to the bottom of the garden from the catchment tank/pond. I will want faucets at each major row of the Garden.

✓ Two small structures. Type and size can be determined later, but my initial idea for these is to use a Star Plate connector kit that can be purchased for about $50 (see the Resources Appendix). It allows you to connect 2-by-4's into a pentagonal dome-like structure.

✓ Raised beds and paths between them. Will we have enough rocks from the initial clearing to make beds? If not, what can be used to create these beds? The size and shape of the beds will be determined by the natural contours of the land.

✓ The plants themselves. This will be an ongoing project and is not a part of this plan. All I want to do with this project is to create a suitable environment for growing the plants that will be planted later, over a period of time, as I am able to acquire seeds, and start and purchase plants.

Without a plan, you leave yourself open to confusion and disappointment. A plan clearly communicates your vision and wishes to your contractor. It can also open a lot of discussions about what can and should be done, what should NOT be done, how things are done, and how much it will cost.

Designing Your Dream

When you sit down to define your thoughts on paper, it's helpful to think of a few things about the layout and design of your garden space or property. The book *Introduction to Permaculture* (see the Bibliography) is the classic study of how to design a garden that makes sense in terms of placement of plants, outbuildings, and other components of your garden, so I recommend it. For now, here are a few considerations to keep in mind:

- When you first buy a plant at the nursery, it is small. Remember, trees often become very large in a short amount of time, so be sure to research their growth habits and plant them accordingly.
- Plant large trees where they will provide shade for things that need shade. It's nice to have shade over your house, but consider the kind of tree you're planting: will it drop lots of leaves, flowers, seedpods or fruit onto your roof and into your rain gutters when it gets large? It's a good idea to think about locating larger trees toward the back of your property.
- Think of convenience when designing your garden and planning where the plants will grow. For example, a small culinary herb garden near your kitchen door makes it easy to pop outside and snip a few fresh, tasty herbs for your dinner salad or for dishes like spaghetti. If your herbs are too far away, believe me, you'll be inclined to make excuses for not going out to pick them, as I often do! People in France call a garden that combines vegetables, flowers and herbs a "potager" (pronounced poe-tah-JAY). I like that concept a lot. When designing your garden, keep the French idea in mind: all veggies don't need to planted in the same area in tidy little rows, separated from flowers, herbs, and other plants. A potager garden is lovely to look at and serves the dual purpose of giving you easy access to ingredients for your dinner and a bouquet for the table all in one convenient location. Plus, many of the flowers that you'll be growing in a potager attract beneficial insects that can help to control some of the more troublesome insects that might feast on your prize plants. Chapter 6 tells you all about beneficial insects and suggests many ideas for plants that can attract them.
- Don't overlook access: how will you get from one part of the garden to another? Pathways are an important component of any garden and can be very attractive. Paths can be as simple as bare dirt or rock, or you can lay down landscape fabric, gravel, cinder, or pebbles. Cement paths never need weeding and look very tidy, so you might want to think about paving your paths.
- Even the smallest suburban back yard has enough room for a compost pile. It's fun to recycle your yard waste and kitchen scraps, and that can also help our over-crowded landfills. Leave a corner of your yard as a utilitarian area, where a compost pile and a small "stick pile" can exist. See Chapter 5 for details.
- Along the same lines, think about creating a work area. It might include a potting table and an area to store your seed flats, pots, bags of potting mix, wheelbarrow and other tools. Especially for

windward gardeners, it's nice to have a covered area that protects you from the rain, so you can continue to garden even when the weather is not conducive to gardening in the wide-open spaces.

Chapter 2
Undesirable Plants To Know About

This chapter includes information about the following 14 nasty, invasive plants that you should know about if you are thinking about buying a home or property in Hawai`i or if you are already a landowner:

Miconia
Albizia
Australian tree fern
Autograph tree
Fountain grass and pampas grass
Guavas (strawberry guava and yellow guava)
Kahili ginger
Lantana
Maile pilau
Melastoma, tibouchina and Koster's curse

You'll learn how to eradicate all of these plants, mostly by natural means, and perhaps use them as nourishing mulch or in your compost pile. I'll also tell you which plants you should not use in mulch or compost.

For each plant, you'll see and learn the following information:
✓   An illustration
✓   How its invasiveness is rated by environmental groups and governmental agencies
✓   The elevation(s) where it grows
✓   What it looks like and other pertinent information
✓   How to control it

Let's Abolish the Term "Weed Tree"

Even before I moved to Hawai`i, I heard people using the expression "weed tree." Although I understood what it meant -- a tree that is undesirable, drops seeds everywhere and creates an entire forest of its offspring in no time — it just didn't seem quite right that any tree was thought of as a weed. They are all good for something in their native environments, such as providing food and shelter for birds, or shade for humans. Even some trees that are considered undesirable can be chopped up, ground to a pulp and used as compost and mulch. But be careful — some trees have seeds that stay good for years. I'll tell you all about this and more in the descriptions that follow.

But I think the main reason I don't like this term is because I have heard some of our native trees referred to as "weed trees" by people who don't know what they are. Perhaps they do not provide a spectacular display of flowers or foliage and people think they're kind of boring. Whatever the reason, I believe it's important for all island residents to learn what trees exist on their properties before we start condemning them to the status of "trash." Just because a plant doesn't have lush foliage and big huge dripping, scented flowers doesn't make it a "weed": Many of our natives fall into this category and I believe they are far more important to the environment and to our Hawaiian heritage than the pretty ones.

I choose to use the word "undesirable" instead of "weed tree." Most plants that fall into this category are invasive.

What Makes a Plant Invasive?

This information comes from the Maui Invasive Species Committee (MISC).

✓ Outcompetes desirable plants

✓ Rapid growth

✓ Early maturity

✓ Production of many seeds

✓ Short germination periods

✓ Lengthy seed viability

✓ Effective seed dispersal methods

✓ Ability to reproduce vegetatively

✓ Ability to use local pollinators (bees and such)

✓ Produces dense shade

✓ Produces a dense root mass

Many of the plants that we consider invasive weeds today have been introduced in the past by well-meaning people who thought they would look pretty in landscapes or would provide a useful fruit. Then some of those plants "went bad," or rather wild, because they liked it so much here that they joyfully reproduced. They were so well suited to their new environment that they became very successful in forming whole populations of themselves. That's fine with some plants, like coconut palms — if you want them. But others, things such as maile pilau ("stink" maile vine), can strangle a tree, and plants such as tibouchina can crowd out other plants in an area, making it impossible for many native plants to thrive. And others, such as the autograph tree, schefflera and strawberry guava, can actually kill our native `ohi`a trees when they grow at the base.

A Quick Vocabulary Lesson

Here are some terms that are sometimes confusing:

Native species are plants and animals that occur naturally in a given area. In Hawai`i, this refers to the plants and animals that arrived without human help—either on the wind, the waves or via the wings of birds, which often carry seeds in their intestines.

Endemic refers to plants that grew in an area before humans arrived and which evolved into their present forms in their native locations. MISC adds that because the Hawaiian islands are the most geographically isolated landmass in the world, many plants and animals "are found here and nowhere else in the world." I'll be using the term "native" interchangeably with endemic because it's easier for me to remember what native means.

Indigenous plants are also native, but they never changed or evolved after they naturally arrived in their new island homes by natural methods such as the wind and animals. Here's a good trick to help you remember the difference between endemic and indigenous plants: endemic plants *end*ed up here and the form we see today is the *end* of their current evolutionary cycle, while indigenous plants came *in*, either on the ocean or carried by birds or other animals. (Thanks to Heidi Bornhorst for her explanation of these terms in her book *Growing Native Hawaiian Plants.*)

Introduced or **alien** plants came to our islands with the help of humans, either in the distant past in the canoes of the first Polynesian settlers, or in more modern times, by other means and for whatever reasons. Not all of them are bad and not all of them negatively affect the environment. The familiar plumeria falls into this category.

Invasive species are "alien plants that cause ecological damage by out-competing native species, which reduces biological diversity and changes ecological function," according to the Maui Invasive Species Committee. They go on to cite the example of Miconia, a tree from South America that is the number one undesirable plant in Hawai`i because it spreads very rapidly and shades out and kills other plants that try to grow under it. This causes erosion and it degrades Hawai`i's healthy watersheds. These are the plants I'm calling "undesirables." Many dedicated people throughout our islands are working very hard to control and eliminate the plants such as Miconia that threaten our environment.

Wisdom from the Maui Invasive Species Committee

Plants from around the world are arriving daily in Hawai`i. They arrive by plane, through the mail, and by boat. Airline travelers bring them in either intentionally or accidentally (seeds can stick to the soles of shoes!). Visiting boats and ships can even contribute to the introduction of invasive species. It's simple to order plants and seeds through the Internet and mail order catalogs. You can make a difference by first thinking about the impact alien plants have on our unique Hawaiian environment before you bring in any plants.

Tools of the Trade for Dealing With Undesirables

If your property, or a property you are considering buying, has any of the undesirable plants described in this chapter, you would be wise to have the following tools on hand if you plan to be involved with their removal and control.

✓ Good leather gloves: a smart form of preventative medicine.
✓ Weed whacker: Get a powerful one with replaceable heads for clearing both grassy weeds and small branchy plants like waiawi, or strawberry guava. You'll use it often, for many years.
✓ Chain saw: You can tackle many smaller tasks yourself.
✓ Machete: Buy a good machete and a sharpening stone to keep it in tip-top condition.
✓ Large loppers: for chopping up small branches that are a bit too large for a machete, but not large enough for a chain saw.

Tips for using pruning tools:

✓ Loppers: Hold them right side up, with the cutting blade on top and the hook under the branch you're cutting. Cut all the way to the base of the branch without cutting into the plant's main trunk.
✓ Hand-held tree saw: For sawing off smaller branches that are hard to reach.
✓ Pole pruner: Extends to about 10 feet, making it possible to trim high branches without a ladder.
✓ Protective eyeware: Good preventive medicine. You can buy special glasses at your hardware store.

A chipper/shredder or grinder is a wise investment

A chipper/shredder is a valuable investment that will continue to pay for itself in usefulness over many years. By grinding up some of the undesirable plants after you cut them down, a chipper/shredder allows you to use them as compost or mulch.

Before you use your ground-up plant material as nourishing mulch around desirable plants, first check to see if the plant you have removed has seeds. If it does, do not use it directly as mulch because those seeds will undoubtedly sprout and continue to perpetuate the problem you are attempting to solve. For example, papaya seeds will form a carpet of baby papaya trees if you spread compost containing them around your garden areas. That's good news for people who want to grow papaya trees, but not for the home gardener who has more limited space.

To kill the seeds of many undesirables, stack your chopped-up plant material and simply throw a sheet of black plastic over the pile for about three months. It will heat up and kill or inactivate many kinds of seeds. Not all seeds are cooked during the composting process, however, so you might want to use a small amount of your finished compost in a trial area and wait to see what comes up before you use it in widespread areas. Turn to Chapter 5 for complete instructions on composting.

Pruning Primer

You can control many undesirables by keeping them pruned back, but if those plants are over 10 or 15 feet tall, it is best to hire a professional arborist.

Basic pruning rules

The book *Gardening for Dummies* states, "pruning is part maintenance, part preventative medicine and part landscaping." Here are the pruning rules that they recommend:

☞ Don't prune unless you must: many native trees do fine without pruning, but if you want to control an undesirable tree, of course this is an instance where you will want to prune and keep on pruning to keep it under control. You can manage its sprouts or keikis more easily than you can the parent tree.

☞ Remove dead or diseased wood as soon as possible. I prefer to take such yard waste to the local recycling center's compost operation rather than composting it on my own property.

☞ Cut off branches that rub against each other.

☞ If a tree is less than 10 feet tall and less than about 8 inches in diameter, you can coppice it, which is a simple method of chopping off the top 5 to 6 feet of the tree, leaving a 5 to 6 foot "stump." This is a good method to use with wiliwili: you can chop up the top part and simply stack it around the base of other plants, which then serves as both mulch and nutrient.

Tips for pruning trees

Be careful! The tools you use for this activity are sharp. I don't want to harp on this, but if you've got a big tree or a big job, seek the help of a professional tree trimmer.

☞ If you're pruning small to medium limbs, you can cut them off in one whack at the trunk with large loppers or your tree saw, especially small branches.

☞ It's not necessary to treat pruning wounds with tar or asphalt or other commercial products designed for that purpose. Most pruning cuts will heal just fine by themselves and some gardeners believe that applying sealing products to open wounds does nothing but seal in bacteria.

The University of Hawai`i's College of Tropical Agriculture has a free book called *Woody Plant Control for the Home, Pasture and Forest.* They say that controlling woody plants by mechanical means requires "hard labor and persistence to achieve permanent control. You have to attack woody plants again and again before they will succumb to mechanical control."

Selecting an arborist

If you need to prune or remove any tree that is over 10 or 15 feet tall, it's best to rely on a professional arborist. Arborists are professional tree people who will make sure that tree care is done safely and in a way that will maximize your investment, "minimize injuries and liability and extend the use and beauty of trees," according to the U.H. College of Tropical Agriculture's Fact sheet, "Selecting a Tree Care Professional."

Your Yellow Pages and local newspapers include listings for arborists under Tree Service and Arborists. Better yet, get referrals from friends or neighbors who have used tree care professionals in the past.

How to choose an arborist

1. Make sure the company is licensed.
2. Ask whether the International Society of Arborists (ISA) certifies the tree workers.
3. Ask for proof of insurance, both personal and property damage.
4. Request references for similar work done by the company.
5. Get more than one estimate.
6. Get it in writing in the form of a contract.

USE CAUTION AND COMMON SENSE! Invest some time and your trees will thank you for it by thriving as healthy, long-lived and valuable members of your property.

All About the Undesirable Ones

The following plants are included because the various islands' Invasive Species Committees have singled them out as problems or because they are very widespread in large parts of Hawai`i. Most of them are plants that you might encounter in or around your property. It's important for all of us to learn about them so we can help to control them and support the work of environmental groups that are involved in their control.

For all of the plants included in this chapter, you can help to reduce their spread by doing the following simple things:

✓ Never purchase or plant them.
✓ Encourage your friends not to buy them or other undesirables so nurseries will stop selling them.
✓ Mention this problem to the folks at your neighborhood nursery and ask them not to sell any of these undesirable plants.

Here are the plants that are included in this chapter:

- Miconia
- Albizia
- Australian tree fern
- Autograph tree
- Fountain grass and Pampas grass
- Guavas (strawberry guava and yellow guava)
- Kahili ginger
- Lantana
- Maile pilau
- Melastoma, tibouchina and Koster's curse

17

In the descriptions of these plants, we'll include the designation that the University of Hawai`i Weed Risk Assessment (WRA) Protocol has determined, or ratings from other sources, such as PIER (Pacific Islands Ecosystems at Risk), the Division of Land and Natural Resources (DLNR), or the various islands' Invasive Species Committees (ISC), which have provided "Top 5" lists of their biggest problem plants.

- The WRA rating H (HPWRA) indicates that the species poses a high risk of becoming a serious pest.
- The WRA rating H (Hawai`i) indicates that the species has been documented to cause significant ecological or economic harm in Hawai`i.
- The INVASIVE rating is included from PIER and DLNR: it means that the plant is well known to spread uncontrollably.
- The WRA rating EVALUATE simply means that the species in question has been assessed but that no assessment of risk can be provided at this time.

Let's start discussing the undesirable plants with the worst one first (Miconia). After that, the plants appear in alphabetical order rather than by the order of their invasiveness potential.

Miconia (Miconia calvescens)

WRA designation: H (Hawai`i)
DLNR designation: INVASIVE
PIER designation: INVASIVE
Hawai`i State Department of Agriculture designation: NOXIOUS WEED
ISC Top 5 for O`ahu, Kaua`i, Maui and the Big Island.
Elevation: Sea level to 5000 feet

Illustration 2.1: Miconia's distinguishing feature is its large leaves with a purple underside.

Miconia, known as the "purple plague," is the number one worst invasive plant in all of Hawai`i. It is a fast-growing, attractive tree from

South America that grows to 50 feet or more and shades out other plants in native forests, pastures and farmlands. It has destroyed 70% of the forest growth in Tahiti and is a major threat in parts of Hawai`i, especially along the eastern coast of the Big Island, where it is found on approximately 110,000 acres. One Miconia tree can produce millions of seeds each year, which birds help to disperse.

Malama O Puna destroys thousands of Miconia trees

René Siracusa is a true environmental crusader. Her Malama O Puna non-profit organization in Pahoa has been highly instrumental in gathering volunteers to trek into the forests of the Puna district on the Big Island and pull, poison and otherwise eradicate the "purple plague" that is Miconia.

A tree climber and gardener since early childhood, René says she was greatly influenced by the Disney movie "Johnny Appleseed" as a child. She went on to earn a Master's degree in linguistic anthropology from the University of Hawai`i at Manoa, but says her life changed forever when she attended a course taught by the legendary ethnobotanist and author Beatrice Krauss.

René's dedication and hard work have helped to control the Miconia populations on the Big Island, and her educational efforts have reached many people. She advises that a young Miconia tree will set seeds at age three, and thereafter it will flower and produce seeds three times every year. And these seeds will remain viable for at least 10 years, possibly longer. Her volunteer expeditions use an herbicide called Garlon-4, mixed with forest crop oil and red dye, which enables other volunteers to clearly see which trees have been treated. Products such as RoundUp are ineffective against Miconia, based on René's experience.

You can reach Malama O Puna at 965-9254.

How to control Miconia

The Coordinating Group on Alien Pest Species (CGAPS) reports that roughly $2,000,000 has been spent on Miconia control efforts every year since 1999, with undoubtedly much more yet to be spent in order to achieve success.

Aggressive eradication efforts are underway in parts of Hawai`i in the hope that this extremely prolific introduced species can be stopped. If you have it or find any trees, call your island's Invasive Species Committee so they can use the global positioning system (GPS) to chart the location and continue to monitor the area for years to come. They also need to gather lots of information about the plant and the area where it is found, says the Kaua`i Invasive Species Committee. After you report any Miconia trees, make sure that you destroy them, as described earlier.

🖐 **CAUTION:** Do not compost ground-up Miconia trees because of the sand-sized seeds, which can remain viable in the soil for 10 years or longer.

Albizia (Paraserianthes falcataria, also known as *Albizia falcataria*)

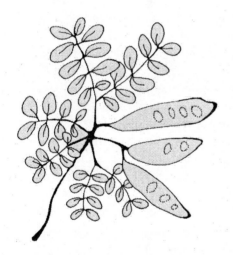

WRA designation: H (HPWRA)
PIER designation: INVASIVE
ISC Top 5 for the Big Island
Elevation: Sea level to over 1000 feet, perhaps as high as 5000 feet

Illustration 2.2: Albizias grow to be very large trees and provide habitat for such undesirable creatures as the invasive coqui frog.

The problem with many invasive undesirables is that they are attractive. This is certainly the case with Albizia, which was introduced in 1917 as an ornamental tree and for reforestation. Its ferny, spreading branches form an appealing canopy over roads in the Puna district of the eastern Big Island. When visitors first drive south on Highway 130 after the town of Pahoa, they are enchanted by the large, delicate trees that form a tunnel through which you drive in dappled sunlight. But driving through Lava Trees State Park during a stormy, windy night can be a terrifying and dangerous experience because the brittle branches and entire trees often snap off and crash to the pavement below.

As with many undesirable life forms, the Albizia does have some redeeming qualities. It is a nitrogen fixer for other plants that grow nearby and its fallen leaves improve the soil. The leaves also provide food for certain animals. It has good, lightweight wood that is used for veneer, lightweight pallets, boxes and shelving. It also provides good pulpwood.

How to control Albizias

Do not bulldoze until you are ready to use your property because Albizia grows quickly in bulldozed areas. Leave your natural vegetation untouched if you are not going to build your house or landscape your property right away. But it's smart to weed out Albizia seedlings and small trees before they get large and become much harder to remove.

If you have small Albizias that seem manageable to you, you can chop them down yourself and place them in the crotch of another tree, where the roots will shrivel and die. The seeds are incredibly prolific, according to René Siracusa of Malama O Puna.

🖐 **CAUTION:** The practice of grinding plant parts with a chipper/ shredder and composting the results is not recommended for Albizia cuttings because the seeds will sprout, even years later.

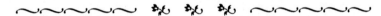

A practice called coppicing is often used by the folks at permaculture farms, such as Pangaia on the Big Island. There, they cut off young trees halfway up the trunk and then chop the top portion into smaller lengths, which they then use as nitrogen-rich mulch around the base of other plants. However, if you leave Albizia cuttings on the ground, they will sprout, says René Siracusa. She has learned that girdling a tree can be an effective way to kill it.

☞ How to girdle a tree:
1. Strip the bark from the ground level all the way around the tree, up to 18 inches from the ground.
2. It will take time, but eventually the tree will wither and die.

🖐 **CAUTION:** If you decide to use the girdling method, be very careful, especially with large Albizia trees, because the tree will start to fall down in big, heavy pieces, which can endanger people, other valuable plants and nearby buildings.

Goats love to eat Albizia leaves and bark, and their munching can girdle the tree, resulting in its eventual death. So if you live in the country and have lots of Albizia, you can use it to nourish some useful animals. But keep your eyes open for dead and dying trees, because they can start falling down in chunks after the goats girdle them for you.

Australian Tree Fern (Sphaeropteris cooperi, also known as Cyathea cooperi)

WRA designation: H (Hawai`i)
PIER designation: INVASIVE
Elevation: 1800-3700 feet

Illustration 2.3: It's difficult to distinguish Australian tree ferns from the desirable native hapu`u tree fern.

The Australian tree fern looks a lot like the native hapu`u, or Hawaiian tree fern (*Cibotium* species). However, it is a serious invader of rainforests and can literally take over, causing the native ferns to dwindle in numbers. It is sometimes mistakenly sold as the hapu`u. Two distinguishing characteristics of the Australian invader are the light colored scales on the frond bases and the frond scars on the trunk. Also, the new growth that appears on these ferns is white and hairy looking, which helps to differentiate it from the native hapu`u, whose new growth is typically red. If you look closely, the Australian tree fern's spores (on the underside of the leaves) are rectangular shaped rather than round, like the hapu`u.

The Australian tree fern has a growth rate about five times faster than our native hapu`u, it is highly adaptable, it has prolific spore production, and it can actually modify its habitat to make it more favorable to itself, which is a trait common to the most dangerous invasive species.

How to control Australian tree ferns

According to HEAR (Hawaiian Ecosystems at Risk Project; www.hear.org), "eradication efforts on Maui take two forms: large Australian tree ferns are felled, then their growing tips are severed" and "set above the ground to avoid contact with the soil, where they might resprout," according to the Kauaʻi Invasive Species Committee. HEAR concludes that "smaller plants are removed entirely." If you live in an area where these ferns exist, check with your local nursery or your island's Invasive Species Committee to learn the differences in appearance between them and our native hapuʻu. When they're young, it's simple to dig them out of the ground and destroy them so their spores do not stand a chance of creating more keikis.

Autograph Tree (Clusia rosea)

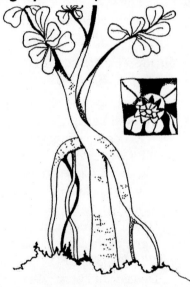

WRA designation: EVALUATE
DLNR designation: INVASIVE
PIER designation: INVASIVE
Elevation: Sea level to 3000 feet

Illustration 2.4: Children especially like to carve their names in autograph leaves, but these invasive trees can kill our native ʻohiʻas if left growing at their base.

The familiar West Indian "autograph tree," or copay, is a mildly invasive small tree that often occurs in areas close to the shoreline. You might know it for its leaves, which are fleshy and can be used to write on. The wood is actually hard and strong and might be useful for building, plant stakes or other purposes, but it's rarely used. Why not dream up a use for this wood instead of trashing it?

Autograph trees like to grow at the base of ʻohiʻa trees, so they can be hard to remove — you certainly do not want to use herbicides on anything that is so close to one of our native trees. But that's how they start their life: by beginning on another plant. In time, after its roots reach the ground, the autograph tree will strangle its host and will replace it. I have changed my attitude about these trees as I discover more of them sprouting at the base of my `ohi`a trees: now, instead of leaving "just one" autograph tree, I have become diligent in removing them whenever I see them, because the seeds contained in their fruit will make the problem much worse if they are allowed to germinate and grow into more destructive trees.

How to control autograph trees

To control autograph trees, cut them back at their base before they get too large and try to keep them cut back from time to time. We paint full-strength horticultural vinegar on the stumps after we cut them down. Then we repeat this application when we see new growth forming. For details about using horticultural vinegar, turn to Chapter 3. If you have larger, older autograph trees that you cannot remove, pick and destroy the fruit when it develops, so seeds cannot form and contribute to the spread of this invasive species.

Fountain Grass and Pampas Grass (Pennisetum setaceum; Cortaderia selloana and C. jubata)

Fountain grass:
WRA designation: H (Hawai`i).
PIER designation: INVASIVE
ISC Top 5 for O`ahu and Maui County (including Lana`i and Moloka`i)
Hawai`i Department of Agriculture designation: NOXIOUS WEED
Division of Forestry and Wildlife of the Hawai`i Department of Land and Natural Resources designation: one of Hawai`i's most invasive horticultural pests
Elevation: Sea level to 7000 feet

Illustration 2.5: Fountain grass forms large clumps that quickly take over an area.

Pampas grass:
WRA designation: Not yet evaluated
PIER designation: INVASIVE
Hawai`i Department of Agriculture designation: NOXIOUS WEED
ISC Top 5 for O`ahu, Maui and Moloka`i
Elevation: approximately 2000-7000 feet in dry, open sunny places

More than 100 species of the grasses we see in Hawai`i have been introduced to the islands by well-meaning people who just wanted their homes to look like the homes they knew and loved in other places. Unfortunately, grasses prolifically spread their seeds and many species spread by runners, such as Bermuda grass. The *Poaceae*, or grass family of plants, contains about 10,000 species, according to Dr. Mark Merlin in his book *Hawaiian Coastal Plants*. Only 39 of these are native to Hawai`i and many of the others have become very serious invasive weeds. Fountain grass and Pampas grass, introduced as attractive ornamentals, are two of these.

Introduced from its native Africa, fountain grass has taken over large areas on the leeward side of many islands. Dr. Merlin writes that "it's an aggressive colonizer of arid, open spaces, often out-competing native species." It also creates a wildfire hazard and is the main fuel for perennial wildfires in West Hawai`i. You'll see a lot of it along the sides of Highway 190 between Waimea and Kailua-Kona on the Big Island.

Pampas grass is a giant bunchgrass from South Africa that is especially prevalent on O`ahu, Maui and Moloka`i. The narrow leaves have sharp, serrated edges and it has white to purple flower plumes. This plant grows to over 13 feet tall and its seeds are spread by the wind. Seeds can be viable for at least six years.

Pampas grass forms dense stands and spreads rapidly. After it's established, pampas grass can crowd out native plants, damage grazing lands, and create a fire hazard.

How to control fountain grass and pampas grass

The Hawai`i State Alien Species Coordinator, which is part of the Department of Land and Natural Resources (DLNR), includes both fountain grass and Pampas grass on its list of the worst invasive horticultural plants in Hawai`i and urges that they not be grown anywhere in Hawai`i. Although the young shoots of fountain grass are a common forage plant for cattle, it has escaped from their fields and should not be introduced to areas where it doesn't yet occur.

If your property is on the leeward side of any of the islands, you'll want to check for fountain grass and try to control the population before it becomes a serious problem. Burning it is not the answer: "it is strongly adapted to fires, re-establishing itself very quickly after a burn," says Dr. Merlin. So you can try covering it with cardboard or black plastic, try digging it out by the roots if you don't have too many members of this species, and keep on pulling the keikis as they appear. But what should you do with the seeds? Perhaps if you cover them with cardboard you can prevent them from sprouting into a million new plants. Experiment and see what works best for you in your microclimate.

I had some pampas grass in my yard in California and tried to remove one after it had grown into a large plant. What a job! The leaves are serrated and I ended up with a lot of cuts on my arms. If you tackle it, be sure to remove all of the underground rhizomes. Control is easiest, of course, if you can pull and destroy these plants while they're still small. The horticultural vinegar mentioned in Chapter 3 might be helpful for widespread infestations.

Guava and Strawberry guava (Psidium guajava and Psidium cattleianum)

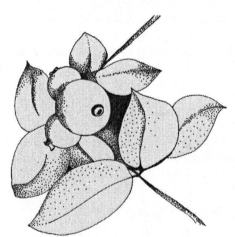

The designations for both species of guava are:
WRA designation: H (Hawai`i)
PIER designation: INVASIVE
Elevation: Sea level to 4000 feet

Illustration 2.6: Although yellow guavas are delicious, the trees can take over an area when their roots spread, even your lawn!

The strawberry guava, called waiawi `ula-`ula in Hawaiian, is the most serious invasive plant in moist rainforest areas of the windward sides of all the main Hawaiian islands, second only to Miconia. The Hawaiian name, waiawi, is pronounced "Vi-VEE." It is extremely fast growing and can become 20-50 feet tall. It has fine-textured, moderately heavy wood used

26

only for fuel wood in Hawai`i, but we have discovered a great use for it as plant stakes and supports for the signs in Hi`iaka's Garden (see below). The invasiveness danger comes from the fact that it sends up hundreds, in time potentially thousands, of seedlings, resulting in an impenetrable clump of invasive stalks. Although it was introduced in 1825 for the edible fruit, the fruit flies often get it before I do, so if you want to eat one, be sure to open it up first and check for wormy inhabitants.

The yellow guava, or kuawa, is an evergreen shrub or small tree to 30 feet in height, introduced into Hawai`i early in the 19th century. It is cultivated for its rounded yellow edible fruits, which are very rich in vitamin C. It has become widely naturalized in lowland thickets. It has larger flowers, larger fruits and different leaves than strawberry guava (waiawi). The hard, strong, heavy wood of guava has been used for tool handles and other implements. If you let it dry out and chop it up, it makes a great fuel for open fire barbecues. And the flowers make a beautiful, delicious garnish for fruit salads and other dishes. For the most part, you'll probably want to control the wild guava population in your yard by keeping it pruned and contained.

If you like guava and want to plant a tree, a cultivated variety is recommended: it bears larger, better quality fruit than the wild types and is less invasive.

Extracts from guava leaves, bark, roots and buds have been used in Hawaiian folk medicine. It was widely used to remedy such ailments as dysentery, diarrhea, stomachaches and other digestive problems. If you pinch off the tip of a leaf bud and eat it, it is said that your stomachache or gassy feeling will quickly disappear. In Tahiti, young guava shoots are pounded into a paste and applied to wounds that won't stop bleeding. Other Polynesian islanders use guava for sores, boils, cuts, sprains, and rashes.

I can't repeat enough how invasive guavas can become: cattle, wild hogs and birds scatter and spread its seeds. Guava thickets in pastures destroy forage plants. Eradication is difficult because of the sprouts that pop up from the roots.

How to control guava

Feral pigs are a major source of spreading this plant; so if you can control the swine by hunting them or fencing your property, that's a good first step in controlling waiawi. You can also continually cut it back. You could dig it out by the roots or bring in a bulldozer to dig it up, but its seeds can remain in the soil and will eventually sprout and form a new stand of this hard to control, very invasive plant. Plus, birds that eat the fruit of nearby guava will undoubtedly drop some onto your property. If you live in the country and have a major problem with invasive guava, goats and sheep like to eat the newly sprouted shoots and can help to control it.

The Kaua`i Invasive Species Committee has had success in controlling waiawi with a 20% solution of the herbicide Garlon-4 mixed with Forest Crop oil. They apply it to the base of the trunk, and they recommend notching trunks that are over 5 inches in diameter before applying the herbicide. Later, the waiawi trees decay and provide filtered shade where native plants can germinate and stand a chance of starting a successful life.

The Nature Conservancy's web site reports this information about waiawi control: "Manual and mechanical control measures work reasonably well and are recommended where practical. Seedlings and saplings originating from seed can be uprooted. Stems up to two inches can be uprooted with a weed wrench, although some roots may need to be cut once the plant is partially uprooted. Uprooted plants may resprout or reroot in areas with greater than 2000 mm (about 80 inches) of rain per year or drier areas after prolonged rain, especially if the plants are set on the ground. Manual and mechanical methods are less effective on root sprouts."

☞ If you have a small amount of waiawi, here's a method for eradicating it:
1. Strip off all of the leaves of all the upright branches.
2. When new leaves grow back, strip them off and continue doing this several times until the sapling gives up its attempts to survive. Without the photosynthesis that the leaves provide to the plant's respiration and nourishment, it simply cannot continue its existence.

Using waiawi for stakes and furniture

At Hi`iaka's Garden, we have found a great use for some of the waiawi that grows on our property: we soak it in a solution of Borax and water, which deters twig borer beetles, and then use it for our garden signs and even for furniture. It holds up better indoors than outdoors, of course, but our waiawi plant stakes normally stay standing for about two or three years.

☞ Recipe for treating waiawi sticks:
1. Cut waiawi stalks to the ground with a saw or large loppers, depending on the diameter of each stalk. You probably don't want stalks larger than about 2 inches in diameter if you plan to use them for plant stakes. Put them into the Borax soak immediately (see below).
2. Cut each stalk to a manageable length, cutting off the top end, which gets skinny and would not provide any support for plants if you were

to use it as a plant stake. If you have a stick pile, you can toss the tops in there or chop them up in your chipper/shredder. But beware of the seeds and don't spread any chopped up waiawi containing them on your property or you will just make the problem worse.

3. Use a large garbage can or wading pool: for each 30 gallons of water, add half a box (about two pounds) of 20 Mule Team Borax and stir thoroughly.

4. Prop your waiawi sticks into the liquid and allow them to sit and soak it up for at least one week. If you leave one or two entire sticks with the leaves still attached to the top, you'll know your sticks are ready when those leaves turn yellow.

5. After the soaking period is over, remove all sticks and prop them up in a dry place for at least four weeks.
   You can then cut them to size, Verithane or paint them if you like, and then lash them together to use as plant supports, furniture or other creative projects.

☞ **NOTE:** Insects can still affect the outer bark even after you soak your sticks. Because the bark will peel off in time anyway, you can shave it off with a knife while the sticks are green. This also gives it a more tidy appearance.

Kahili Ginger (Hedychium gardnerianum)

WRA designation: H (Hawai`i)
DLNR designation: INVASIVE
PIER designation: INVASIVE
Elevation: Sea level to 5500 feet
in wet habitats on all islands

Illustration 2.7: Although attractive, Kahili ginger can quickly dominate rainforest landscapes.

How could a beautiful flowering ginger be considered an undesirable invasive? It's a matter of too much of a good thing with kahili. Although it is attractive with its large, showy flower spikes, it spreads voraciously by runners and seeds, making it very difficult to eradicate and control because its roots cover the ground and prevent saplings of other plants from growing by choking out the native forest plants. And its flowers are said to be poisonous, so it's a good thing to eradicate, especially if you have curious children.

This showy ginger grows just over 3 feet tall. Birds as well as humans disperse the conspicuous, fleshy, red seeds. It is so hardy it can even survive a forest fire.

Major infestations of kahili ginger exist near Volcano, Hawai`i.

How to control Kahili ginger

Their fleshy rhizomes make mechanical control of kahili ginger very difficult. If you have a large patch of it and can bulldoze, that might get rid of it, but be sure to dispose of the rhizomes where they won't regrow. University of Hawai`i field tests have shown that yellow ginger was extremely sensitive to Metsulfuron and also that this same herbicide worked well on kahili ginger. You can also help to solve the problem of this invasive species by asking your local nursery not to carry this plant.

Lantana (Lantana camara)

WRA designation: H (Hawai`i)
PIER designation: INVASIVE
Elevation: Near sea level to 3500 feet

Illustration 2.8: Thorny lantana can be difficult to remove.

Introduced from the West Indies, some varieties of this invasive, thorny weed are actually sold as bedding plants in nurseries. It infests over 400,000 acres through the state of Hawai`i and is especially bad in Koke`e State Park on Kaua`i.

How to control lantana

If you have a field of lantana and can get a herd of animals to trample it that might help in controlling it. Otherwise, you must pull it out by the roots. Try to remove it when it is small, because large plants are thorny and spreading. When you pull it, be sure to get out all of the lateral roots. Mowing or weed whacking gives you only a temporary remedy, as it will come back from the roots. Burning does not always provide an effective treatment, and can actually increase the population.

Several insects can help to control lantana: the defoliating caterpillar, or *Hypena strigata*, can be effective. Do NOT introduce what might sound like a beneficial insect because it can also get out of control and eat other plants in your garden that you had no intention of controlling.

Maile pilau (Paederia foetida)

WRA designation: H (Hawai`i)
PIER designation: INVASIVE
Elevation: Sea level to 6000 feet

Illustration 2.9: Do not let the attractive flowers convince you to leave "just one" maile pilau, because it will quickly become a serious invader.

Known not so affectionately as "stink maile," this vine is horribly invasive and can reach lengths of 20 feet or longer. Don't be tempted to leave "just one" because of its pretty flowers! If the property you're considering buying is overrun with this stuff, think twice before you buy it: you'll never get rid of it all. It smothers all trees and smaller plants that happen to be in the same area where it grows. And it smells nasty!

How to control maile pilau

If you learn to recognize the keikis, they're easy to pull out by the roots. But because it grows quickly, and the vines can be two inches in diameter (or more), you'll need a saw to cut it off at the base when it is climbing up a tree. The stump can and will sprout and even if you cover it with black plastic, this is not effective in killing it because it grows in total darkness as well as full sun. The folks at Pangaia permaculture farm on the Big Island use a horse to control their maile pilau when it is young and succulent. And they do a lot of hand weeding.

Melastoma, Tibouchina, and Koster's Curse (Melastoma candidum and related species; Tibouchina urvilleana and related species; Clidemia hirta)

Illustration 2.10: The melastoma flower is pretty, but the plants can choke all other plant life on entire acres.

- The designations for melastoma are:
  WRA designation: H (Hawai`i)
  DLNR designation: INVASIVE
  PIER designation: INVASIVE
  Hawai`i State Department of Agriculture designation: NOXIOUS WEED
  ISC Top 5 for O`ahu and the Big Island

- The designations for tibouchina are:
  WRA designation: H (HPWRA)
  DLNR designation: INVASIVE
  PIER designation: INVASIVE
- The designations for Koster's curse are:
  WRA designation: Not yet evaluated
  DLNR designation: INVASIVE
  PIER designation: INVASIVE
  All three species occur from near sea level to 4000 feet in elevation.

Melastoma is an attractive shrub with pink or lavender flowers. Called by several common names including glory bush, princess bush, and false azalea, it creates dense thickets that do not allow anything else to grow in the same environment. They grow especially well in wet pastures and forests and completely shade out the understory plants. Gentle bulldozing works well to rip these plants out of the ground, but if they cover the properties that surround yours, you'll never completely get rid of them because they spread by seeds that are dispersed by the wind and the many birds that live here.

In the same plant family as melastoma, tibouchina is the predominant plant in higher elevation gardens such as the Volcano area of the Big Island. Pretty with its purple, azalea-like flowers, it is spread by birds and can form dense stands that shade out all other plant life.

Also called soap bush, Koster's curse can grow to about 9 feet tall and has rounded, hairy branches and oval-shaped leaves with berries that are 1/4 inch to 1/2 inch long. It is an aggressive invader and shades out all vegetation below it. Birds disperse the seeds, but any animal moving through the thickets can carry seeds away with it. It is probably not resistant to fire, but it rapidly colonizes burned areas. It thrives in both open grassland and in deep shade.

This plant is a serious pest in mesic and wet environments on O'ahu and South Kona on the Big Island. It has also become established on Kaua'i, West Maui, and Waiakea, Hawai'i. Plants flower and fruit prolifically all year, producing sweet, pulpy, dark-blue berries filled with tiny seeds. It can create an impenetrable stand with its densely branching habit. It's a pioneering species after bulldozing has disturbed land, and it can displace native plants.

How to control melastoma, tibouchina and Koster's curse

Pull out young plants when you see them and keep the larger bushes well pruned. Just keep cutting them if they are a problem on your property and never introduce them purposely, even though they are prized as houseplants in less temperate climates.

Never import or plant melastoma, tibouchina or Koster's curse. If you have any of them or see them growing or for sale, call the Invasive Species Committee on your island. (Refer to the Resources Appendix for their phone number and other contact information.)

Chapter 3
Controlling Weeds Without RoundUp

If you want to reduce your use of herbicides such as RoundUp to control small weeds and other problem plants, this chapter is for you. If you need to control undesirable trees and larger plants such as shrubs, we cover them in Chapter 2. Here you will read descriptions of a number of weeds that most land stewards will not want on their properties. However, some of the weedy plants we'll describe are actually beneficial to you or your property, so perhaps we'll change your opinion about them. You might even develop the old "if you can't beat 'em, join 'em" kind of attitude. We will conclude with some techniques, such as mulching, for controlling those nasty weeds.

Cardboard Is Next to Godliness

It's simple to use flattened cardboard boxes instead of herbicides to control weedy areas. When I first saw cardboard being used by some folks at a nearby permaculture farm, I thought "why didn't I know about this terrific, easy method a long time ago?" How well I remember digging out a 2-foot by 12-foot strip of lawn in my back yard in San Jose, California, in order to expand my vegetable garden. If only I had known that by simply placing sheets of cardboard over the area it would suffocate the lawn, I would have saved myself several back-stressing hours of digging out the unwanted grass. Since that discovery, I have used flattened cardboard boxes and newspaper extensively to prepare garden beds and to kill weeds in pathways.

In the past, I've used black plastic and landscape fabric, but plastic gets ragged and trashy looking in time and then it can be hard to remove. It costs money to buy and when it starts to disintegrate, where else are you going to take it but to our too-full landfills? Cardboard and newspaper are free and eventually they break down, contributing to the formation of humus to nourish your plants.

Super simple recipe for using cardboard to control weedy areas

Chapter 4 gives complete directions for building a raised bed with a foundation of cardboard, but for now here are the super simple getting-started directions.

1. If the weeds in an area are tall, mow them or weed whack them down as close to the ground as possible. No need to remove the cut weeds, pull them out by the roots, level the ground, or remove any rocks unless they're big ones.
2. Mark the area with stakes or string or simply sprinkle some flour to mark the edges.
3. If you're going to use the area for planting later on, sprinkle the ground with bone meal and/or blood meal, or a bucket or two of compost. If you have seed-filled weeds that you want to get rid of, spread them here.
4. Cover the entire area with cardboard, newspaper, or old non-synthetic carpet, overlapping the pieces so you leave no holes for weeds.
5. If you're intent on just eliminating some weeds, such as in path areas, you can cover the cardboard with palm fronds, fern fronds, small tree branches, or whatever. This helps to keep the cardboard from blowing away and makes the area look a little more attractive. Be careful that you don't create tripping hazards, however.

Mulching Is the Answer

Mulch is basically anything that you lay on the ground around your plants that keeps the soil moist, cool, weed-free and nourished. Mulch can be black plastic, landscape fabric, or natural ingredients like leaves, chopped-up branches, compost, cardboard, or whatever other brilliant material you can dream up. I prefer to use naturally occurring materials because they're free and in time they break down, adding to the soil around my plants.

Living mulch is just a groundcover that gives more

If you're going to add naturally occurring materials to the ground around your plants, why not consider some living mulches? Living mulches are simply plants that help to control weeds, nourish the soil, and stay alive for prolonged periods of time.

Here are descriptions and growing instructions for growing perennial peanut and fo-ti, both of which can serve as wonderful living mulches.

Perennial peanut (*Arachis pintoi*)

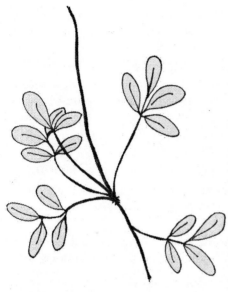

Illustration 3.1: Perennial peanut spreads quickly and makes a great lawn substitute that keeps weeds at bay.

It sounds odd to think of a peanut as a lawn alternative, but that is exactly what the perennial, non-edible peanut is used for at permaculture farms such as Pangaia on the Big Island. Its attractive, low-growing habit with pretty small yellow flowers fills in areas of the garden where you want to discourage weeds. It looks great, is drought tolerant and is non-invasive, according to the University of Hawai`i's Weed Risk Assessment. It requires no mowing, no weed whacking, and it doesn't climb up other plants. If you live in a rural setting and love honey, you might consider setting up a beehive because honeybees love the sweet yellow flowers. Because it grows well in shady areas, it makes a great cover crop for dryland taro, coffee, bananas, macadamia nut trees and other trees. And you can plant vegetable seedlings right into an established perennial peanut bed, which will help to suppress weediness and prevent erosion.

☞ Here are some particulars about this plant:

• If you live in town, perennial peanut makes a great lawn substitute. It's attractive and never needs mowing. You can walk on it and it won't crowd out other plants that live near it.
• If you live in the country, it's an effective way to control weeds in orchards, pathways, and other problem areas.

How to grow perennial peanut

Perennial peanut does best in areas that receive 40 inches of rain a year, or more. It can be a bit tricky to get established in your garden, according to the folks at Pangaia permaculture farm and can take several months to become established. They advise that it becomes established faster when you start it from seed rather than from cuttings. Seed can be difficult to find, so cuttings from a friend might be the only way to acquire this plant.

☞ Starting perennial peanut from seed

1. Prepare the area where you want this plant to grow by covering the ground with cardboard or plastic to kill existing weeds.
2. Leave the cover in place for three to four weeks, then remove it and keep it weeded until you plant.
3. When the young plants are about two inches tall, transplant them to the area where you want them to grow: plant two to three individual plants together in holes about one foot apart.
4. Keep your plants well watered for the first few months until they begin to spread and become at home in their new home.

Hints and tips:

✓ In leeward gardens, be sure to keep it well watered for the first six months.
✓ In windward gardens, keep an eye on it during droughts: it might need some hand watering, especially during the first six months.
✓ If you live below 300 feet in elevation, make sure that it gets enough water because of the drier conditions near sea level.
✓ If you live above 300 feet, it should flourish with very little additional watering and care.

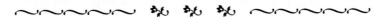

Perennial peanut seeds and plants are available at select nurseries and farm supply stores throughout the Hawaiian islands, or you can order them over the Internet. KM Seed in Waimea on the Big Island sells them. Refer to the Resources Appendix for contact information.

Starting perennial peanut from cuttings

1. Prepare the area where you want this plant to grow by covering the ground with cardboard or plastic to kill existing weeds. Leave the cover in place for three to four weeks, then remove it and keep it weeded until you plant.
2. Cut as many 4 to 8 inch long sprigs of an existing perennial peanut plant as you want, remembering that you might get only about a 50% success rate.

3. I recommend starting cuttings in small pots in a protected area out of direct sunlight, but you can try to root them right in the ground, especially if you live in a rainy area.

4. Whether you start with previously rooted cuttings or unrooted sprigs directly, bury them so that only the top inch of the stem is above the soil surface.

5. If you want to encourage a dense cover crop, plant your cuttings about 10 to 15 inches apart.

6. If you have a low-fertility soil, it's a good idea to apply a small amount of a nitrogen-rich fertilizer or compost tea at the same time you plant your cuttings.

Fo-ti (*Polygonum multiflorum*)

Fo-ti is called He-shou-wu in Chinese medicine. The root is used as a rejuvenating tonic and it grows like a weed wherever I've introduced it into my garden.

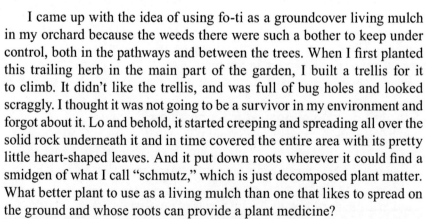

Illustration 3.2: Fo-ti quickly covers the ground and has beneficial qualities when the root is used in medicines.

I came up with the idea of using fo-ti as a groundcover living mulch in my orchard because the weeds there were such a bother to keep under control, both in the pathways and between the trees. When I first planted this trailing herb in the main part of the garden, I built a trellis for it to climb. It didn't like the trellis, and was full of bug holes and looked scraggly. I thought it was not going to be a survivor in my environment and forgot about it. Lo and behold, it started creeping and spreading all over the solid rock underneath it and in time covered the entire area with its pretty little heart-shaped leaves. And it put down roots wherever it could find a smidgen of what I call "schmutz," which is just decomposed plant matter. What better plant to use as a living mulch than one that likes to spread on the ground and whose roots can provide a plant medicine?

Fo-ti plants are available from some mail order catalogs, such as Horizon Herbs. Check the Resources Appendix. After you get one plant going, it starts very easily from cuttings.

How to grow Fo-ti

1. Prepare the area where you want this plant to grow by covering the ground with cardboard or plastic to kill existing weeds. Leave the cover in place for three to four weeks, then remove it and keep it weeded until you plant.
2. Cut as many 4-inch to 8-inch long sprigs of existing plants as you need. The success rate is normally very high for fo-ti.
3. I recommend starting cuttings in small pots in a protected area out of direct sunlight, but you can try to root them right in the ground, especially if you live in a rainy area.
4. After your cuttings are nicely rooted, plant them in your garden.
5. If you want to encourage a dense cover crop, plant your cuttings about 10 to 15 inches apart and keep them watered for the first several weeks if it doesn't rain.

Other Non-Chemical Remedies

You can also control weeds by pruning and pulling them, weed whacking, and by using a new product called horticultural vinegar. Read on for details about these three useful practices.

Pruning and pulling

Pruning and pulling out your unwanted plants out by their dirty little roots are the easiest and most effective methods for getting rid of weeds. Remember to use garden gloves when you pull weeds because you'll save your hands from not only thorns but from biting insects as well. After you have been attacked by an anthill full of biting red ants for the first time, it won't be so difficult to remember to put your gloves on the next time you go out on a search-and-destroy mission of the weeds in your garden.

When you pull weeds, normally you want to get the entire plant, including the entire root system. Here are some tools that can be helpful in your weeding adventure:

✓ Hula hoe. Sometimes called a stirrup hoe, this is a wonderful tool for easily scooping small weeds out by their roots. It works best in areas covered by dirt or cinder, but is not effective on solid rock.

Illustration 3.3: My favorite tool, the "hula" or "stirrup" hoe, pulls small weeds right out of the ground so easily.

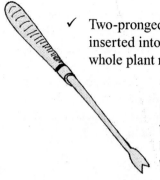

✓ Two-pronged hand weeding tool. The prongs, when inserted into the soil at the base of a tricky weed, pop the whole plant right out of the ground very easily.

Illustration 3.4: The two-pronged weeding tool is a great help for those hard to pull medium-sized weeds, especially those with a taproot.

✓ Trowel. For larger weeds with more extensive root systems, a trowel or hand spade is often the right tool for the job. It allows you to get right in there and dig out the problem plant from its roots.

Illustration 3.5: No garden would be complete without at least one trowel.

✓ Spade. Regular pointed-end shovels are very helpful when you need to remove larger plants. Stick your shovel into the soil in a circle about one foot from the base or trunk of the plant you want to dig out and gradually dig deeper around the plant. If it's a weed, or something you consider to be a weed, you'll want to get as much of the root system as possible. And if you're digging out a valuable plant to replant in another location, you'll want to dig out as much of the root system as you can to prevent transplant shock or harm to the plant. In either case, try to get as much of the rootball as possible. There will always be hairy little rootlets that don't come up with the majority of the roots, but that's usually all right.

Illustration 3.6: The spade is another "must have" tool for digging and planting.

Weed whacking

Weed whacking permanently solves very few problems. But what are you going to do when you have a half-acre of invasive grassy weeds? We strive to pull all of our unwanted plants out by the roots, but until we do (perhaps when Hawai`i freezes over), using a weed whacker keeps the garden looking tidy and it creates job security for the person wielding the whacker!

When you whack, be careful! Here are some safety tips to follow every single time you head out with that fun toy:

- Wear long pants, covered shoes and a long-sleeved shirt. You would be surprised how much damage one small rock can cause.
- Keep your fingers and other body parts away from the string when it is moving.
- Consider at least wearing sunglasses. Official protective eyeware, available at your local garden supply or hardware store, is an excellent idea.
- Be sure the cutting string is the correct length.
- Check the area to be whacked before you begin and remove any string, rope, or vines, because they can get tangled up in the whacker's head and damage it.
- Stop your machine if it gets clogged with grass or other plant matter. Clean it out because the additional stress on the head can cause it to break.
- In tall grassy areas, start high, near the tops of the plants, and work your way down in layers.
- When you're moving from one area to another with your machine running, be very careful of the rotating head and make sure you don't accidentally press the throttle button.

Horticultural vinegar

When you think of vinegar, you think of salads, right? This strong vinegar isn't edible, but it can provide an inexpensive, environmentally safe herbicide for spot treatment on organic farms. It can also be useful in the control of unwanted vegetation along roadsides and range lands, as well as in the control of weeds around yards, brick walls, patios and cracks in pavements.

Research has been conducted to determine how well vinegar controls weeds. The results tell us that a strong version of vinegar (10, 15 or 20% acetic acid concentration) can kill many important weed species at several growth stages. This vinegar provided an 80-100% percent kill of selected annual weeds, including giant foxtail, common lambsquarters, smooth

41

pigweed, and velvetleaf. At Hi`iaka's Garden, we have conducted tests with this vinegar in a dilution of 1 part vinegar to 3 parts water, and have had immediate success in killing *Mimosa pudica* ("sleeping grass"), spurge, oxalis, guava, vervain, young melastoma, several grasses, and many others in one or two applications.

However, the strong concentration of acetic acid contained in these new vinegar products should not be taken lightly.

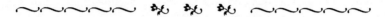

🖐 **CAUTION:** Vinegar with acetic acid concentrations greater than 5% may be hazardous and should be handled with appropriate precautions.

Check the Resources Appendix for contact information for Greenergy's Blackberry and Brush Block.

Some Insidious Small Weeds

We'll talk about the smaller weeds that are commonly found on Hawaiian properties next:
- Clover and wood sorrel
- Sleeping grass or sensitive plant
- Spurge
- Wild morning glory

Clover and wood sorrel (*Oxalis repens* and *O. corniculata*)

Illustration 3.7: The pretty flowers of wood sorrel make it a desirable "weed."

There are a couple of different species of *Oxalis* that occur in Hawai`i. The most common one is a tiny-leafed clover-type plant that spreads by underground runners and seeds. A larger variety, called `ihi, is a type of wood sorrel and is quite attractive. This *Oxalis* was an early Polynesian introduction and is considered a creeping perennial weed in open, disturbed places, from close to the ocean to about the 1800-foot elevation. It was also used in Hawaiian plant medicine for the treatment of constipation and for asthma and tuberculosis. I have a patch of it in my orchard and enjoy its presence and beauty, so I don't want to remove it and would welcome it if it were to spread. Where "wonderful weeds" grow, many other less desirable weeds cannot find a foothold.

When the small form of our local *Oxalis* started creeping from one garden bed into the surrounding path areas, we had to make a decision: would we try to control it through pulling it out every time we saw it popping up? Or would we learn to accept it and live with it? It's not bad looking and it does discourage other weeds from growing in its wake. I think the jury is still out on this issue, however, because I don't want to see this *Oxalis* creeping into nearby garden beds and choking out my more important plants.

Sleeping grass (*Mimosa pudica*)

Illustration 3.8: Often called "sleeping grass" in Hawai`i, Mimosa can be almost impossible to eliminate.

Sleeping grass is called pua-hilahila in Hawaiian. Morning grass, sensitive plant, and "that damn weed" are just some of the nicknames for this highly invasive member of the legume family. PIER (the Pacific Island Ecosystems at Risk project) has assessed it as invasive and recommends that it not be imported from Australia and other countries where it is native. It occurs in many tropical areas of the world and is used for treating insomnia in Belize, in the Mayan tradition described by Dr. Rosita Arvigo and Nadine Epstein in their book, *Rainforest Home Remedies*. There, it is called sleepy head, twelve o'clock prickle, and xmutz.

The "prickle" part of the name should name should help to explain why it can be such a problem in landscaped areas: the small thorns, which cover all parts of this nasty little invader except the roots, can not only poke you, but can become infected if you don't pull them out and treat your small wounds.

Making good use of a bad weed

Rosita Arvigo speaks of mimosa as "an adorable little plant." With all due respect, I believe she must not have it growing in her gardens in Belize, Central America! Some visitors to my garden think it's cool the way the leaves fold up when you touch them, but to anyone who has struggled to keep this pest weeded and controlled, it is not so amusing after about the 900th time you touch it!

Here is Rosita's recipe for a Mimosa Sleep Aid:

"Some Maya toast the leaves and stems, then reduce them to a tasteless powder by passing the mixture through a sieve. They sprinkle the powder into the last meal of the day. Others like to smoke the powdered leaves in a corn husk."

Recipe for fresh Mimosa tea:

Gather 10 fresh sprigs of Mimosa about 6 inches long, and then chop them into 1-inch pieces. You can include the flowers and seeds if there are any. Place your plant material into a 1-quart teapot and then pour boiling water over it, cover it and let it steep (just let it sit) for at least 10 minutes. Then strain it and drink it hot or chilled.

Mimosa has small purple puffball flowers that turn into seedpods that are chock-full of spiny little seeds, each of which seems to form a new thorny invader close to its parent.

I control mimosa by putting on a pair of gloves and pulling it out by the root. This can be tricky because the root can spread widely and can easily break off while you're trying to pull it, leaving a piece that has the potential for growing new above-ground foliage. Thus, the cycle is perpetuated. I've learned to recognize this plant when it is very small: this is the time to get rid of it because if it hasn't flowered and formed seeds, it hasn't had the chance to form keikis that make the problem worse. But as its name suggests, it IS sensitive and its ferny little leaves close up as soon as you touch them, making it almost impossible to see the little devil. To dispose of the plants that I pull, I toss them onto my gravel road and allow them to dry out before I put them under a sheet of cardboard. I don't think that a compost pile will ever get hot enough to kill the seeds, and like some other plants, the heating process might actually encourage the seeds to sprout.

Goats are said to like the stuff, so if you live in a rural setting, adding one of these cute animals to your roster of pets might be something to consider if you are constantly fighting a mimosa problem.

Spurge (*Euphorbia hirta* and *E. heterophylla*)

Spurge is called koko-kahiki in Hawaiian and to me is one of the ugliest, most invasive and hateful of weeds. The darn stuff seems to form flowers and seeds almost as soon as it sprouts, so unless you learn to recognize the plant in its cotyledon stage (when it first sprouts) and crawl around on the ground the rest of your life pulling those keikis, you're just going to have spurge forever, so matter what you do.

Illustration 3.9: Spurge is a truly ugly weed. I believe I have five species of it in my garden and will always be pulling it out.

✍ **CAUTION:** This plant is "somewhat poisonous," according to Dr. Arthur Whistler in his book *Polynesian Herbal Medicine.* He states that spurge "has no economic significance other than being a weed. The only reported Polynesian medicinal uses are from Hawai`i, where this plant is used commonly as a laxative. This practice calls for crushing the leaves and stems in warm water, and drinking the liquid." So it does have a little redeeming value, but the fact that it is considered mildly poisonous would certainly deter me from trying any on an experimental basis, and I caution you to heed the same advice.

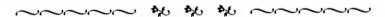

The only control for spurge is to keep on pulling it out by the roots or cover it with cardboard if it's in an area where that is possible. After I pull it, I don't like to use it directly as mulch around the neighboring plants because of its tiny, energetic seeds that will cause about 1,000 more spurge plants to grow in a 6 square inch area (or so it seems). I also don't like to throw it into a compost pile for the same reason -- I just don't know if the compost will ever heat up to the point that it will kill or inactivate spurge seeds.

What, then, should you do with the weedy carcasses of spurge after you have joyfully yanked them out of the ground? If you have chickens, their coop is the perfect place to dump an armload of spurge or other seedy weeds. They will eat what they like and the rest of the plant material will decompose in the straw and chicken poop. If any seeds sprout, the chickens will either stomp on them or pull them up with their beaks and eat them. A perfect balance! Another option is to use the pulled-up spurge underneath cardboard, in that first layer I described in step 3 of the recipe for using cardboard to kill weeds earlier in this chapter.

Wild morning glory (*Ipomoea indica* and *I. congesta*)

Illustration 3.10: Wild morning glories come in several different forms. They can form quite a tangled mess.

The several varieties of native morning glory that are found in Hawai`i are called either koali or kowali `awa. Koali grows near the ocean to about 2,000 feet in elevation and likes full sun. Although some members of the morning glory family have very beautiful flowers, such as the Heavenly Blue morning glory, some wild varieties of koali have insignificant flowers. You might not even see them unless you crawl around in the morning and look for them. The vines tangle their way around your lanai furniture and any plants that happen to be in their way. And they grow very fast: we burned some brush and scrap wood in one area in September, and by January the charred ground was invisible underneath an absolute mass of wild morning glories. But a sheet of black plastic took care of that.

Traditional medicinal uses of koali

The early Hawaiians used koali as a laxative, and it was one of the best known of their medicinal plants. They also crushed parts of the plant with salt and applied the mixture to sprains and fractures as a poultice.

In spite of its redeeming medicinal properties, I choose to keep this vine pulled out by the roots. It's all right to use it as mulch around other plants: I have not seen uprooted koali take root and when it drops its seeds the keikis are easy to notice and uproot.

Chapter 4
Building a Raised Garden Bed In One Afternoon

I highly recommend that you read this chapter! Whether you have built 100 gardens before or none at all, it will give you useful advice and information about how to easily create raised beds with free or cheap, commonly found "stuff" that is probably already around your yard or that's available at your local garden center.

What Is a Raised Bed?

Raised beds are a fairly time-honored concept. The raised bed, or biointensive, method of growing vegetables started in 1972 at Stanford University in California, where a group called Ecology Action began a 1/2 acre research, demonstration and teaching garden. It was so productive that it produced a complete vegetarian diet for one person in just 2800 square feet of garden. In 1980 the method was taken to India, where it improved local nutrition. Since then, biointensive farming techniques have been used in China, Brazil, Africa, Mexico, the Philippines and other countries. If you're interested in reading all about it, check out the books *How to Grow More Vegetables Than You Ever Thought Possible On Less Land Than You Can Imagine* by John Jeavons and *Lasagna Gardening* by Patricia Lanza. (See the Bibliography.)

"Lasagna gardening doesn't mean growing your own lasagna," Lanza says in her book. It's based on a permaculture technique called sheet composting, which is just a fancy name for this easy, organic layering method you can use to create better soil while keeping your garden neat and attractive. Through this method, you can build and maintain a garden without digging, tilling or removing sod or lawn. Lanza adds that "using no power tools, heavy equipment or expensive additives, one person can easily create and enjoy a healthy, productive garden" right on top of solid rock, as is the case in parts of Hawai`i. And if you have a patch of old, weedy lawn, it's the perfect way to transform the area in a few hours.

Before You Start, Be Kind To Your Body

"Because gardening is terrific exercise in the fresh air and rewarding on so many levels, we often underestimate the time and effort it will take and overestimate our physical abilities," says Dr. William Madosky of the Madosky Chiropractic and Acupuncture Center in St. Louis, Missouri. The ThirdAge Health Newsletter (www.thirdage.com) has created a nice little list of tips and advice for gardeners called "Back Tips for Gardeners." In it, Dr. Madosky relates "gardening-related pain is one of the most common complaints we get in our office in the springtime." He says you can greatly reduce your chances for pain and injury while gardening by tuning into your body and observing the following techniques:

✓ Treat gardening as a sport. Begin gardening by warming up as you would before any sports activity. Stretch the most frequently used muscles in your upper and lower body so they become more flexible and able to handle the tasks at hand. Don't forget to stretch after you're done to help relax muscles and reduce soreness later.

✓ Carefully plan how much time is required. Realistically assess how much you can accomplish. Most injuries occur from doing too much too quickly.

✓ Keep good body mechanics in mind. Carefully lift heavy bags of dirt or mulch by keeping your back straight, bending at the knees, lifting with the strength of your legs and holding the bag as close to your body as possible. When you dig with a shovel, lift the dirt and turn your entire body before emptying the contents. Avoid lifting, twisting and throwing, especially if the soil is wet or clay.

✓ Alternate your activities so you use different muscle groups. Vary your activities to minimize the repetitive stress placed on your spine and muscles.

✓ Use a cushion, stool or small bench when weeding. This helps to avoid strain on your knees and lower back.

✓ Take frequent breaks. Minimize the chance of injury by taking breaks every 30 to 60 minutes. Take a few minutes to stretch, get a drink of water and evaluate what you want to do next.

✓ Stop gardening before you become fatigued. Most injuries occur when you are trying to do "one last thing." If you feel stiff, sore or experience pain, use ice on the affected area for 15 to 20 minutes. If the pain persists or becomes more intense, stop gardening and consult you health care provider.

All the Dirt About Dirt

To use topsoil or not to use topsoil, that is the question. You don't really need it and introducing it can run the risk of introducing nematodes to your property. Nematodes are microscopic wormy little things that can destroy the roots of some plants, causing them to die. Skip ahead to Chapter 6 for more information about nematodes.

A good planting mix is half black lava cinder and half macadamia nut compost. Be sure you use black cinder and not red cinder because the red is not a good growing medium for most plants. It's good to use as fill material for house pads and roads, however. You can also add purchased ingredients such as peat moss and vermiculite to "lighten" the soil and help it retain moisture. These ingredients are good for small projects, but the cost can mount if you are creating larger garden areas. Check your local phone book for soil delivery services: many companies will make a custom potting mix for you.

Topsoil or its equivalent (compost or cinder) is normally available by the yard. A yard refers to a cubic yard of material and it generally fills a normal size pickup truck's bed.

Rock Walls and Borders Are Nice, But...

With the raised bed method, you don't really need them. Although rock borders look attractive, a properly prepared raised bed doesn't need them to keep the soil in place. When we created some beds on top of lava mounds, we encircled them with rocks to keep the soil from escaping, but weeds will grow sideways from between the rocks and that makes it hard to keep the area looking tidy.

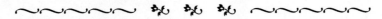

Wisdom About Building Your Garden from *The Herbalist's Garden*

Concentrate on building one step at a time; with perseverance, your grand vision will come to life. Remember that you are creating a legacy. The trees or herbs you plant today may become the enjoyment of generations beyond your lifetime.

Curves are more appealing than straight lines, and in gardens they're more productive. Gardens that are long and straight usually experience an energy loss at the ends of the rows, and plants there do not do as well. Round gardens maintain their energy throughout. The shape of your garden may also be dependent in part on the materials you are building your bed with. More fluid, curving shapes are easier to create when using stone or just raised mounds of soil.

Creating Your Raised Bed Garden

Start small! A 4-foot by 8-foot area will make a nice bed and won't require many ingredients. One of the basic principles of raised bed gardening is that you never want to step on the beds, so consider access when you're planning your raised bed: you should be able to reach into the middle of it from either side without stepping on the bed. This keeps it light and fluffy and doesn't compact the soil. Four feet wide is a good size. My orchard consists of two huge raised beds, each 4 feet wide and about 100 feet long, containing a mix of 45 yards of black cinder, mac nut compost and topsoil. Some of our garden beds are round: to allow access into these beds, we have created "keyhole" paths into the center of such beds.

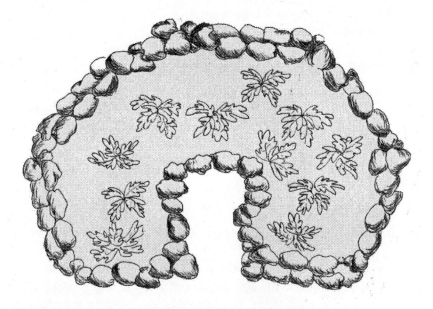

Illustration 4.1: Keyhole paths allow you to get into garden areas without stepping on the soil and compacting it.

☞ Here's all you need to know to create your first raised bed garden area:
1. If the weeds in an area are tall, mow them or weed whack them down as close to the ground as possible. No need to remove the cut weeds, pull them out by the roots, level the ground, or remove any rocks unless they're big ones.

2. Mark the area with stakes or string or simply sprinkle some flour to mark the edges.

Illustration 4.2: I'm completely sold on the lasagna bed method because it's fast and super simple.

3. Sprinkle the ground with bone meal and/or blood meal, or a bucket or two of compost (this adds nitrogen, which starts the process of reducing the carbon in the following layers). If you have seed-filled weeds that you want to get rid of, spread them here.
4. Cover the entire area with cardboard, newspaper, or old non-synthetic carpet, overlapping and leaving no holes for weeds. Water this layer well.
5. Spread a thin layer of manure or compost. Chicken manure works well: you can buy it at your garden supply store.
6. Spread alternating layers of peat moss, topsoil (if you want to use it) or black cinder, wood ashes, chopped leaves, grass clippings, and/or compost. You can vary the ingredients according to what you have: for example, you can use plant rubbish like chopped-up tree trimmings, pine needles, hay, old tomato stems, corn husks, small branches, etc. Water your new bed thoroughly.

7. Plan the depth of your bed depending on what you want to grow. Small plants such as herbs and flowers need little root space, while large plants like trees need much more. Keep this in mind while building your bed: it could be from 3 inches to 4 feet deep, like in my orchard.
8. Cover your bed with a cosmetic layer of chipped bark, leaves, or sawdust. Water everything well. The bed is done!
9. You can plant in your new bed right away. With your hand, dig a small hole to the base of the loose top mulch. Plant your plants close together, and mix the plants, as nature does. No need for straight rows, either.

Notes from the experts
✓ If your bed is shallow and you have built it on an area containing soil, root crops might not do well the first year, but by the second year, the ground underneath the bed will be revolutionized -- full of worms and microorganisms.
✓ Sprinkle a little bone meal and blood meal each year and add mulch and compost to keep up the level. The soil is so rich that you don't need to fertilize: the bed supplies everything your plants need.
✓ Water newly planted seedlings frequently.
✓ You don't need to rotate plants or rest the ground in this system.
✓ Because you never hoe or dig, you can plant closely.
✓ Don't bury sawdust or wood chips: leave them on top so the atmospheric nitrogen breaks down the wood. Keep the mulch loose and don't let it mat.
✓ Raised beds can provide a rich habitat for slugs, sowbugs, etc., so protect tiny seedlings with beer traps, diatomaceous earth or iron phosphate granules, sold as Sluggo. Refer to Chapter 6 for more information on natural insect control.

☞ NOTE: I never transplant tiny seedlings directly into my garden beds because of the danger presented by bugs and slugs. If you keep young plants in small pots until they're bigger, you'll be giving them a head start on a long and healthy life.

Drip Irrigation Is Simple and Conserves Water

Plants that are suited to your environment won't need you to provide a lot of watering, over and above what Mother Nature gives them for free. However, even the most drought tolerant native plants need to be watered on a regular basis their first year in the ground, until they're established.

If you live on the windward side of an island, many of your plants will rely on you to water them when Mother Nature decides not to provide rain for a couple of weeks or longer.

Most plants do best when they have a regular, consistent source of water. This can be hard in Hawai`i, especially on the windward sides of the islands, where we sometimes get many inches of rain in a short period of time, then droughts that can last a month or more. Drip irrigation is an easy, effective way of giving your plants water when and where they need it: at their root zone. Drip watering prevents wasted water in areas that don't need it, and by denying water, you can prevent habitats for weeds to flourish. When you use this method, the water from soaker hoses or emitters slowly drips around the base of plants and provides the optimum amount of water, with little or no wasteful runoff. All you have to do is turn on the hose that connects your drip system to a faucet and let it run for an hour or so when needed. You might even think about investing in a timer so you never have to remember to turn on the faucet. But don't forget to turn off your timer when it has rained a lot! Too much water is one of the main causes of plant death, and can be just as bad for a plant as not enough water.

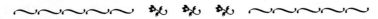

What is drip watering?

The concept of drip watering is simple: it's simply the slow, regular delivery of water directly to the root zone of your plants, keeping the ground moist but never saturated. Your plants receive the ideal amount of water at the ideal rate. They retain their proper air and water balance and avoid the stress and shock of the "drench and dry out" cycle associated with conventional watering methods. This results in optimum growth and healthy plants.

☞ Slow, even watering directly to the root zone will:

✓ Save water -- up to 70% less water than conventional sprinklers.

✓ Reduce plant stress -- resulting in earlier production, up to 49% faster growth, healthier and more beautiful plants and up to 84% greater yields.

✓ Reduce weed growth -- you only water the plants, not the weeds.

✓ Reduce water evaporation -- by as much as 70%.

✓ Prevent water run-off and soil erosion.

✓ Reduce thatch in your lawn, which results from shallow, infrequent watering.

From the Guide *Drip Watering Made Easy* by the Raindrip company

You can get really fancy with drip irrigation or you can keep it truly simple. It can appear confusing when you first shop for your drip watering system: there are so many little gadgets to learn about and choose from. But the basics of drip watering are really just the following ingredients:

✓ 1/2 inch black hose that you cut into the correct lengths and punch holes in for emitters and other parts, such as 1/4-inch hose.

✓ A hole punch, specially made for piercing the black hose used in drip irrigation.

✓ Emitters, which are small plastic pieces you plug into the black hose. They disperse water at a determined number of gallons per hour.

Illustration 4.3a: These drip irrigation parts are: (top) hole punch; (middle) emitters; (bottom) 1/2-inch black poly hose.

✓ Connectors, which can be straight, angled or "T" shaped. Just plug them into the holes you have punched in the main black hose and then connect other things to them, such as:

✓ 1/4-inch hose that you can weave through your plants, connecting emitters where they are needed.

✓ 1/4-inch laser-drilled soaker line is my favorite because you don't have to fuss with emitters at all. The only disadvantage is that the small holes are spaced every six inches, so you don't have as much control over where the water comes out. But you

Illustration 4.3b: Barbed fittings can be T-shaped (top), 90-degree corners (middle), and straight (bottom).

can connect 1/4-inch non-soaker line to the drilled hose with straight connectors for areas where you don't want to water, such as over paths.

✓ Sprinklers and misters are fun to use but are not necessary. I feel that they negate some of the benefits of keeping your irrigation water at the base of the plants.

✓ Flow restrictor is the name of a little plastic piece you insert at the beginning of your system, at the faucet end of the line. This regulates how much water goes into the system: you can buy them in different sizes that will allow more or less water to pump into the hoses.

Drip watering kits make it easy to create your first system

For your first drip system, consider buying a kit that includes all the pieces you'll need to set up a small, basic system. Kits are a good introduction to drip watering and include all the directions you will need to get started and easily create your first system. Maybe you'll get hooked on creating your own system with drippers and emitters and soaker lines going all over your yard: you can even install drip watering for potted and hanging plants. Then all you need to do is turn on the faucet and sit back and enjoy your bountiful garden instead of running around with a watering can and worrying about whether you have given each plant the water that it needs. Check your local garden center or garden supply catalogs. Our Resources Appendix lists the phone number and web site for the Gardener's Supply Catalog, and there are many other sources on the Internet for garden-related equipment.

Soaker hoses simplify drip watering even more

There's an even easier way to apply many of the benefits of drip irrigation. My simple solution to all of the hoses, emitters, connectors and such is to simply use soaker hoses. You can buy them at any garden store or garden department at large stores such as Wal-Mart. They're relatively inexpensive, too. The normal length of a soaker hose is 50 feet: you can connect up to three of them together for widespread coverage of your plants in an area. If you have more than 150 feet of hoses, it usually results in significantly reduced dripping at the end of the line.

Because water oozes out from the entire soaker hose, it is not as efficient a use of your water as "proper" drip irrigation systems provide. I like this method because it's easy to set up, and it does give a more efficient way of watering your plants than squirting your plants with a hose or using sprinklers. And the problem of clogged emitters, which can happen in time with a proper drip system, is nonexistent with a soaker hose system. I've found that soaker hoses survive about five years before they start to spring leaks.

☞ **Hints and tips**

✓ How often should you water your plants with a soaker system? I typically run my soaker hoses every other day for about an hour at a time when the weather is dry.

✓ If you want to customize your soaker hose system, just buy some hose repair pieces at your garden center. Then you can cut the soaker hose, insert a plastic mender piece, and to the other end of the mender connect a piece of regular garden hose. This is useful if you need to string your soaker hose across a path: the water flows through the regular hose and doesn't get wasted on the path. This method also works well if you don't need the entire length of a soaker hose. Just be sure to close up the end of the line with an end cap that comes with each soaker hose you buy.

✓ If you only have one water faucet in your yard, no problem! You can buy plastic or metal "Y" connectors to automatically turn your faucet into two faucets, each of which can have a separate hose attached to it. Simple switches turn each side off and on. You can get fancy with these and add more than one connector to your faucet if you like. Some of the soaker hose systems we have set up in Hiʻiaka's Garden have five or six connectors and lots of hoses running off of them like crazy spaghetti. You can buy "Y" connectors at the same store where you get your hose repair pieces.

✓ For both types of drip systems -- "proper" drip systems and soaker hose systems -- the hoses can pop up and not lie flat on the ground when you first lay them down. "Earth staples" are a good solution to this problem. They are long, U-shaped metal stakes that you simply insert into the ground at intervals to secure your hoses, wherever they're needed. Earth staples are available through the Gardener's Supply catalog and at garden stores. (Turn to the Resources Appendix.)

Super Simple Guide To Starting Seeds and Cuttings

So many people I've talked to admit to being afraid of failure when it comes to starting seeds from scratch. Perhaps they have had unsuccessful experiences in the past or simply don't know where to begin the process.

In this section, I'll give a quick and easy primer for how to start seeds and take cuttings to make more plants.

What are heirloom varieties?

Tomatoes are red, corn is yellow, and string beans are green -- right? Not necessarily true! Common commercial varieties of string beans are green, yes, and that's what we mostly see and eat. "But they can also be purple, maroon, or yellow. Tomatoes can be orange, yellow or purple. Many familiar fruits and vegetables grow in a rainbow of colors," says Rosalind Creasy in her book *Blue Potatoes, Orange Tomatoes.* Just look through a seed catalog, like Richter's Herbs, to discover 40 naturally occurring varieties of basil, or the Thyme Garden's to discover 70 varieties of thyme alone. The 2004 Seeds of Change catalog lists 50 varieties of tomatoes! How does an ambitious gardener make a decision about which seeds to buy? Well, that's where the fun begins!

Do you want a tomato with a thicker skin that will discourage fruit flies? It already exists: just read the heirloom seed catalogs' descriptions and order a pack of seeds through one of them. You won't have much success in finding heirloom varieties at your local garden center or nursery because most people want familiar varieties and that's what the companies who provide plants and seeds to retail nurseries concentrate their efforts on. So if you're interested in trying some wonderfully tasty or beautiful old-fashioned varieties of plants, you'll need to become a bit of a gardening Sherlock Holmes. Our Resources Appendix lists a number of seed companies that specialize in heirlooms, so check them out and maybe you'll discover a wonderfully delicious purple tomato that does well in your microclimate.

☞ Starting seeds

Putting seeds into soil feels almost like a religion to me... what power I feel when I participate in a life-creating exercise! Most seed packets or seed catalogs include specific instructions for starting the particular seed contained inside the envelope, but here are some general rules, hints and tips.

You'll need these items to begin your seed-starting adventure:
✓ Seeds (obviously)
✓ Potting mix, which can be purchased mixes (like ProMix or Super Soil) or a blend you make yourself with peat moss, compost, vermiculite, black cinder, and so on.
✓ Flats or large, shallow pots. The black plastic flats you can get at nursery stores for a dollar or less work just fine.

✓ Perhaps a trowel or shovel and gloves, if you want them.
  The Hi'iaka's Garden recipe for potting mix is:
  For a 20-gallon trash can, mix the following in a wheelbarrow:
✓ 1/2 bag of a 2-cubic foot of purchased potting mix
✓ 7 quarts of peat moss (a 4-cup measuring cup equals 1 quart)
✓ 3.5 gallons of black cinder (use a 1-gallon black plastic nursery pot
  to measure)
✓ 4 quarts of Vermiculite or Perlite (gives the mix porosity and helps
  to retain water)

This mix makes about six flats and seven gallon pots. We use it for starting seeds and for all of our potted plants. If you don't have one of the ingredients, chances are your seeds will start just fine without it.

Super simple seed planting steps

Because of the humidity in Hawai'i, many kinds of seeds go "pau" (bad) fairly quickly. I always try to use seeds very soon after I buy them and also use an entire seed packet whenever I start any seeds. If all of them do well, you'll have plenty for yourself and lots of extras to give to friends and relatives as nice little gifts from Mother Earth. And if worst comes to worst and you simply can't find homes for all of your keikis, just add them to your mulch or compost pile. Continue reading for our simple directions for starting seeds.

1. The first thing to do after making your potting mix is to fill your flats or pots. Make sure that you give the seeds plenty of room: if a seed packet has 300 seeds in it, for example, you'll want to use an entire flat. Some packets have very few seeds in them: in this case, you can use a black plastic nursery pot. I prefer the 1/2-gallon size for many seeds because it gives plenty of root space and uses less potting soil than a gallon pot. After you fill your flat or pot with soil to about 1 inch of the top, gently pat it down to compress it a bit. Then give it a gentle shower with the hose.

2. How deep do you plant seeds? In general, the bigger the seed the deeper you need to plant it. For example, seeds for green beans are quite large and need to be planted at least 1/2 inch deep, while carrot seeds are tiny and should be planted with just a scattering of potting mix over them. Some seeds are called "light-dependent germinators," which just means that they need sunlight in order to sprout. Your seed packet will mention this if it's a requirement. In

this case, all you need to do is scatter the seeds over the soil surface and then gently pat them into the soil with your palm.

3. For larger seeds, poke holes of the correct depth into your potting mix. You can use a screwdriver or pencil to make your holes. Then drop one seed into each hole. Cover with soil, gently pat the soil down with your palm, and then water it again. Place the flat or pot in a protected place where it will get plenty of sun. I prefer to put my seed starting pots on a table so any ground-crawling critters like snails and slugs are less likely to find my succulent salad to feast upon.

4. For smaller seeds, scatter the seeds on top of the soil in your flat or pot. Then sprinkle a small amount of potting mix over the entire surface. Pat it down gently with your palm and give it a gentle shower. Place the flat or pot in a protected place where it will get plenty of sun.

☞ **NOTE:** Some instructions might mention that it's good idea to cover your seeds with clear plastic to keep them moist and warm. However, I have found that this can cause new sprouts to burn, shrivel and die. For the most part, it's a little too warm here to make covering your seeds with plastic necessary. Be sure to water them frequently, especially if they're small seeds, because the surface layer of the soil can dry out quickly.

Starting cuttings

This is a great, easy way to get free plants from many of the varieties you already have, and it's also a great way to meet your neighbors. You can't cut off the top of a palm tree and put it in soil and expect it to form roots (actually, this will kill a palm tree), but you can start other plants like mint and many others by simply cutting off a sprig and putting it into a glass of water or a little pot with some soil in it.

Use the potting mix recipe that's in the seed starting section of this chapter, but instead of using gallon or 1/2 gallon pots and flats, you can use smaller pots if you have just a couple of cuttings you want to start.

Super simple steps for starting cuttings

1. With clippers or scissors, cut 6-inch to 8-inch pieces of the plant you want to root. For most plants, take green, fleshy, succulent new growth that does not have flowers at the tips. Woody branches are harder to start. You may get only a 50% success rate with all cuttings, depending on the plant, so be sure to start more than you need. If you get too many, potted plants are always welcome gifts for your plant-loving friends and family.

2. Strip off the lower leaves, leaving a nice stalk or trunk on each piece.

3. If you want, you can dip each cutting into a product like Rootone, which is a rooting hormone that helps the plant develop roots. Rootone is not considered strictly organic, so you might want to keep that consideration in mind.

4. Fill small pots with your potting mix, water them well, and then poke a hole that's large enough for each cutting.

5. Carefully place each cutting into the hole you have made. Then gently press soil around the base.

6. Sprinkle with water, being careful not to displace any of your cuttings from the soil.

7. Put your finished pots in an area that does not get hot direct sunlight. Keep the pots moist, but not swimming in water.

8. In a short time, you'll know which of your cuttings are going to survive because they will continue to stand upright and stay green. They might even start to get some new growth at the tips. You can gently empty the soil out of the pot if you want to see if the plant has sprouted roots. When the roots start appearing at the hole at the bottom of your pots, it's time to transplant them.

☞ **NOTE:** There are other methods of starting plants, such as air layering, that we won't cover in this Guide. This information is available in many books, so if you're interested, a trip to your library or bookstore is always a fun adventure.

Super simple steps for transplanting young plants

After your seeds have sprouted and the young plants are two to three inches tall, it's time to transplant them into pots of their own. I do not recommend that you transplant keikis directly into your garden beds when they're still small and fragile because so many insects and other critters can eat them or stomp on them. They're just keikis, after all!

The same thing goes for young, newly rooted cuttings: after they have formed a good number of roots, transplant the survivors into larger pots. When they are large and robust, that's the time to transplant them into your garden.

☞ Here are the simple transplanting steps:

1. When I transplant small plants, I use three-inch plastic pots or grow bags that are available at any nursery or garden center.
2. Fill your pots or bags about 2/3 full with your potting mix.
3. Water your pots or bags well.
4. Carefully uproot your keikis with a small trowel or weeding tool. Be sure to transplant them right away.
5. Pick up each plant by its leaves, not the stem.
6. Carefully place the keiki plant into the 2/3 full pot or bag.
7. Hold the plant upright by its leaves with one hand and with the other, gently scoop in more potting mix around the base of the plant.
8. When the pot is full, gently pat down the soil mix around the base of the plant.
9. Water gently and keep your keikis out of direct sunlight for the first few days to avoid transplant shock. You can use products like Vitamin B-1 or Super Thrive to reduce transplant shock, but if you have done the transplanting gently and keep your keikis out of the hot sun, most types of plants should be all right without needing special products to help them.

When your plants are big and strong in a month or two (or longer, depending on the plant), that's the time you can safely transplant them into your garden. Just be certain to protect them against bugs and critters while they're still young, and keep them well watered if it doesn't rain.

Chapter 5
Making Free Fertilizer From
Mother Nature's Bounty

When you go for a hike in the Hawaiian wilderness, whom do you think is fertilizing all of the `ohi`a trees, kului, `a`ali`i and other wild native plants? No one. No one human, that is! The plants take care of themselves: their leaves drop to the ground and form a natural mulch that decomposes to nourish the parent plant. If they endure dry spells, they are selected, in the Darwinian scheme of things. Remember "survival of the fittest"? That's how I view the plants in my garden: the hardy ones that are well adapted to my microclimate are the ones that survive. If a plant doesn't survive, it tells me that plant didn't like it in my garden; it does not mean that I am a lousy gardener!

This chapter is a "must read" if you think that all plants need you and "Triple 16" fertilizer. You'll learn how to easily create natural nourishment for plants through composting and mulching and perhaps you might even adopt a more philosophical attitude about the life and death of plants in your garden.

Fertilizing With the Help of Mother Nature

Living in harmony with Mother Nature is so much easier than trying to *make* things grow and happen in the garden. I like to tell visitors to my garden that I am definitely NOT the one in control, because it just isn't possible to fight Nature and win. If you use homegrown, natural methods of feeding and nourishing your plants, you are contributing to the ageless tradition of living compatibly with the Earth, just as your great-grandparents and their ancestors did.

"In nature, living things die, and their death allows life to be reborn. Both animals and plants die on forest floors and in meadows to be composted by time, water, microorganisms, sun, and air to produce a soil improved in structure and nutrients. Organic plant growing follows nature's example. Leaves, grass, weeds, prunings, spiders, birds, trees, and plants should be returned to the soil and reused--not thrown away. Composting is an important way to recycle such elements as carbon, nitrogen, magnesium, sulfur, calcium, potash and trace minerals. These elements are all necessary to maintain the biological cycles of life that exist in nature. Composting has a dual function. It improves the structure of the soil and provides nutrients for plant growth. Fewer nutrients leach out in a soil with adequate organic matter. Improved structure and nourishment produce a healthy soil. A healthy soil produces healthy plants better able to resist insect and disease attacks."

--*How to Grow More Vegetables... Than You Ever Thought Possible On Less Land Than You Can Imagine,* by John Jeavons

Permaculture Techniques Offer Many Creative Solutions

A permaculture movement is happening in Hawai`i. If you're not familiar with the concept of permaculture, it is simply "permanent agriculture," a method of creating and growing gardens that are compatible with the earth, convenient for the humans who use them, and sustainable for providing food for humans, animals and other plants. In his groundbreaking book, *Introduction to Permaculture,* Bill Mollison writes, "permaculture is a design system for creating sustainable human environments. On one level, permaculture deals with plants, animals, buildings and infrastructure. However, permaculture is not about these elements themselves, but rather about the relationships we can create between them by the way we place them in the landscape."

Hack, whack and stack

Perhaps your community has a yard waste recycling program that allows you to dispose of tree branches, grass clippings, bags of leaves and any other plant material you might collect while pruning and cleaning up your property. If it does, I encourage you to use such services. But why go to the extra trouble of hauling your yard waste to a special place when the plants in your very own garden can benefit from it?

Permaculture pioneer Ano Tarletz, of GaiaYoga Gardens on the Big Island, coined the term "hack, whack and stack." (Turn to the Resources Appendix for Ano's contact info.) This permaculture technique is easier than traditional composting, provides nutrients for your valued plants and gives them a rich food source from other plants that you need to control. It's a simple type of passive composting. All you need to do is to "coppice" plants and trees that you don't want getting too tall. To do this, you saw or "hack" off the top several feet of a plant like wiliwili. Then "whack" the pieces into one- to two-foot pieces and "stack" them at the base of the tree or plant you want to nurture. Wiliwili is great for this: many people grow it as a natural fence or privacy barricade. It grows quickly, it's tall and straight, and it even gets attractive flowers in season. It has many valuable nutrients like nitrogen, so that means you can use it to help feed other plants.

When I first saw this practice being done at a farm on the Big Island, I thought it looked a little messy, and it can, especially if you're doing it in your home garden. If you've seen palm fronds stacked at the base of coconut palms, you'll understand what the hack, whack and stack method can look like. To tame the appearance a little, you can chop the pieces into smaller parts and perhaps cover them with lawn clippings, sawdust or leaves that you have raked up. It will eventually break down and create nice, rich humus around the base of the plant that you want to nourish. And it will look tidy when the in-laws visit.

Composting and Mulching

We are a nation of plenty and we should give thanks for that. Imagine... you can easily make your own free fertilizer by turning food scraps and yard waste into compost that will benefit fruit and vegetable crops and keep on giving you more food.

Even if you don't have a lot of property, you can help the environment and our too full landfills by building a small compost pile to take care of your moldy bread and wormy papayas. An added bonus of composting your food waste is that you won't see any more maggots in your garbage cans! Read on to learn about several simple methods of creating an abundant, environmentally friendly, non-stinky compost pile.

Creating a simple compost pile

It's so simple to create a compost pile that you don't even need to build one. Here are three ways of composting that you can do for very little money or for free.

Method 1: Do it on the ground

Just pile your plant material on the ground. I like to start with a layer of broken-up twigs, perhaps some old tomato plants, green bean or squash vines. Then follow these super simple steps:

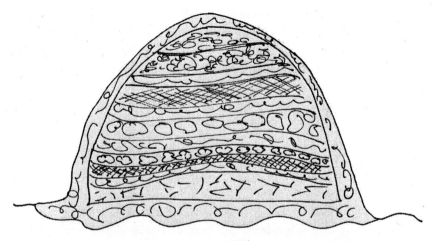

Illustration 5.1: You can build a traditional compost pile by simply dumping layers of organic material on top of each other.

1. Dump your leaves, twigs and other plant material into an area about four feet by four feet around. I start my compost piles on top of weedy pahoehoe lava, but if you have soil or even lawn, all the better.
2. Add other organic materials like grass clippings.
3. Toss your food scraps on top of this and then add some cinder, wood ashes, or straw. Whatever you have works fine.
4. If you want, you can cover your pile loosely with black plastic to keep out four-footed critters. But it's not necessary. If you use it, poke some holes in the plastic to provide some airflow -- this will help to break down the compost materials. It will also prevent anaerobic decomposition from happening (this can cause a compost pile to smell nasty). The holes will allow a little rain to get in -- a compost pile needs some moisture in order to do its work.
5. When you get more food scraps, uncover your pile and add them, making sure to cover them with more cinder, ashes, leaves, or whatever. Or just bury them a few inches deep.
6. As the final layer, spread some dry plant material (dry leaves, straw, etc.) on top of your pile. Or you can use torn-up newspaper.

The John Jeavons recipe for compost uses alternating layers of dry vegetation for the carbon that is needed for composting to happen and green vegetation, for nitrogen, interspersed with kitchen waste, peat moss, and so forth. This combination of carbon and nitrogen is the key to successful composting: the proportions don't need to be exact, as long as you include alternating layers of dry brown plant material and fresh green plant material. I'll sometimes do some pruning of my invasive guavas while I'm building a new compost pile, then strip off the leaves and use them for a green layer. Two birds with one stone: I do some needed pruning to keep an invasive species under control, and make good use of the results for fertilizing my other plants and garden beds.

Stick piles use larger plant parts

What should you do with the sticks that you wind up with after you strip leaves off of the branches? You can "hack, whack and stack" them around the base of other trees and plants, or you can devote an out-of-the-way area of your yard to a "stick pile." A stick pile is simply a pile of branches and other woody or weedy materials that you don't want to chop up--for whatever reason (laziness is usually mine!). For aesthetic reasons, you might want to cover your stick pile with black plastic, landscape fabric or shade cloth. I like shade cloth because it's good looking and it lets rainwater get through to help accelerate the breakdown process. If you use black plastic, be sure to poke some holes in it to prevent anaerobic decomposition.

Method 2: Poultry wire

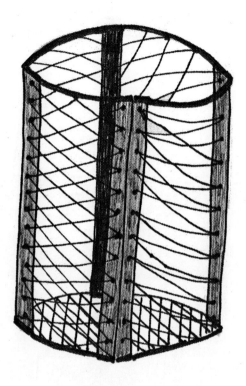

Illustration 5.2: This wire compost bin is a good way to keep your compost tidy.

With the second method, you use poultry wire. It's tidy and doesn't require a cover of black plastic. I bought $14 worth of poultry wire, which is small steel mesh fencing. It made a cylinder 3 feet in diameter and four feet high. I used 6-inch pieces of metal clothesline to attach it to itself at the top, middle and bottom, secured it with sticks into the ground, and started tossing in food scraps and the other items that go into a compost pile. Simple, clean, compact. As with other types of compost piles, you should alternate layers of dry plant material with fresh green leaves or other fresh plant material. The stuff on the bottom will be ready to use within three months. Just unlatch your bottom latch and shovel some out, leaving the uncomposted materials on the top.

Method 3: Commercial composters

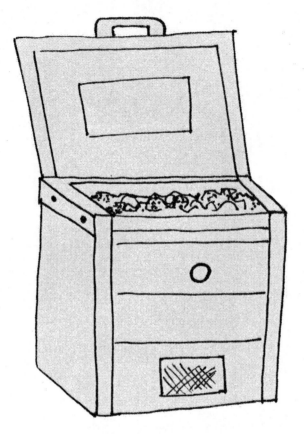

Illustration 5.3: This purchased compost bin is good looking and super simple to use.

    With method number three, you use a commercial composter. The price can be $20 or more, depending on the size and how fancy it is. Check the Gardener's Supply Catalog (www.gardeners.com) for a good selection of commercially available composters. Black plastic composting cubes are great because they look tidy and attractive and have no odors because of the fitting lid. You assemble this type of composter by popping it together then placing it anywhere you want. It's almost cute. And because it has a tight lid, you don't have to worry about adding a layer of straw, cinder or leaves every time you add food scraps. With this method of composting, you open one of the lower doors and scoop out finished compost from the bottom of the heap when you need it.

Turn it if you want

After your compost pile is about three or four feet high, stop adding things to it and let it "cook" for two or three months. This is the simple part: just cover it and forget about it. The composting gurus say to turn your pile periodically, but sometimes I forget. It turns into nice, fertile compost anyway. When you choose not to turn your compost pile, this is called the "passive" method, meaning that you do nothing--the compost process happens all by itself. When you turn your compost, that's called the "active" method. Compost happens faster when you turn it once every week or two. When your compost is ready, it will look like rich, crumbly soil and will smell pleasant and earthy. You can then dig it into your garden beds, surround plants with it as mulch, or plant a tree right there in your finished pile.

Do's and don'ts of composting

You can compost so many different kinds of materials--it's a great way to recycle in your own home and back yard.

Here are some examples of nitrogen-rich materials that you can and should use in your compost. Thanks to Piper Selden of Recycle Hawai`i for the following information:

- ✓ Grass clippings and disease-free plants
- ✓ Weeds before they form seeds
- ✓ All fruit and vegetable matter, including seeds
- ✓ Egg shells and nut shells
- ✓ Tea bags with the staples removed
- ✓ Coffee grounds and filters
- ✓ Seaweed, but rinse it with fresh water first to get rid of the salt, which can damage plants when you use it

☞ **NOTE:** Seeds from tomatoes and papayas will almost always sprout after you use your finished compost in the garden. Although compost piles heat up, they never get hot enough to kill certain kinds of seeds. This can be a blessing... or not! The first time I used my homemade compost in Hawai`i, I ended up with a carpet of baby papaya trees. Perhaps you could start up a papaya nursery with all those keikis, but I weeded them out and threw them back into the compost pile.

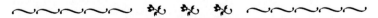

☞ Here are some examples of carbon-rich materials that you can and should use in your compost:
- Trimmings from trees and shrubs
- Dry grass clippings and leaves that you have raked up
- Strips of newspaper (yes, the ink is okay, as it's soy-based nowadays)
- Shredded paper plates, paper towels and napkins, especially if they have food waste on them

☞ Never include these items in your compost pile:
- Meat, fat, bones and fish
- Dairy products
- Cooking oil
- Pet litter or feces (however, manure from farm animals is not only okay, it's an excellent addition to compost)
- Human feces (may contain pathogens and is not recommended for backyard composting)
- Ashes from charcoal used in your barbecue; ashes from wood fires are very good to use in compost
- Glossy paper, such as magazines and newspaper inserts

Composting with wonderful worms

Although the idea of worms might sound yucky to some people, worm composting is very clean, odor-free and simple. You can keep a worm bin under your kitchen sink or on your lanai if you have qualms about worms sharing your indoor living space. But don't worry--they won't escape from the bin!

Worm manure is called worm castings, and it's the end product of worm composting. All it takes is a teaspoonful of castings in a gallon of water, and you have a super-duper compost tea that you can use to water all your plants. Read on for our recipe!

☞ **NOTE:** It is against Hawai`i state law to import compost worms from another state. The worms you must use for worm composting are called red wigglers, and there is a local Hawaiian variety of this worm that you can purchase from reliable sources in Hawai`i. Piper Selden of Hawai`i Rainbow Worms in Hilo has them for sale. You can reach her at (808) 959-7257 or visit her web site at www. hawaiirainbowworms.com.

How to build a simple worm bin

Piper Selden gives these instructions for building a super simple worm bin:

1. Use three plastic storage bins with snap-on covers. They can be 7 inches by 12 inches or the larger size available at drug stores and hardware stores.
2. Drill a lot of small holes in the bottoms of two bins and along the top edge of both bins. Piper uses a rotary drill with a 1/8-inch bit. Make sure that the holes are big enough for your worms because later on when you swap the order of the bins, they will crawl up into the bin above.
3. Paint the outside of your two drilled bins a dark color with a non-toxic type of paint.
4. Fill one of the bins in which you have drilled holes half full of the following: damp strips of newspaper and/or boxboard (example: cereal boxes). Just pack it loosely.
5. Stack the bins so the one with no holes is on the bottom and the one with the shredded paper is on top. This is also the bin that will hold your worms. The third bin goes in the middle and will be empty.
6. Add your worms to the top bin that has the shredded paper and tuck them in under the "bedding." Be sure to keep them in a place that does not get hot, direct sun.
7. Feed your worms kitchen scraps such as papaya rind, banana peels, or the core of a tomato. They won't eat a lot, so don't overload the bin with too much food at first.
8. Don't feed the worms anything more for about 2 weeks: this will put them into a reproductive phase, which will help to populate your bin.
9. After 2 weeks, feed your worms every other day. Tuck the food scraps under the bedding to prevent fruit flies.
10. Keep the compost material moist but not soggy and turn it every once in a while to keep the temperature at a bearable level for your wigglers.
11. After about 3 months, take the active bin and put it in the middle position. In the empty bin that used to be in the middle, add new bedding made from damp strips of newspaper and boxboard.
12. Add food scraps to the new top layer. Within 2 weeks to one month, the worms from the middle bin will have crawled up into your new top bin. You can then use the worm castings in the middle bin.

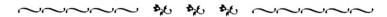

☞ **NOTE:** If you would prefer to purchase an affordable ready-made worm bin complete with local starter worms, you can contact Piper's company, Hawai`i Rainbow Worms, at (808) 959-7257.

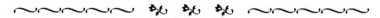

Recipe for worm compost "tea"

My favorite way to use worm compost is to make compost tea:

1. Put 1 teaspoonful of your finished worm compost into a 1-gallon bucket or watering can.
2. Fill it with water and let it sit for no longer than 24 hours.
3. Water your prized plants that you want to fertilize with the worm compost tea and watch them respond with vibrant growth!

"In place" composting

When we first created our orchard in 2001, we encircled each tree with a 6-foot long cage of 2-inch steel mesh fencing to protect it from marauding dogs or (Heaven forbid) wild pigs, wind, or anything else that might threaten a young tree. As we pruned and weeded in the new orchard, the wire cages provided a handy place to "hack, whack and stack" the leaves, branches, and other plant material that we might have otherwise discarded or gone to the trouble of hauling to one of our "proper" compost piles. The stuff stayed inside the circular cage and formed nice mulch for the tree, and then eventually it broke down and contributed to a nice nutritious, loamy bed. I call this method "in place" composting because it conveniently places the compost material where it is needed: right at the base of the plant you want to nourish.

Creating an "in place" pile

☞ To create an "in place" compost pile, follow these super simple steps:

1. Cut approximately 6 feet of wide gauge steel mesh fencing (sometimes called "hog wire") or any size chicken wire.
2. Attach the wire to itself by looping the cut ends over and around the wire at the other side of your cut piece: you only need to attach it at the top and bottom and perhaps at one spot in the middle.
3. Place your finished "cage" over the plant you want to protect and nourish.
4. If you're using chicken wire, you'll need to provide stakes to hold the wire in place. Weave two wood or metal stakes through the wire at

opposite sides of the circle it forms, then pound them into the ground around the tree or other plant you want to nourish.

5. Every time you rake, weed, or prune in the general vicinity, drop the leaves, weeds, small branches, or whatever you have into the cage.

In time, the materials you have added to this compost pile will break down and will nourish your prized plant. Even before the compost material completely breaks down, it will help to keep down weeds, keep the soil around your plant cool and moist, and benefit the plant in general.

"Next to" composting

Another method of composting that we have developed at Hi`iaka's Garden is what I call "next to" composting. This method is working nicely in the area just behind our orchard, where we dump palm fronds, seedy weeds, old cardboard that we pick up from other areas, and other stuff and junk that we don't have the time or motivation to chop up for the regular compost pile.

☞ **NOTE:** The "next to" technique works best if you have a fairly large amount of property.

Creating a "next to" pile

☞ It's simple to create a "next to" compost pile:

1. Lay branches and other plant material on the ground next to an area that it will serve to fertilize and nourish after it breaks down. It's a passive composting technique: that is, you don't need to turn it. My "next to" piles are generally long and narrow.

2. After you get some stuff piled up, cover it with black plastic.

3. Poke several holes in the plastic with a pitchfork or spading fork to allow some rainwater to get into the pile and to give it air circulation.

4. As you gather more ungainly plant material or dig out seedy weeds from other parts of your property, you can lift the plastic and add it to the cooking pile. It will take longer to break down these larger materials than a regular compost pile, but in time they will decompose and will form a nice, loamy pile.

5. When your "next to" pile has broken down, shovel or rake the resulting treasure around your prized plants that live next to it.

The chicken method of recycling food waste

If you live in a community that allows you to keep a couple of chickens, they're great for getting rid of your kitchen scraps. I keep a large plastic jar right on my kitchen counter, into which I put all food scraps except fish, chicken and meat bones. It fills up every day with orange peels, wilted lettuce, papaya rinds and seeds, two bites of sandwich I didn't have room for, etc. Instead of putting my kitchen scraps into the compost pile, I like to give them to the chickens: they're adorable little creatures that provide not only nutritious eggs but incredibly rich manure. What they don't eat rots in their yard, and then every couple of months we rake out the muck and throw it into a compost pile. This method is simple and satisfies me because it's such a beautiful "full circle" approach to living lightly on the Earth.

Using your finished compost

I wish I had more compost because it makes such wonderful mulch to put around my plants. Mulch is so important in the garden because it keeps the soil cooler and moister than if it were bare, and the nutrients in the compost leach out into the soil and enrich my cherished plants.

☞ There are several ways to use your completed compost.

✓ Mulching is the super simple way to provide nutrition for your plants. When you have rich, crumbly compost, it's the perfect material for using as mulch. Ano Tarletz, of GaiaYoga Gardens on the Big Island, says that we should strive to be "mulch millionaires," a goal I feared I would never attain when I first began my garden. It does take time to create compost and other types of mulch that your plants will appreciate, but in time, you'll start seeing mulch opportunities all around you. What about all those messy leaves from the invasive guava that perhaps you rake up and take to the dump? They make excellent mulch--by using them, you are building your "mulch wealth" quotient. You can add dried leaves such as guava to your compost pile for the carbon content that it needs, or you can use them directly in your garden as mulch.

✓ Digging compost into the soil is a good practice when you are creating a new garden bed or re-invigorating an older bed in which the plants have lived out their lifespan. Just spread a thick layer of compost on top of your garden bed and dig it in with your shovel or spading fork.

✓ Compost tea is simple to make and fun to use. I like the name "poop soup." It's just a liquid fertilizer that helps to revitalize your plants. It's very safe to use and you can actually control the strength of your compost tea by adding more or less water.

☞ To make compost tea just follow these super simple steps:
   1. Half fill a bucket with finished compost
   2. Then fill it up with water. I use a plastic garbage can if I want to make a large quantity of compost tea.
   3. Stir your mixture and let it sit overnight.
   4. Then simply water your plants with it.
   5. After the liquid is gone, you can make more tea from the leftover compost another couple of times with equally good results.
   6. Use the remnants of the compost as mulch.
✓ Compost makes an excellent addition to purchased potting mixes, but don't use it for starting seeds because it can contain a fungus that's bad for seedlings.

Take a class

There are starting to be good classes on how to build compost piles and create your own natural fertilizer. Keep your eyes open for announcements in your local newspaper or check with a botanical garden near your home. If your community has an Outdoor Circle group or community garden, they often teach or sponsor composting classes. On the Big Island, Recycle Hawai`i is doing a great job sponsoring classes. Check the Resources Appendix for contact info.

Chapter 6
Getting to Know Your Insect Friends and Foes

When you take a walk outdoors in Hawai`i, you won't find anyone wandering through the jungles or forests with a spray can to control the insects that are simply sustaining their lifecycles by munching on plants. Insects form an important part of the ecology of gardens--however we feel about them, it's a good idea to learn to recognize and deal with some of the most common bugs you're likely to see in your own garden.

You'll want to read this chapter if you think that all bugs are bad bugs and that all plants need you to help them fight off nasty insects. You'll learn to use some safe, natural remedies for bothersome insect pests and how to tell the difference between our insect friends and foes.

When visitors express alarm that a plant such as my ma`o hau hele, or native yellow hibiscus, has bug-chewed leaves, they often ask, "what are you going to do about this problem?" I reply, "nothing. The plant is healthy; it is putting out new growth, forming flowers, and then seeds. It is successfully achieving its mission in life, which is to reproduce itself. In nature, there is a harmonious balance between plants and insects." One attitude that I have let go of in gardening is my perfectionism--if a plant has a few chewed-up leaves, it's all right with me--I don't expect all of my plants to be beauty queens! Ever since I've been an organic gardener, I've had the attitude that I should grow a little more than I need so there's "some for them, some for me." If a plant is valuable and is in danger of dying from an invasion of insect pests, I can then use a number of organically tried and true methods for controlling those pests.

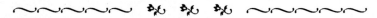

A healthy soil produces healthy plants better able to resist insect and disease attacks. Most insects look for sick plants to eat. The best way to control insects and diseases in plants is with a living, healthy soil rather than with poisons, which kill beneficial soil life.
--*How to Grow More Vegetables... Than You Ever Thought Possible On Less Land Than You Can Imagine,* by John Jeavons

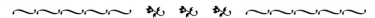

The Buddhist Approach Toward All Living Things

I changed my attitude about killing bugs and slugs one day when a Buddhist nun visited the garden. I was surprised when she avoided stepping on a line of ants, saying under her breath, "mustn't kill them." At the end of our tour I asked her if, from the Buddhist perspective, it would be all right for me to gather slugs and throw them into the chicken coop for those critters to feast on. She replied, "oh, no... you must take them to a wild place and release them!" Right, I thought, as if they're not going to crawl back onto my prized plants. But I did change my habits after that and decided to let the chickens run free part of the day: now when they find and eat slugs on their own, that's all right and makes me feel more in harmony with nature. Although I still continue to "hand pick" (or squish) certain troublesome insects, I always remember the wisdom of my gentle visitor.

Why Shouldn't I Use Chemical Pesticides?

Shunyam Nirav includes a tidy little list of good reasons for avoiding the use of chemical remedies for insect pests in his book, *Hawaiian Organic Growing Guide*. Here's what he says:

✓ Pesticides accumulate in the environment, which affects humans as well as other species. "An alarming study showed that virtually all mother's milk in Hawai`i contains traces of agricultural chemicals."
✓ In many cases, insects have become resistant to chemicals, so they just don't work.
✓ Chemical pest control is expensive. You must use them year after year, usually in increasing amounts.
✓ Chemical pesticides can also kill beneficial insects such as honeybees that are so important to pollination. Some of them also kill insect parasites and predators such as wasps, praying mantids, and other insects that naturally control the populations of destructive insects.

Controlling Those Darn Bugs the Natural Way

Just as with fertilizing the natural way, I believe in natural pest control--or no pest control at all. Preventive maintenance of your garden is the first step toward keeping problem insect pests to a minimum. Here is some good advice from Rodale Books' booklet *Good Bug, Bad Bug*:

✓ Build up your soil. Adding compost works wonders to improve the health of your plants. If you overfertilize with a nitrogen-rich fertilizer, it will actually encourage certain insects such as aphids to infest the succulent new growth that this type of fertilizer promotes.

✓ Attract predator and parasite insects by planting pollen and nectar plants, such as ʻohiʻa lehua, wiliwili, daisies, cosmos, marigolds, carrots and other vegetables that you allow to flower. Dill and many other herbs can also help to attract beneficial insects. Examples of some predator insects are ladybugs and certain types of wasps and flies. We'll talk about some of them in this chapter.

✓ Rotate your crops. Don't plant your tomatoes or green beans in the same place every year.

✓ Grow a wide variety of plants. Monocrops attract diseases and pests, so if you mix many types of flowers and vegetables, as in a "potager" garden (see Chapter 1), you'll likely confuse the pesky bugs and have fewer problems with them.

✓ Plant healthy plants. Avoid "bargains" at the garden center because they might be old and tired, rootbound, or might already be infested with some type of insect.

✓ Select resistant varieties. Varieties of such vegetables as tomatoes are available that are resistant to common diseases such as tobacco mosaic virus. Check seed catalogs to see which varieties are disease- or insect-resistant. Be aware, however, that we still do not know the long-term outcomes of genetic engineering. I am avoiding the use of genetically engineered seeds until I see the results of studies and we learn more about possible adverse effects to the environment and our bodies.

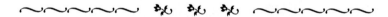

White Wave's opinion about genetic engineering

I found the following on a carton of soy milk, of all things:

"Genetic engineering is a science that takes plant breeding methods a step further. With it, scientists can insert specific genes from one species into another. This results in combinations nature could never create. Some believe that this will solve a host of agricultural issues. No one really knows what the long-term effects of this will be on our health or the food supply. We don't discount the possibility that the method may ultimately lead to some benefits for humankind. We just don't think it's wise to experiment with the world's food supply without understanding what the outcomes could be."

From White Wave, Inc., Boulder Colorado

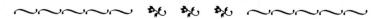

Keep the garden clean

Every once in awhile it's a good idea to rake up old compost, leaves, stalks and dead plants to minimize the number of hiding places you're providing for bugs and slugs, especially if you start noticing an invasion of any particular insect pest.

Get rid of pests before you plant

If you examine your garden site and destroy all of the pests that you find before you plant in a new area, you can control some of the existing insects and give your plants a head start in surviving. Look under rocks, boards and any surface debris and then squish the bad bugs and slugs that you find. It's also wise to check nearby plants for such pests as whiteflies that might infest your new plantings. If the problem is bad, simply pull out the infested plants and spray some insecticidal soap around the area.

Put up barriers

One of the tricks many gardeners have discovered is the use of floating row covers, called by brand names such as Remay. This gauzy fabric is super light, it allows light and moisture to penetrate, and it doesn't cost much. When you drape the fabric over your crops and weight it down with rocks along the sides, you'll be protecting vulnerable plants from the hungry insects that love to munch on them. Copper strips are another type of barrier that effectively keeps slugs and snails out of your planting areas. Check our Resources Appendix for contact information for the Gardener's Supply catalog.

If all else fails and a plant's life is being threatened by some kind of bug or slug, here are some effective natural remedies you can try.

Hand-picking

Hand-picking is the technical term for killing bugs. It works especially well with larger insects, slugs, and snails. Oh, that satisfying "crunch" when you step on a snail's shell! It would be difficult to hand pick the hundreds of aphids that can infest large plants, so for this problem, consider spraying the infested plant with a solution of soap and water or an ultra-fine oil. Read on for information on how to do this.

Insecticidal soap and other natural sprays

For widespread infestations of such insects as aphids and scale, a soap spray can help to keep their population under control. I've found that a few aphids or scale on a plant don't usually kill it, but the numbers of these insects can quickly get out of control.

Insecticidal soaps that you can buy commercially are selective and have little effect on beneficial insects like honeybees and ladybugs, according to Shunyam Nirav in the *Hawaiian Organic Growing Guide*. He goes on to say "the sprayed-on soap penetrates the bodies of insect pests, bringing destruction of membranes and resulting death." You can buy natural insecticidal soap at your garden center or make your own, based on the recipe below.

Easy Homemade Bug Soap Spray
Most conventional soaps contain cleaning agents and perfumes, which can injure plants and be generally ineffective for pest control. However, Ivory Liquid has been found to be effective. Here's the recipe:
1. Pour a small amount of Ivory Liquid dish detergent into a spray bottle and fill the bottle with water. I've also heard that Dr. Bronner's peppermint oil soap is very good for insect control.
2. Shake it up and then spray it on your infested plants.
3. Repeat the process often, especially after it rains, until you see a reduction in the number of problem insects.

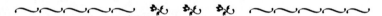

Garlic and pepper sprays
Some gardeners believe that a spray made from garlic and/or hot peppers deters or kills certain insects.
☞ To make this type of natural pest control spray, follow these simple steps:
1. Peel several cloves of garlic and put them in a blender. You can also add a couple of Jalapeño or Nioi hot Hawaiian peppers, but be sure to wash your hands after handling them!
2. Fill the blender jar 1/2 full with water.
3. Whirl the contents around on the "blend" setting for one minute.
4. Strain your mixture through a sieve, cheesecloth or panty hose.
5. Empty your strained mixture into a spray bottle.
6. Blast your infested plants with your super garlic/pepper spray.

☞ **NOTE:** If you have leftover spray, you can keep it in the refrigerator for up to a week. After that, discard it in your compost pile and make a fresh batch for optimum effectiveness against your insect foes.

Ultra-fine oils and dormant oil

Using a special type of highly refined mineral oil on your plants is an environmentally friendly practice that has been used for centuries to control the toughest garden pests such as aphids, spider mites and scales. You can purchase a product called SunSpray Ultra-Fine, which is easier to use than chemicals because you apply it less frequently than other pest remedies. You just spray it on your susceptible or infested plants to coat pests and their eggs: this interferes with the insects' respiration and membrane function. You can use it on plants in your house, garden or greenhouse, as well as on vegetables and trees. And it's safe to use up to the day of harvest.

Ultra-fine oil is sometimes called summer oil. You can use it at any time of the year, provided that the daytime heat does not exceed a temperature that is stated on the product. It is made from paraffinic oil and has little potential of being toxic to plants. It helps to control aphids, leafminer larvae, mealybugs, mites, scales, thrips, whiteflies and other insects.

You'll read about dormant oil in this chapter as well. The difference between this and ultra-fine oil is that horticultural dormant oils are more potent and are designed for use on deciduous trees in the winter when the leaves are gone and the tree is dormant. While some trees can tolerate dormant oil during the warmer time of year, others will react to it adversely if it is applied during the growing season and especially on hot days. Be sure to follow the instructions on the product label.

IGR (insect growth regulators)

Insect growth regulators are important pest management products that interrupt or inhibit the life cycle of pests, thus reducing or eliminating the need for pesticides wherever pests are not welcome. Sometimes called "birth control for roaches and fleas," IGRs inhibit the insect's ability to reach maturity, thus stopping the life cycle and resulting infestations. IGRs are not insecticides (in the bug-killing definition) but are man-made proteins that only affect certain insects or groups of insects.

Methoprene, Hydroprene and Nylar are the most common ingredients in insect growth inhibitors. The Methoprene products are sold under the brand name of Precor. Hydroprene is an IGR that was first introduced to help prevent or control populations of indoor roaches. It is sold under the brand name Gencor IGR.

If your dog or cat is on "Program," this is technically an IGR. After you apply this product, a chemical in your pet's bloodstream stops the baby fleas from hatching out of their eggs.

Get 'em drunk

If wandering around your garden at night with a flashlight searching for slugs and snails doesn't sound like fun to you, there's still hope for controlling these slimy creatures with natural methods. Beer is the answer. What a way to go for the snails and slugs that party in it, then drown! It's super simple to use:

1. Fill a small jar about one third full with beer. I use the cheapest rotgut I can buy.
2. Dig a small hole in your soil and place the jar at an angle, leaving one side of the opening at ground level so the critters can ooze into it without having to work to crawl up and then down into it.
3. After it rains, you'll need to replenish your beer in the jar, but it really works, especially if you put several beer traps around susceptible plants or entire garden beds.

BT for wormy visitors

Many caterpillars and other wormy creatures will become beautiful butterflies or other flying insects that don't harm a thing. I stopped killing hornworms when I learned that they might be the larval stage of the endangered hummingbird moth, also called the Blackburn's Sphinx moth (*Manduca blackburni*). Look under "Hornworm" later in this chapter for more information.

If you have an infestation of small leaf-eating worms, bacillus thuringiensis (BT) works wonders. It's a naturally occurring type of soil bacteria product that you spray on, but it is effective mainly against young and small wormy creatures. BT is safe for the environment--it kills only the larvae of pests such as mosquitoes, some caterpillars, and other insects through a toxin that the BT secretes. It's available as a powder or liquid at garden stores everywhere. Just follow the directions on the label. As with all products that you use in the garden, use caution and keep your BT away from children, pets and ponds, and avoid unnecessary exposure to yourself.

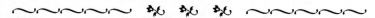

In 1994 the *Journal of Pesticide Reform* printed an article that stresses the importance of proper BT usage:

"Large-scale applications of BT can have far-reaching ecological effects. BT can reduce dramatically the number and variety of moth and butterfly species, which in turn impacts birds and animals that feed on caterpillars... There is no reason to use it [BT] indiscriminately. Its environmental and health effects, as well as those of all other alternatives, must be thoroughly considered before use. BT should be used only when necessary, and in the smallest quantities possible. It should always be used as part of a sustainable management program."

Controlling ants, aphids and scale with Tanglefoot

Did you know that ants are farmers? They are very hard-working insects who actually transport certain insects like aphids and scale insects onto the leaves of plants, where they tend them and feed off of their sweet secretions called "honeydew." If you can keep the ants off of a plant, you'll have a lot fewer problems with aphids and scale. It's simple to do and natural too: a product called Tree Tanglefoot is what you need. It's a very sticky substance that you can smear onto tape you have placed around the stalk of a plant to prevent ants from getting past the barricade. Aphids and scale often attack lemon trees and other citrus; Tanglefoot works very well on this type of fruit tree. It's available in spray cans or tubes at your nursery or garden center. You can even smear it around the posts that hold up your house to deter ants from invading the indoors. I prefer to use tubes of this product rather than sprays because it gives a thicker application. When you apply it to trees, be sure to smear it high enough on the trunk so that it will be protected by the shade that the plant provides: otherwise, it can melt in the hot sun.

CAUTION About Tanglefoot Use

Do not apply Tanglefoot directly onto tree trunks. In time, it can become toxic because it is a petroleum-based product. Instead, first wrap the trunk with polyester pillow stuffing. Then cover that with some duct tape, over which you can smear your Tanglefoot in a line like toothpaste.

If you have a problem with ants in your house, *Herbs for Health* magazine reported in their August 2004 issue that you can "try a mix of 1/4 cup dried peppermint leaves, 1/4 cup powdered cayenne pepper and 1/4 cup borax. Sprinkle the mixture liberally around the area where ants are entering your home. Another option is to use essential oils. Try placing a few drops of peppermint, spearmint or citronella oil on a cotton ball. Put this in areas where you have seen ants. Renew the oil every two days to keep the scent strong. You can also make a homemade ant trap. In a screw-top jar, mix 3 cups of water, 1 cup of sugar and 4 teaspoons of boric acid.

Poke holes in the jar lid and place it near ant trails (keep it out of the reach of children and pets)."

Pruning and destroying infested parts

One good way to control an infestation of a pest such as aphids or scale is to prune the affected branches of the plant. Citrus trees are a good example of this: the pruning gets rid of many of the insects and encourages new growth. Just don't prune off developing fruit unless you really feel it's necessary: why waste it? Insects such as scale and aphids suck out the leaf juices but don't harm the fruit. If you can control the insects on the leaves, you'll still get plenty of fruit. And if you find any insects on your fruit, simply wash them off before you eat it.

I like to take heavily-infested plant parts that I have pruned to my local green waste recycling center rather than encouraging those insects to continue existing and reproducing on my own property. If you live in a community that allows you to have an open fire, a bonfire is a great and fun way to ensure that all of the insects on your pruned branches are destroyed.

Consider chickens or ducks

Of course, many cities and housing developments don't allow farm animals in the backyard! But if you live far from the madding crowd, you might consider adding some adorable birds to your family. I have a few chickens that I allow to roam freely a few hours each day. The number of slugs and snails that I see has definitely diminished since I set my chickens loose to forage. The birds love to eat these gastropods and are doing me a huge favor by keeping their population under control. Chickens are also an excellent source of natural fertilizer and their eggs are healthy and delicious. I can't imagine life without them at my garden.

Know Your Enemy: A Quick Guide To Common Insect Friends and Foes

I have many opinions and attitudes about insects. I'll bet you do too. Icky, gross, slimy, creepy and yucky are just some of the words that come to mind when I start thinking of bugs. But this is another area of gardening where I have had to give myself an attitude adjustment: many insects, as you probably already know, are helpful because they eat and control other insects that might not be so nice. And even some of the less beneficial insects have a valuable place in the ecology of our back yards--and on each of our islands.

The rest of this chapter describes over two dozen insects commonly found in home gardens in Hawai`i. Much of the information contained in this chapter comes from a little book called *Good Bug, Bad Bug*, by Rodale Press (see the Bibliography), but I also consulted with an entomologist to ensure that the information I'm presenting here is as accurate as it can be for our islands.

Hawaiian insects are unique, like many other plant and animal species found in our remote island chain. And prepare yourself for a shock--there are about 10,000 species of native insects here! And some of those species are listed as endangered, along with the many species of plants and animals that we also recognize as threatened. How many alien insects live here? An incredible 3400 species exist in Hawai`i, plus about 560 other land arthropods (segmented invertebrates, like many of the insects, snails and spiders). The Hawai`i State Department of Agriculture has introduced another 383 species for the biological control of insect pests. That's a lot of bugs! But don't worry; you'll only need to know about a few common insects in order to make sure that your garden is as healthy and robust as it can be, without the use of chemicals or pesticides.

☞ I want to emphasize two important points before we move into the discussions of the insects:

✓ Not all insects are our enemies. The familiar ladybug, or ladybird beetle, is a good example of a beneficial insect. It's even cute. Ladybugs have been introduced into Hawai`i and are common in some areas. They eat aphids and other small destructive insects like scales, mealybugs and spider mites. Never kill a ladybug! They definitely are our friends in the garden. I'll let you know whether each insect in the following descriptions is a friend or a foe so you can learn to save the ones that are only doing good.

✓ Never order any insect from a catalog or the Internet. It is illegal in Hawai`i for private citizens to import any insect species, even good ones like ladybugs. If you were to bring an insect into Hawai`i, you might be introducing a species that's new here, because what the companies send to customers is not always exactly what they advertise.

☞ In the descriptions that follow, I'll include this information:

✓ The name of the insect, including its common name and scientific name (genus, species). If multiple species exist, we include the higher classification of order, class or family. For example, there are so many species of whitefly that we're including only their family name, *Aleyrodidae*.

✓ An illustration of each insect
✓ Whether it's a friend or a foe
✓ Where it lives
✓ A description of the insect
✓ How to control the foes without poison or how to encourage the friends

Aphid (family *Aphididae*)

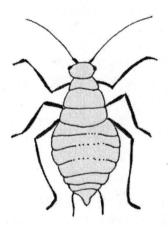

Illustration 6.1: Hungry aphids can literally suck the life out of a plant in short order.

Friend or foe: Foe
Where it lives: On plant stems and the underside of leaves, especially at the leaf terminals.

Description: Aphids are small, hungry insects that can suck the life right out of certain plants, like your vegetables and palms. They are usually green, but can range in color from pink, yellow, or black to gray. The queens and males have wings. Ants "farm" aphids for their sweet excretions, called honeydew, which can promote the growth of sooty mold and other fungal diseases.

How to control aphids without poison:
✓ Be careful to maintain healthy plants, but don't over-fertilize with nitrogen because aphids are attracted to the succulent new growth it promotes. This means avoiding fertilizers such as "Triple 16" because the amount of nitrogen (the first "16") is very high.
✓ Soap and garlic sprays can provide a temporary remedy for aphids, but in areas with a lot of rainfall the effects of such sprays are short-lived.

✓ Control ants, which feed on the aphids' honeydew, or excretion, by applying Tanglefoot around the base of your affected plants after you wash the ants off the plant with a sharp stream of water. Please remember the caution about using Tanglefoot earlier in this chapter.

Banana root borer (*Cosmopolites sordidus*)

Illustration 6.2: The small banana root borer can kill a banana tree in time.

Friend or foe: Foe
Where it lives: In the corms or pseudostems of banana trees, at ground level.

Description: The banana root borer is actually a weevil that in time causes the death of banana plants. Their eggs are white and sausage-shaped, about 1/2 inch long. Grubs are about 1/2 inch long, with reddish-brown heads and no legs. Although the adults have wings, they rarely fly. They hide under debris or in the soil around banana plants during the day and are active at night.

How to control banana root borers without poison:
Because banana root borers have become resistant to certain insecticides, the University of Hawai'i Cooperative Extension Service recommends that homeowners and farmers take these preventative steps to control and trap this insect:
✓ Clean plant clumps or mats of plant debris.
✓ Because the adults are attracted to freshly cut trunks and corms, you can make a split-log trap with fresh stems that you cut into 1- to 1-1/2-foot lengths. Split the stems lengthwise and place the halves with the cut surfaces on the soil. Place your traps at several locations around your banana plants. Check for insects every two or three days and hand pick the ones you find.
✓ Remove plants that you have harvested from the field at least once every week to eliminate the places where adult borers hide. Also be sure to remove stumps of banana plants by cutting them into four to eight pieces. If you chop them up even smaller, they make a good addition to your compost pile.
✓ Do not transport planting material from infested fields to uninfested ones. Check young plants that you are moving for pencil-sized holes at the base of the plant and the corms.

✓ Under no circumstances should you move young banana trees from one island to another.

Bees: Honeybee and Carpenter bee (*Apis mellifera*; *Xylocopa sonorina*)

Illustration 6.3: The familiar honeybee is a great friend in any garden.

Friend or foe: Friend, although the carpenter bee can sting humans and it also drills holes in wood

Where it lives: In hives, generally away from populated areas

Description: Honeybees are plump, usually black and yellow and fuzzy, and about 1/2 inch to 1 inch long. They are so important to pollination in the garden that we have developed an expression to describe their powers: "the birds and the bees." Without them, many plants would not be able to set fruit or seed. Bees normally sting humans only when we provoke them; otherwise, they are just busy doing their job and couldn't care less about us. The common honeybee was introduced to Hawai`i.

How to encourage honeybees in your garden:
✓ Protect these insects by not using insecticides.
✓ Plant pollen-rich and nectar flowers that have small flowers such as dill, lemon balm, mustard, parsley, yarrow and other herbs. Honeybees love the Holy basil (Ocimum sanctum) and other basils in Hi`iaka's Garden and their numbers have increased greatly since we began the garden in 2000.

The Sonoran carpenter bee is a big, scary-looking bee that is often mistaken for a bumblebee. They are very large (up to 1 inch long). The females are black and can inflict a painful sting for which you should seek medical treatment, while the males are yellow and stingless. They actually bore tunnels into wood with their strong jaws. You can tell if carpenter bees have been at work on the eaves of your house or elsewhere by the round half-inch diameter holes on the underside of boards. The telltale evidence is sawdust on surfaces below affected areas. They don't eat the wood; they just excavate tunnels for nesting sites. Although they rarely cause severe damage, except to unpainted redwood, you don't want to encourage them around your property. Read on!

How to discourage carpenter bees:

Although they can cause damage to wooden surfaces, especially redwood, carpenter bees are beneficial pollinators of various types of plants. Pesticides don't have much effect on carpenter bees: preventive measures are what work best against these big buzzers. Here are a few hints and advice, thanks to the UH "Urban Pest Press" series and the University of California at Davis web site:

✓ If the exterior wooden areas of your home are made of hardwoods, these bees are discouraged from trying to tunnel into them, as opposed to homes that are built from softer woods such as redwood, which carpenter bees just love.

✓ Filling in any crevices or cracks in the wood outside your home with a wood putty product will make the wood less attractive to the bees.

✓ Painting or varnishing outdoor wooden surface is important to prevent weathering, which opens doors (and holes) for the bees. Painted wood is much less likely to become a nest for carpenter bees. They especially like redwood, so make sure you paint any exposed redwood surfaces.

✓ After you see a carpenter bee leaving a hole, plug it up with steel wool and then apply caulk over it to prevent the insect from coming back.

✓ Protect rough areas, such as the ends of timbers, with wire screening or metal flashing.

Centipede and millipede (orders *Chilopoda* and *Diplopoda*)

Illustration 6.4: The centipede (top) is an unwelcome resident in many areas. The millipede is less dangerous and more beneficial to the garden.

Friend or foe: Friend (believe it or not!)
Where it lives: In dark places, such as under houses and in compost piles

Description: Adults of both types of these arthropods are slender and segmented with many legs. Centipedes are by far the larger of the two, up to 5 inches long. They also have fewer legs than millipedes. Many people think that centipedes are creepy, and they can deliver a painful bite. Avoid them at all costs! They prey on soil-dwelling pests, cockroaches, possibly slugs, and can sometimes eat earthworms, which is not such a good thing. Millipedes eat mostly decaying plant material, so they can help the decomposition process in your compost pile.

How to control centipedes and millipedes in your garden:
✓ Do not use pesticides. If you're finding too many of them, deter them by sprinkling wood ashes, diatomaceous earth or cinders along rows of seeds that are germinating. Stake your plant branches to keep fruit and vegetables off the ground.
✓ Keep garden beds clean by raking up leaves and other organic matter: this discourages centipedes by depriving them of a possible home.
✓ Don't plant anything too close to your home. If you spread gravel around the border of your house, it will discourage centipedes from entering.
✓ Chickens love to forage for centipedes and can help to keep the population under control.

Chinese rose beetle (*Adoretus sinicus*)

Illustration 6.5: These hungry fellows leave a telltale "lace" pattern on the leaves they have eaten.

Friend or foe: Foe
Where it lives: Larvae live in leaf litter around plants. Adults hide in the daytime and appear on your plants mostly in the early evening hours.

Description: The Chinese rose beetle is a sturdy brown beetle that is flecked with white. They are about 1/2 inch long at maturity. Their presence is obvious, as they create a lace-like or shotgun-like design on leaves, eventually causing them to turn yellow and drop. They are an introduced species of insect that just love to munch on the leaves of roses, grapes, beans, cabbage, and many other native and introduced plants. They especially like the various hibiscus species, including the Red Zinger tea hibiscus and the Ma'o hau hele, our beautiful endangered native yellow hibiscus.

How to control Chinese rose beetles without poison:
✓ These critters come out in the evening, up until about 10 o'clock. Setting up a light over the affected plant deters the beetles.
✓ You can also hand pick them in the evening.
✓ Another option is to purchase chips of the neem tree and sprinkle them on the ground surrounding your prize plants. I don't know where the beetles go, but they must leave the area. You'll need to repeat the application of neem chips from time to time.

Fruit fly (*Bactrocera* spp.; *Ceratitis capitata*)

Illustration 6.6: The Oriental fruit fly looks like the other fruit flies that attack orchards and home gardens.

Friend or foe: Foe
Where it lives: Orchards, kitchens and anywhere there is fruit (although the melon fruit fly is a pest of cucumbers, melons, squash, pumpkins, eggplant, tomatoes and peppers). Fruit flies occur in dry leeward areas as well as wet lowland areas on the windward sides of all the islands.

Description: Fruit flies are small white and yellow flies with clear or marked wings. Hawai'i is host to four major species of damaging fruit flies, all of which have been introduced: members of the *Bactrocera* genus include the Oriental fruit fly, the solanaceous fruit fly and the melon fly, while the Mediterranean fruit fly is classified as *Ceratitis capitata*. Another reason for keeping wild guava under control is that it serves as a host plant for Oriental fruit flies. Their habit is to mass and congregate on ripening fruit. The larvae are obvious white, wiggly things that hatch inside of your favorite fruit, and are a clear indication that fruit flies have been at work on the outside of that fruit.

How to control fruit flies without poison:

✓ Keep damaged or rotten fruit cleaned up from under trees. It's a perfect addition to your compost pile or worm bin, but be sure to cover it with a layer of dry leaves, straw, or shredded newspaper to discourage even more fruit flies. Better yet, give rotten fruit to chickens or ducks if you have them.

✓ Soap and garlic sprays can provide a temporary remedy for fruit flies, but in areas with a lot of rainfall the effects of such sprays are short-lived.

✓ Sticky traps (available at nurseries) can catch a good number of fruit flies if you hang them around your kitchen or in the trees whose fruit they love.

✓ Harvesting fruit while it's still slightly green prevents fruit flies from stinging it before you can eat it. This practice also deprives them of a place to lay their eggs. I always check for larvae inside of fruit such as guavas and papayas before I take a big bite.

✓ Keep invasive host plants such as wild guava and ivy gourd (for the melon fruit fly) under control as much as possible.

✓ If you want to grow full-size tomatoes, bell peppers, cucumbers and many other vegetables, it's hard to keep the fruit flies from eating them before you do without growing these crops in a greenhouse. If you want to grow these crops in the wide-open spaces, you can tie paper bags or floating row cover (Remay) over ripening fruit to prevent flies from stinging it.

✓ The HAW-FLYPM (Hawai`i Area Wide Fruit Fly Integrated Pest Management Program) is a USDA-Agriculture Research Service funded partnership with the University of Hawai`i Cooperative Extension Service and the Hawai`i State Department of Agriculture. They provide packets of a pheromone that attracts male fruit flies, and all you have to do is prepare plastic jugs that you hang around your yard. The male flies are attracted to the pheromone, enter the jug, and cannot escape, thus reducing the number of available males that are available to breed with the females. Fruit fly populations have shown dramatic reductions on farms and in yards that have joined this service. Refer to the Resources Appendix for contact information so you can become a "cooperator" in this free program.

Hornworm and Hawk moth (family *Sphingidae*)

Friend or foe: Sometimes a friend, sometimes a foe

Illustration 6.7a, 6.7b: The ugly hornworm turns into the spirited hawk moth.

Where it lives: Hornworms live on the plants they eat: they have specific tastes and eat only certain plants, such as sweet potatoes, morning glories, or tomatoes, although tomato hornworms do not live in Hawai`i. This type of worm can decimate plants very quickly: you'll see evidence of them by the large holes they chew in leaves and fruit.

Description: If you look at hornworms closely, after getting over your initial disgust, they are actually quite pretty: the sweet potato hornworm is primarily green with a white diagonal stripe along each side. All types of hornworms can grow as long as 5 inches. The telling feature is the single large horn on this worm's tail. They do not bite humans. Many species also have a spot that looks like an eye on each side of their front end. They can completely destroy both young and older plants during an infestation. They can also affect some ornamentals, such as caladium.

☞ **NOTE:** The moth that hatches from certain hornworm eggs can be an endangered native Hawaiian moth called the Blackburn's Sphinx moth (*Manduca blackburni*), which is Hawai`i's first federally-listed endangered insect. Its wingspan is up to five inches, and when it flits and hovers from flower to flower like a hummingbird, it sucks nectar from ginger blossoms and other plants with its long proboscis. It truly looks and behaves like a hummingbird!

How to control hornworms without poison:
✓ I no longer kill any hornworms I find on my property. If there is a large infestation, I heed the wisdom of my Buddhist visitor and take them to a "wild place" away from my susceptible plants.
✓ If you grow nectar or pollen plants, they attract parasitic wasps, which provide some control of hornworms.

- ✓ I do not recommend that you use BT for hornworms, because they might be the larval stage of an endangered moth.
- ✓ If you see hornworms on any maile pilau, let them eat as much as they want!

Ladybird (Ladybug) beetle (family *Coccinellidae*)

Illustration 6.8: Everyone loves ladybugs.

Friend or foe: Friend
Where it lives: On the leaves of plants where other insects like aphids occur. Both the adult beetles and their larvae feed on soft-bodied pests and insect eggs, such as mealybugs, spider mites and young scale.

Description: These shiny, round beetles are usually red or orange with black polka dots. They can be from 1/16 to 3/8 inch long. They are extremely beneficial and very cute.

How to encourage ladybugs in your garden:
- ✓ Plant pollen and nectar plants, especially dill and angelica.
- ✓ Although ladybugs are very beneficial, do not order them from a catalog or the Internet because this might introduce new parasites.

Leafminers (*Liriomyza* spp.)

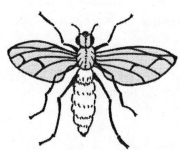

Illustration 6.9: Although leafminer damage can be ugly, they rarely kill a plant.

Friend or foe: Foe
Where it lives: All of the Hawaiian islands have leafminers. Their larvae tunnel through the leaves of such plants as tomatoes, beans, cucumbers, onions and other vegetables, flowers and weeds, leaving hollowed-out or curved "mines." When heavy infestations occur, the affected leaves are filled with mines, which cause the leaves to turn yellow and die. They threaten mainly young plants and usually present only a nuisance on older plants without killing them.

Description: Larvae are the main culprits. They are yellow to orange legless maggots. The adults are black or black and yellow flies about 1/10 of an inch long. The citrus leafminer is a problem for many kinds of young citrus trees in nurseries on O'ahu, Kaua'i and Maui county. Its larvae are elongated, pale colored, and translucent. Adult citrus leafminers are tiny silvery moths with a black spot at the tip of each wing.

Much of the time, the damage done by leafminers is cosmetic and not serious. And thanks to a number of beneficial parasites that the Hawai'i Department of Agriculture has introduced, the population of leafminers in Hawai'i has been controlled to a certain extent. So if you don't mind a little cosmetic damage on some of your plants' leaves, leafminers should not be a huge problem in your home garden.

How to control leafminers without poison:

✓ It's important not to use pesticides for leafminer control because these products can kill the beneficial predators of this insect. And they just don't work.

✓ IGRs (insect growth regulators) are a good choice for leafminer control if you have a major infestation and feel that an aggressive control is necessary.

✓ If you cover your seedlings with floating row covers (Remay), this will prevent the flying adult leaf miners from gaining access and laying their eggs.

✓ Do not remove the damaged leaves from your plants or you might accidentally kill the beneficial parasites that are inside leafminer larvae.

✓ Parasitic wasps are natural predators of both the regular leafminer and the citrus leafminer. You can attract these beneficial insects, which do not sting humans, by planting nectar and pollen-rich plants.

✓ A spray made from neem extract can also be helpful in heavy infestations.

Mealybug (family *Pseudococcidae*)

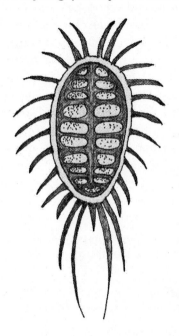

Illustration 6.10: You'll never see a mealybug as clearly as this drawing because they're very tiny.

Friend or foe: Foe

Where it lives: Primarily on the new growth of plants such as flowers, avocado trees, ornamentals, oleanders, poinsettias, citrus and other fruit trees

Description: Mealybugs are tiny insects with soft pink, oval bodies and are only 1/10 of an inch long. They are also covered with white, powdery or waxy fluff. They suck the plant juices from all parts of affected plants, causing the leaves to wither and turn yellow and the fruit to drop prematurely.

How to control mealybugs without poison:
✓ Rinse plants with a sharp stream of water.
✓ Use insecticidal soap or ultra-fine oil every 10 to 14 days to make sure you are killing the next generation of young mealybugs.
✓ Encourage parasitic wasps and possibly ladybugs by growing pollen and nectar-producing plants.

Nematode (Phylum *Nematoda*)

Friend or foe: Can be either, but in Hawai'i it is usually considered a foe.

Where it lives: In the soil around the plants whose roots it eats.

Illustration 6.11: Nematodes are another insect you probably won't see because they're very small.

Description: Over 15,000 known species of nematodes exist, according to the University of California at Berkeley web site. They are sometimes called roundworms. Nematodes are tiny and you will probably never see one. But if you were to look at a harmful nematode under a microscope, you would see that they are slender, translucent and unsegmented worms, usually only 1/50 of an inch long. Beneficial species are larger--from 1/25 of an inch to several inches long. But if you look at the roots of affected plants you'll see root knots ("galls"), injured root tips, and/or excessive branching. On the leaves of affected plants, you'll see lesions of dying tissue and twisted, distorted leaves. Nematodes especially like corn, lettuce, peppers, potatoes, tomatoes and other vegetables.

Beneficial nematodes are parasites of some soil-dwelling pests such as root weevils, stem borers, corn rootworms and other lawn and garden pests. They are about 1/4 inch long and are good for the compost pile, as they help to cause the decomposition of organic materials.

☞ **NOTE:** Although parasitic insects exist that can provide control of nematodes, it is against the law in Hawai`i to import them through mail order catalogs or the Internet.

How to control nematodes without poison:
✓ Practice crop rotation by alternating nonsusceptible crops with those that nematodes typically attack.
✓ Marigolds are helpful in suppressing nematode infestations. A variety called Mexican marigold (*Tagetes minuta*) is said to be the most effective anti-nematocidal of the marigolds. Check the Resources Appendix for seed sources.
✓ If you solarize your soil where you know that nematodes live, it will heat the soil to a temperature that's high enough to kill the pests that are living there. To solarize, simply cover the area with clear plastic and let it "cook" during the summer months. Firmly secure the plastic with a number of rocks or boards around the edges.

Scale (Families *Coccidae* (soft scales) and *Diaspididae* (armored scales)

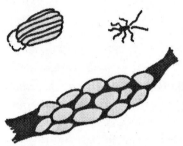

Illustration 6.12: Top left: cottony cushion scale female with egg sac; right: single scale insect in its crawler stage; bottom: scale colony on a stem.

Friend or foe: Foe
Where it lives: On plant stems and on the tops and undersides of leaves.

Description: Adults are generally oval or round, and look like 1/4 to 1/2-inch "bumps" or barnacles on your plants. You might not even recognize them as insects. Young larvae are very small and are crawlers that look like miniature mealybugs. There are two major kinds of scale: soft-bodied and armored. You can control soft scale with insecticidal soap sprays or ultra-fine oil, but you must hand pick the armored type, especially when they become adults.

Hawai`i has many different species of scale. Four that present problems are:

☞ Green scale: a soft scale that affects coffee plants, gardenias and many other plants.

☞ Coconut scale: this is an armored scale that affects coco palms and many other plants.

☞ Cottony cushion scale: this scale is easy to recognize because of its cottony-looking egg sac and its profuse production of honeydew. Females are bright orange, red, yellow or brown, but their most distinguishing feature is the elongated, fluted white cottony egg sac that is attached to the insect's body.

☞ Sago palm scale: this scale is also called the cycad scale. Infested sago palms, when infested, look like they have been whitewashed. Leaves become yellow-brown and eventually die. This type of scale is especially problematic in the windward and central areas of O`ahu and has also been found in Kona and Waiakea on the Big Island. Infestations usually begin on the undersides of leaves, but spread to the upper surfaces, the terminal portion of the sago palm, and even the trunk. A white circular disk covers mature female sago palm scales, about 1/16 inch in diameter. Juvenile males are also white, but much smaller. Adult males are orange-brown and look like tiny flying midges.

98

How to control scale insects without poison:

✓ Use soap spray or ultra-fine oil to control young scale and soft scale. Young scale move around and are sensitive to soap. If you have a plant like a potted palm that has scale, you can spray it with insecticidal soap, but don't expect all of the scale to vanish: only the soft scale and the armored juveniles will perish. Adult armored scale will continue to suck the plant's juices and will not die unless you hand pick them. The formula is to spray every 10 to 14 days, in order to make sure you are killing the next generation of young scale.

✓ Hand pick armored scale. You can also dip a soft brush or cloth into insecticidal soap and then use it to "wash" the scales from your plants.

✓ Prune and destroy infested branches.

✓ Control ants, which feed on the soft scale's honeydew, or excretion, by applying Tanglefoot around the base of your affected plants after you wash the ants off the plant with a sharp stream of water. Please remember the caution about using Tanglefoot that we talked about earlier in this chapter.

✓ Predatory beetles and some parasitic wasps can be helpful in controlling scale. You can attract them to your garden by planting nectar and pollen plants.

✓ Use dormant oil sprays on fruit and ornamental trees.

✓ For sago palm scale, some people have found that if they clip off all the leaves of their plants this eliminates many of these pests. However, if you do this, you run the risk of also getting rid of beneficial ladybugs (and their larvae, which are white and look like mealybugs) that might be feasting on the problematic scale insects.

✓ A tiny black lady beetle and several other ladybird beetles are predators of some types of scale, but no predators have been associated with the sago palm scale as of this writing.

✓ You can also blast scale insects off your plants' leaves with a sharp stream of water from your hose. Let them dry, then spray with an ultra-fine oil, but don't do this on a sunny day because it can sunburn the leaves.

Slug and snail (class *Gastropoda*)

Friend or foe: Foe

Illustration 6.13a, 6.13b: The semi-slug (left) is becoming very populous in some areas of Hawai`i; the giant African snail is also a hungry invader.

Where they live: In cool, moist places, such as under rocks or pieces of wood. They come out mainly at night and on cool, misty days and feast on tender foliage and decaying plant material on the ground.

Description: Slugs and snails are slimy crawlers with no legs. Snails have a crunchy shell on their backs, while slugs do not. Depending on the species, slugs and snails can range from 1/4 inch in length to over 6 inches, as is the case with the giant African snail. There are many species of both slugs and snails: they can be gray, tan, green or black. Some have darker spots or patterns.

Controlling slugs and snails without poison:
✓ Hand-picking and squishing work well. If you do this, wear gloves and please use caution not to touch slugs or snails because some species can spread disease to humans. The giant African snail (*Achatina fulica*) and the Southeast Asian semi-slug (*Parmarion martensi*) are both introduced species that can cause a type of meningitis in humans, so use extra care if either of these creatures exists on your property.
✓ Beer traps are the most common and effective natural control for both snails and slugs.
✓ A product called Sluggo is very effective. It's an organic product that contains iron phosphate, a naturally occurring ingredient in soil.

- ✓ If you purchase copper strips at your garden center and fasten them around the trunks of your trees and around the borders of your garden beds, this stops both slugs and snails in their tracks.
- ✓ Spread wide bands of cinders, wood ashes or diatomaceous earth along the rows in your garden to protect seedlings. However, please note that some slugs can cross cinder or diatomaceous earth when it is wet.
- ✓ Certain ground beetles eat slugs, so if you make walkways of clover, sod or stone mulch, you'll provide a habitat for those beetles.
- ✓ Chickens and ducks forage for them and can be very helpful in controlling the population. But they sometimes eat your lettuce and other succulent veggies as well!

Spiders (class *Arachnida*)

Illustration 6.14: This female brown widow spider can deliver a painful bite to you as well as to its mate.

Friend or foe: Most of them are friends (see below for information on some that are considered foes).

Where they live: everywhere, even indoors. Widow spiders live primarily outdoors in dark, hidden places, such as under homes, under rocks and among piles of wood, cinder blocks, and items stored on shelves. "Crab" spiders live in open areas and spin their large webs between trees, shrubs, and other plants.

Description: Spiders are our eight-legged arachnid friends. There are hundreds of different kinds of spiders. Aside from a couple of biting spiders, most of them are our friends because they eat many insects that get trapped in their webs.

How to encourage spiders in your garden:

If you mulch your garden areas with hay or dried grass when you first plant, it will attract spiders, which will then live happily and thrive on the insects they eat.

But be on the lookout for "crab" spiders and the three species of widow spiders that exist in Hawai`i. These spiders can inflict bites that sometimes result in swelling that requires medical treatment.

"Crab" spiders, sometimes called "spiny-backed spiders" (*Gasteracantha sp. and Thelacantha brevispina*), look like little crabs. The adults are white with red or orange bumps and they have six 1/8 inch red spines projecting from their 1/2-inch long bodies. They exist on the all of the main islands.

The three species of widow spiders that live in Hawai`i are either brown or black, and they have long legs and the characteristic red "hour glass" marking on their abdomens. They belong to the genus *Lactrodectus* and live on all of the main islands, with the brown widow spider being commonly found in urban areas. The widows are shy and generally avoid contact with humans. If you accidentally provoke a female widow spider and she bites you, it will feel like a pinprick at first and will leave two red puncture marks. More intense pain can follow--it can last for several hours and can spread to your abdomen and legs, eventually causing nausea, fainting, dizziness, and other serious and unpleasant symptoms. Always seek immediate medical attention if you think a widow spider might have bitten you. But take heart--death rarely results! Your symptoms, if left untreated, will last for two or three days and if you're in general good health, you will recover soon. But stay on the safe side and visit your doctor.

How to control unwanted spiders without poison:

✓ Keep webs controlled by sweeping them down with a broom.
✓ If you find egg cases near any of these spiders, you can hand pick and destroy them to control the next generation.
✓ Store things under your house neatly and dispose of stacked-up rubbish on a regular basis: this will discourage the spiders from building webs, nests and dwelling places.
✓ Inspect crawl spaces under your house periodically and destroy any spiders, webs, nests and eggs that you find. Please wear gloves while you're doing this!
✓ Vacuum adult spiders and their egg cases. When you're done, put the vacuum bag into a plastic bag, tie it securely, and then throw out

the bag to prevent the spiders and eggs inside from escaping and hatching.
✓ Certain kinds of parasitic wasps are helpful because they attack the eggs of some spiders.

Spittlebug (family *Cercopidae*)

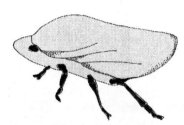

Friend or foe: Foe
Where it lives: Mainly at the junction of leaves and stems inside a foamy mass of "spittle." They like many different types of plants, including basil and other herbs, strawberries, legumes, forage plants and nursery crops.

Illustration 6.15: The cute spittlebug mainly makes a sticky mess but rarely causes a plant to die.

Description: Spittle bugs are oval, yellow to yellowish-green, about 1/4 to 1/2 inch long, with a face that looks a little like a frog. Their presence is easy to see due to the frothy "spittle" that they deposit on the plant stems where they live. They do not normally cause a plant to die and are mainly a cosmetic problem. But be sure to wash your homegrown produce before you eat it!

How to control spittle bugs without poison:
✓ Avoid using pesticides to encourage predatory bugs, both native and introduced.
✓ Use a sharp stream from your hose to blast the spittle masses and insects off your plants.
✓ If you have had a large infestation during the summer months, cut down and destroy the dead plants to kill eggs that will hatch during the next growing season.

Whitefly (family *Aleyrodidae*)

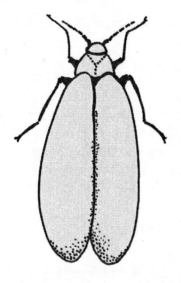

Illustration 6.16: Tiny whiteflies can quickly get out of control; so if you start seeing some, start controlling them right away (see below).

Friend or foe: Foe
Where it lives: In greenhouses and outdoors on such plants as citrus, azaleas, rhododendrons, squash, cucumbers, lettuce, eggplants, peppers, lantana, strawberry, tomatoes and many ornamentals. There are nearly 40 species of whitefly that live in Hawai`i, all of which have been introduced. They're a major pest in both agricultural areas and home gardens.

Description: Whiteflies are very small, powdery-looking white flying insects, only about 1/25 of an inch long. They live primarily on the undersides of leaves. They suck sap from their host plants, which causes the plant to lose vigor and wilt. Eventually the leaves turn yellow and die, and the entire plant can die if left untreated. Large numbers of whiteflies can develop in a very short amount of time. They also secrete sugary honeydew, which is a medium for the growth of sooty mold. They're a bad one.

How to control whiteflies without poison:
✓ Grow lots of nectar and pollen plants to encourage native parasitic wasps, lacewings and introduced ladybugs. Please remember not to mail order any insects into Hawai`i.
✓ If you hang purchased yellow sticky traps around the affected plants, many whiteflies will stick to them and then die.
✓ You can sometimes use a hand-held vacuum cleaner to remove whiteflies from the undersides of leaves. Be sure to put the vacuum bag into a tightly sealed plastic bag before you throw it out.
✓ A spray of neem extract, insecticidal soap or summer oil can be effective against whiteflies. The secret is to spray every 10 to 14 days, in order to make sure you are killing the next generation of young whiteflies.
✓ IGRs (insect growth regulators) are also effective in controlling whiteflies.

Chapter 7
Wonderful Weeds to Encourage

This chapter includes plants that at first sight might not fill your expectations of attractive landscape plants. You might already have some of the plants in this chapter growing in your yard! You might want to weed them out until you know what they are, but as you get to know them, you may learn to love them as I do because many occur nowhere else in the world, yet they are so simple to grow. They are truly wonderful weeds!

You should read this chapter if you want to know about some simple to care for plants that grow naturally in many parts of Hawai`i. It includes descriptions and illustrations of numerous native plants, fruit trees and herbs that might be considered weedy, and which you might not have thought about growing. The plants you'll learn about in this chapter are:

Hawaiian natives and naturalized plants:
    Bamboo orchid
    Ferns
    Popolo
    Pua kala
    `Uhaloa

Fruit and herbs:
    Bananas
    Basil
    Hot pepper
    Passionfruit
    Papayas
    Poha berries
    Sweet potato

Medicinal plants:
    Gotu kola
    Noni
    Plantain
    Purslane
    Vervain

And you will learn the following information about the plants in this chapter:

✓ Illustration
✓ Description of the plant: I'll keep the descriptions general and non-technical.

✓ Climate zone where it thrives: I'll list the appropriateness of growing each plant in windward and leeward gardens and mention the elevation range at which each plant is likely to occur and succeed.

✓ How to grow it: I'll tell you how much water and shade each plant needs and mention how to start some of the plants from seed or cuttings.

✓ Possible insect pests and diseases: Because most of the plants in this chapter are often considered "weeds," and many are naturally-occurring natives, they are amazingly resistant to insects and diseases. That's why I like them so much and want to share them with my readers.

✓ Medicinal uses, invasiveness potential and other special notes of interest: I'll mention whether the plants have medicinal properties and if they were used for building or other practical uses in earlier times. And I'll discuss whether each plant has the potential of becoming invasive, because, as weeds, some of them can create a few too many "wonderful weeds" of their own.

Hawaiian Natives and Naturalized Plants

Remember the old saying? "A weed is simply a plant that is growing where it isn't wanted." That's so true of many Hawaiian native plants and others that have become naturalized yet do no harm to the environment. If you learn just a little about some of these plants, I guarantee you'll change some of your old opinions and attitudes about them. Here are a few plants that you might not have considered growing, or keeping, in your garden.

Bamboo orchid (*Arundina graminifolia*)

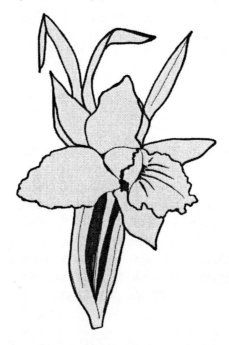

Illustration 7.1: Bamboo orchids are a joy to behold.

- Description: This pretty little orchid is white and lavender with a yellow throat. It's found at the top of foliage that looks like bamboo. It's a wild orchid from the East Indies that was introduced to the Big Island by airplane: they actually dropped seeds over certain areas and it has naturalized beautifully, adding to the name "orchid isle." Fortunately, they are not considered invasive. What a wonderful thing to have wild orchids in your garden! They spread by seeds and also by runners and are simple to pull if you don't want one in a particular area. But I find that they add color and interest wherever they pop up. Unlike other orchids, this beauty blooms prolifically almost year-round with no fertilizer at all. It doesn't have a Hawaiian name as yet, but is so common in places that I wouldn't be surprised if perhaps we'll call it the 'okika 'ohe in the future.
- Climate zone where it thrives:
    Windward areas: yes
    Leeward areas: unknown. I have never seen it in leeward areas, unless someone has intentionally planted it in their yard.
    Elevation: Near sea level

- How to grow it: You can collect seeds from the long seedpods of the bamboo orchid in the fall or winter months when the pods are brown and dry but have not yet opened to disperse their many tiny seeds. Or you might dig up a plant from a roadside area and transplant it to your property. They're also sold at the airport gift shops for people to take home and try to grow on the mainland.

  Like many other orchids, this one does not need soil in which to grow. They thrive in dry, rocky areas--even on bare lava--but they're so carefree that you can introduce them to other microclimates. If you want to grow one in a pot, use small gravel or cinder instead of potting soil. Water it sparingly and apply a high-nitrogen orchid fertilizer if you feel like it, but it should need no special care, as it is truly a wonderful weed.
- Possible insect pests and diseases: none
- Medicinal uses, invasiveness potential and other special notes of interest: I facetiously call bamboo orchids "those damn orchids" because they pop up as wonderful weeds everywhere on my property. If you don't have any, go get some.

Ferns

- Description: Many of the ferns that grow wild in Hawai`i are natives and are quite attractive. Some, however, can become very invasive. We'll talk about four small ferns in this section and include information about their habits that will help you to keep ahead of their advancing growth.
- Climate zone where they thrive: Ferns generally prefer cool, moist climates and are especially prevalent above 500 feet on the windward sides of all islands.
- How to grow them: If ferns are already growing on your property, they are totally low-maintenance. If you want some, it's simple to dig some up from a friend's yard and transplant them into a shady, moist spot on your property. Check Chapter 8 for instructions on growing the hapu`u, or native Hawaiian tree fern.
- Possible insect pests and diseases: Ferns are remarkably disease-resistant and insect-free. A thick clump of ferns, however, can provide a nesting ground for snails and slugs, so keep that in mind when you are working to control those pests. You might want to cut your ferns back to get rid of the nice moist, cool habitat mollusks love. Then when the ferns grow back, it will take a while before the pests re-discover the rich environment the ferns provide.

- Medicinal uses, invasiveness potential and other special notes of interest: None of the ferns described here have been rated as problem invaders. Continue reading for specific information about each of the ferns we're describing.

Laua`e (*Phymatosorus grossus*)

Illustration 7.2a: The maile-scented fern is attractive and native.

The laua`e, or maile-scented fern, is common to all the islands. Visitors to Hi`iaka's Garden always ask what it is: many people do not recognize it as a fern and are curious about the raised spots on the underside of the fronds, which contain the reproductive spores. One form of this fern has a vanilla-like fragrance, similar to maile, and is popularly included in leis.

Sword ferns (*Nephrolepis* spp.)

Sword ferns include five different varieties in Hawai`i, including the popular houseplant, the Boston fern (the *Nephrolepis* genus has several species). The Hawaiian name is kupukupu, but it is not native. It pops up here and there in the garden and looks soft and pretty, but it can spread and choke out other valuable plants. We keep it weeded when it gets to be too much. It's often cultivated for ornamental use around homes, in shady rock gardens, and for houseplants.

Lace fern (*Sphenomeris chusana*)

The lace fern (Hawaiian name pala`a) is very pretty and is not as invasive as the sword ferns or the false staghorn fern (see below). It is one of the most common ferns found in Hawai`i and was used in ancient times for a dark brown dye. Hi`iaka, youngest sister of Pele, the volcano goddess, wore this fern around her hips when she sent the pala`a to trip and entangle the mo`o (dragons) when she fought them in myth and legend. If it starts to overtake our pathway areas, we simply prune back the offending fronds.

Illustration 7.2b: Its delicate fronds make the lace fern a welcome addition in many garden areas.

False staghorn fern (*Dicranopteris emarginata*)

The false staghorn fern (Hawaiian name uluhe) covers many acres of land in Hawai`i with dense thickets. It lives from 500 feet to around 3000 feet in elevation. Although it's a native species, it can be very invasive, so you will probably want to keep it under control in your garden because it smothers vegetation and prevents the growth of other plants.

Popolo/black nightshade (*Solanum nigrum* or *S. americanum*)

Illustration 7.3: It's hard to tell the native species from a toxic introduced species, so be wise and do not eat popolo leaves or berries.

- Description: The popolo might very well be a native plant, as it was found throughout Polynesia before Europeans arrived. It is a member of the nightshade family, and is slightly similar in appearance to a bell pepper plant. It's attractive, gets to be 1 to 3 feet tall and has small white flowers with yellow stamens that typically droop downward. It has small seedy berries that turn black when they are ripe. Be careful if you eat them: they have laxative properties and might be a cross breed of a nearly identical species that has toxic properties.
- Climate zone where it thrives:
    Windward areas: yes
    Leeward areas: yes
    Elevation: sea level to 7500 feet
- How to grow it: If you can find a popolo growing in a friend's yard, collect some ripe berries and scatter them around your yard: it pops up in my garden in many different areas. If I don't want one where it has decided to grow, I simply pull it out and toss it into the compost pile.
- Possible insect pests and diseases: I've seen a few white flies and bug-eaten leaves, but nothing serious seems to threaten its survival.
- Medicinal uses, invasiveness potential and other special notes of interest:
Called the "foundation of Hawaiian pharmacy," the popolo was and still is used for many ailments. According to legend, the Hawaiian god of healing, Lonopuha, hurt his foot with a digging stick one day. The god Kane told him to use popolo leaves to heal his wound, which he did, and his foot immediately healed.
The black berries of the popolo were used for thrush in infants; juice made from the berries and leaves is laxative; young leaves were cooked like spinach and were also used for treating colds, sore throats and coughs. The juice of the leaves and ripe berries were used alone or in compounds for all disorders of the respiratory tract and for skin eruptions. The leaves were pounded with salt and applied to wounds, cuts and abrasions. Popolo also grows on other Polynesian islands, and is used for boils, toothaches, and other ailments.
However, while researching this book, I received the following warning from Dr. Roger Baldwin, author of the book *Hawai`i's Poisonous Plants* (1979): "This plant is highly toxic on the mainland, but Polynesians have used a variety which is both nontoxic and delicious. (I ate many popolos when I was a child.) Until about 40 years ago it was safe to eat wild popolos. Then some fool introduced the toxic mainland variety

to Hawai'i, so now it is not safe to eat wild popolos any more. If a person grows the nontoxic Polynesian variety in a garden it should be perfectly safe to eat, though -- the rule now is: don't eat popolos unless you know they are nontoxic, and don't ever eat popolos in the mainland. You cannot tell toxic from nontoxic plants by looking at them -- I am a botanist and I cannot see any difference between the varieties in the field."

Pua kala (*Argemone glauca*)

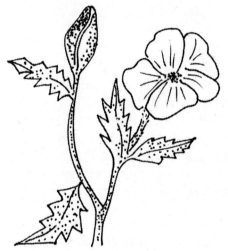

Illustration 7.4: The pua kala thrives in dry areas.

- Description: Pua kala is the Hawaiian prickly poppy, which was introduced around the time that the ancient Polynesians first arrived on our shores. It has pretty white flowers that usually bloom in spring. The flowers are about 2 inches across, and occur at the top of this plant's spiny, pale green foliage that grows to 2 or 3 feet tall.
- Climate zone where it thrives:
    Windward areas: yes, at low elevations, and especially if you can protect it from rain. It likes dry, rocky conditions.
    Leeward areas: yes: it occurs primarily on the leeward sides of all islands except Kaua`i. It also occurs naturally in other dry areas.
    Elevation: sea level to 6000 feet
- How to grow it: Depending on the species, pua kala can behave as either an annual or a biennial. I have not had any luck transplanting it, even plants that I have purchased. But seeds are very simple to start:

1. Collect seeds from dry seedpods in late spring or early summer. Use them right away or store them in a zipper bag in the refrigerator.
2. Prepare a pot or a flat with cinders or sand in the bottom layer for drainage. Then fill your pot with a light potting mix containing cinder. Water it well.
3. Scatter your seeds and barely cover with a small amount of your potting mix, then press the soil down gently with your palm.
4. Water seedlings only once or twice a week, as too much dampness can cause fungal diseases that can kill your keiki plants.
5. They'll grow quickly: when they're 8 to 10 inches tall, you can transplant them to your garden.

☞ **NOTE:** The authors of the book *A Native Hawaiian Garden* advise that pua kala seeds typically sprout in the fall, so if you plant yours in the spring or summer, they might sit in their pot for several months before they poke their little heads above the surface. Don't give up!

- Possible insect pests and diseases: I have seen no insects and have no reports from my sources that insects present problems for this plant. It can get powdery mildew, however, so if your plant or plants start looking "furry," you might want to spray them with a solution of sulfur.
- Medicinal uses, invasiveness potential and other special notes of interest: Pua kala was widely used for toothaches and other forms of pain control: the sap was used to reduce the pain caused by neuralgia, ulcers and warts. A distant relative of the opium poppy, it has a possible mild narcotic effect, according to *Polynesian Herbal Medicine.* In one laboratory study, it tested positive for alkaloids, possibly berberine: when the plant extract was injected into mice, it caused respiratory depression and deep sleep. At higher doses it caused convulsions and death. Obviously, do not eat this plant! I do not believe that pua kala will become invasive in your yard.

`Uhaloa or hi`a-loa (*Waltheria americana* and *W. indica*)

Illustration 7.5: The pale green `uhaloa is a wonderful weed in many lowland areas.

- Description: You might need to get used to this wild amaranth before you develop a love for its appearance. I didn't care for it when I first saw it growing quite abundantly on my newly cleared property, but changed my opinion when I learned that it is an indigenous plant with medicinal uses. It's a shrubby plant that grows no larger than 3 feet tall. The leaves are gray-green and it gets small yellow flowers in clusters.
- Climate zone where it thrives:
    Windward areas: yes
    Leeward areas: yes
    Elevation: sea level to about 4000 feet.
- How to grow it: If I wanted to introduce `uhaloa to my property, I would dig up a plant and move it to a dry spot on my property. Because it's a native, or an early Polynesian introduction, it should fare very well without special potting mix or fertilizer. But as with all newly transplanted plants, do keep it well watered until it becomes established. The flowers and seeds are so tiny I don't know how you would collect them.
- Possible insect pests and diseases: none
- Medicinal uses, invasiveness potential and other special notes of interest: This plant can definitely reseed itself and create a lot of keikis, so it is probably not appropriate for smaller city gardens.

114

However, if your property is larger with rocky areas, this could be an answer for providing some zero maintenance greenery for wild, rocky places.

'Uhaloa was one of the most common medicinal plants in Hawai`i in ancient times: it was made into a tea for asthma, arthritis and other ailments. The root has properties similar to aspirin, so it was used to relieve fevers and other pain.

Fruit and Herbs

Believe it or not, many fruit trees such as papayas and guavas grow so easily that they can become an invasive problem. This section will discuss a few fruit trees and herbs that you can easily grow in your garden.

Bananas (*Musa* spp.)

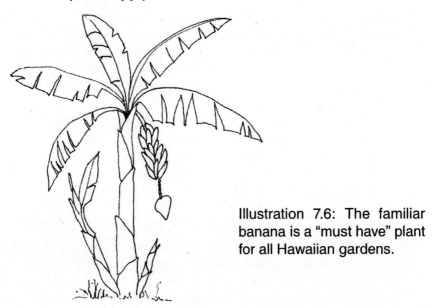

Illustration 7.6: The familiar banana is a "must have" plant for all Hawaiian gardens.

- Description: Nothing says "tropical" quite like a banana tree. Called mai`a in Hawai`i, at least one variety was carried here in the canoes of the first settlers because it was such an important food and fiber plant. Everyone knows what bananas look like: they're tall herbs, actually, that grow in clumps with long pale green leaves. Depending on the variety, bananas can reach 25 feet in height. Each individual

115

plant produces fruit only once. The huge bunch of ripening fruit hangs from the top of each shoot when it is producing.

- Climate zone where it thrives:

  Windward areas: yes, they do best here.

  Leeward areas: yes, but be sure to give them more water than the rain normally provides.

  Elevation: They do best at lower, warmer elevations, but do not care for salty soil or ocean spray. They prosper up to about the elevation of 3000 feet.

- How to grow it: Bananas are simple and I've found that they need a lot less fertilizer than many of the gardening books say they need. Here are some hints and tips about growing bananas:

  1. Be sure to plant bananas in areas that get full sun. If you live in a windy location, plant it where it will get some protection from high winds, such as behind your house or another plant.

  2. Bananas like a fair amount of soil, so prepare your planting area carefully, and try to plant in an area that has several feet of soil so it can form a robust root system. When you buy a young banana plant in a 1-gallon nursery pot, it's hard to imagine how large it will become in such a short amount of time, so be sure to allow plenty of room for this plant to roam. Your baby banana will form a clump of keikis that can get to be 15 feet across--or more! So don't plant it too close to your house, trees or garden beds where you don't want bananas to grow, because it will take over a large area in less time than you can imagine.

  3. Place your young banana plant into a hole that you have enriched with compost.

  4. As your banana grows larger, it will send up shoots, or "suckers" from its base. Mulch the plant heavily with its own leaves, which you can snip off to keep it looking pretty when the leaves turn yellow.

  5. To promote fruit production, growers recommend that you leave only two adult plants and two keiki shoots per clump. You can cut them off or transplant them to another spot to form more plants. Be sure to check the base of any banana plants you move for pencil-sized holes: if you find any, this can indicate that the plant has the banana root borer. You should burn or bury that plant. Never move young banana plants to another island, as this might introduce the borer to an area where it does not already exist. For more information, return to Chapter 6.

6. Frequently add compost, humus, manure or another source of natural nitrogen to the soil around your bananas, as they are heavy feeders. Also make sure that your plant gets plenty of water, especially if you live in a dry area or if it doesn't rain for a week or longer.

7. Harvest your bananas when the first one in a clump (or "rack," as the pros call them) starts to turn yellow. The rest will quickly follow suit and soon you'll have more bananas than you can eat. You can peel them and freeze them, and later, when you have no more bananas, make my recipe for banana-nut muffins (see below).

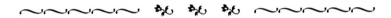

Banana-nut Muffins

1/2 cup melted butter or light salad oil, such as Canola
1 cup white sugar
2 eggs
1 cup mashed very ripe bananas
1 tsp. vanilla
2 cups flour (whole wheat or white)
1/2 tsp. salt
1 tsp. soda
1/3 cup hot water
1/2 cup chopped nuts of any kind (I use walnuts, but Macadamia nuts would be sensational if you have them)
1/2 cup raisins

Blend sugar with oil. Beat in the eggs, bananas, and vanilla and then stir until it's smooth.

Add the flour, soda and salt--no need to sift. Then add the hot water slowly and stir well after each addition. Fold in the nuts and raisins and then pour mixture into muffin tins lined with cupcake papers or a greased 9 by 5-inch bread pan.

For muffins, bake at 325 degrees for about 40 minutes. For bread, bake at 325 for about 70 minutes.

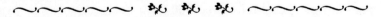

- Possible insect pests and diseases: For information about the banana root borer and how to control it naturally, check back to Chapter 6. The banana bunchy top virus is the latest disease to hit the bananas

of Hawai`i. If you see yellowed, stunted leaves at the growing tops of any of your bananas, report this problem to your local Department of Agriculture.
- Medicinal uses, invasiveness potential and other special notes of interest: Of course, bananas are an important and delicious food. But they also were used for folk medicine in old Hawai`i: juice or sap from the cut flower bud was given to people who felt weak or had stomach cramps. Ancient residents prepared ripe fruit in several ways to treat conditions such as constipation and asthma.

Basil (*Ocimum* spp.)

Illustration 7.7: Every garden should have some basil for its beauty and delicious flavor.

- Description: The Hawaiians know about basil and call it ki paoa. It was introduced by the early European settlers and was used medicinally in earlier times. Many different varieties of basil exist and all of them are simple to grow from seed. Try your hand at growing lemon basil, cinnamon basil, Thai (anise-flavored) basil, or my favorite, "holy" basil (*Ocimum sanctum*), a clove-flavored variety that Hindus call Tulsi. They also consider it sacred. All species look similar: erect, branching herbs that grow to 3 feet tall. The flowers are small and beautiful, edible, and form whorls on spikes up to a foot in length. I call it a wonderful weed because it has naturalized in my garden--I have lemon basil, holy basil and a cross between regular sweet basil and Thai basil growing right out of solid lava rock in the burning sun, with no soil, fertilizer and very little water. Basil is a true survivor!

- Climate zone where it thrives:
    Windward areas: yes
    Leeward areas: yes, perhaps with additional water.
    Elevation: Probably up to about 4000 feet.
- How to grow it: Basil seeds for many of the varieties are available from specialty seed catalogs. You will probably only find regular sweet basil plants and perhaps the Thai basil at your local nursery. I've found that late winter is a good time to start basil from seed. If you'd like to try doing this, just follow these steps:
    1. Fill a pot or a nursery flat with a light potting mix and water it well.
    2. Scatter your seeds over the soil surface, then barely cover with about 1/4 inch of additional potting soil, then pat it down gently.
    3. Keep your pot or flat in a sunny spot and watch for sprouting within several days of planting. Don't let it dry out.
    4. When your keiki plants are about 2 inches tall, transplant them to individual pots. I always choose the largest, healthiest plants and compost the runts.
    5. In a month or six weeks, you can plant them in your garden. I never fertilize my basil and it continues to grow exceptionally well, living for a year or more. When plants become woody, take them out, compost them, and start with new plants.
- Possible insect pests and diseases: spittlebugs, slugs and snails, even fruit flies sometimes affect sweet basil. The other varieties seem fairly insect-resistant, but do expect to see some leaf miner damage.
- Medicinal uses, invasiveness potential and other special notes of interest: Basil is used throughout Polynesia, where the people use its fragrant foliage for cooking, scenting coconut oil, for making leis, and in the past, for embalming. Tahitians use a warm infusion of the leaves for massage and it is commonly used as a "spiritual" herb on many islands, in the belief that its strong fragrance will deter evil spirits and demons, according to the book *Polynesian Herbal Medicine*. Today, we know that basil is a carminative (relieves gas and bloating), diuretic (increases urination) and a febrifuge (reduces fevers). For these purposes, you can brew some of the leaves and flowering tops into a tea. Check the sidebar for my pesto sauce recipe, a delicious Italian use of sweet basil (although I sometimes make pesto with lemon basil, which is very good with fish).

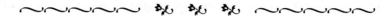

Super Simple Pesto Sauce

Into a blender jar, put:

1 cup olive oil

1 cup loosely-packed fresh basil leaves with flowering tops, if available

6 cloves of garlic, crushed

1/8 cup pine nuts or chopped macadamia nuts or walnuts (optional)

1/2 - 1 tsp. salt

Gradually, add the basil and then blend for a minute until all ingredients are well mixed. It freezes beautifully, so if you make up a big batch, you can save some for the future.

Use it as a dip for crackers or fresh veggies, or toss it with any kind of cooked pasta.

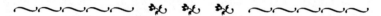

Hot pepper (*Capsicum frutescens*)

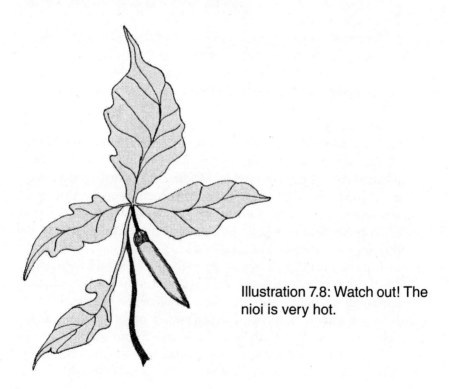

Illustration 7.8: Watch out! The nioi is very hot.

- Description: The Hawaiian name of this small, very hot pepper is nioi. Early European visitors to Hawai`i introduced it from Mexico and Central America a long time ago. Sometimes called a "Thai" pepper, it's a very small, red pepper when ripe, and very hot! The plant self-seeds readily: when overripe peppers fall to the ground many of them sprout. It gets to be 6 feet tall and starts producing the attractive peppers while it's still quite young.
- Climate zone where it thrives:
  Windward areas: yes, near the ocean where it's nice and warm.
  Leeward areas: yes, it seems to prefer hot, dry conditions.
  Elevation: I haven't seen it at high elevations, but believe that it will grow up to about 2000 feet with no problems.
- How to grow it: I actually didn't plant my first nioi: my chickens did the job for me by kicking seeds out of their coop. Now I have several large, productive nioi peppers surrounding the chicken coop fence. If you want to grow it, I think all you would need to do is to scatter some seeds from a dried nioi in the garden bed where you want it. Nioi can often be found at farmer's markets in bags containing perhaps 100 of them. What you would do with so many, I do not know! Aside from the fresh chicken manure that escapes from the coop, my nioi get no additional fertilizer and I have never watered any of them.
- Possible insect pests and diseases: Whiteflies sometimes attack the undersides of the leaves, but I have never lost a plant to them, so I just ignore them. Go back to Chapter 6 to learn about natural controls for whitefly.
- Medicinal uses, invasiveness potential and other special notes of interest: Nioi peppers have not been commonly used medicinally in any part of Polynesia, but the active ingredient that make these peppers hot, called capsaicin, is a superb pain reliever and is used as a topical treatment for arthritis and other internal pain. It produces a sensation of warmth without burning or reddening the skin. The leaves of the nioi, however, are used in Polynesian medicine: in Tonga, Samoa and Tahiti they are "rubbed in the hands or chewed and applied to boils, abscesses and wounds," according to Dr. W. Arthur Whistler in his book *Polynesian Herbal Medicine.*
  After you introduce nioi to your garden, you can expect that more nioi will pop up here and there, whether you want them or not. That's why I call it a wonderful weed. If you get more plants than you really want or need (a little goes a VERY long way), you can pot up the keikis and give them to friends and family. Or toss the extras into the compost

pile. I have heard that the peppers sell for about $5 per pound, so maybe you'll want to bag them up and take them to your local farmer's market to sell.

Spicy Cooking Oil

It's simple to make cooking oil that you can use to sauté or stir-fry veggies and other foods to make a delicious Thai-style dish. It's also an excellent addition to standard salad dressing recipes that will help to spice things up.

1. Use a clean glass jar, such as a mayonnaise jar, either 1-pint or 1 quart, depending on how much oil you want to make.
2. Place several red-ripe nioi peppers in the jar. You can also add some chopped onion, garlic cloves, and perhaps some fresh Thai basil.
3. Fill the jar with olive oil or another good quality cooking oil.
4. Cover the jar tightly and set it in the sun. Let it steep for about one week. Shake it daily.
5. Strain it and transfer the contents to smaller jars for gift giving and storage. Be sure to label it to remind you what's inside.
6. Refrigerate your oil: it will stay good for several months.

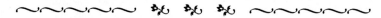

Papayas (*Carica papaya*)

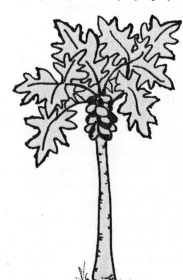

Illustration 7.9: I rarely plant papaya trees, but let the birds drop seeds for me. When I spot a keiki, I look around and ask myself if a papaya tree would go well in that location.

- Description: The familiar papaya, or mikana, is a delicious and common fruit in tropical areas. Early European settlers introduced it to Hawai`i and it quickly became a staple of life. The relatively short-lived trees can reach heights of up to 25 feet. They have hollow trunks and usually no branches. The leaves are large and deeply cut and the fruit forms on the trunk. Papayas produce lots of fruit and are easy to grow. In fact, baby trees pop up in places where you don't expect them! If you love papayas like I do, these volunteer trees can truly be "wonderful weeds."
- Climate zone where it thrives:
  Windward areas: yes: papayas do very well in wet climates.
  Leeward areas: yes: papayas like warm weather, but be sure to give them plenty of water.
  Elevation: Near sea level to approximately 2000 feet.
- How to grow it: Papayas are a very fast-growing fruit tree: you can expect to start harvesting and eating its delicious, nutritious fruit less than one year from the time you plant a tree from seed. Papaya keikis pop up where I least expect them, so that makes them so easy to grow. They do best from seed: I have not had success in transplanting young papaya trees. If I want a tree somewhere, I just scatter some seeds of a papaya I have eaten on the ground and when I see several young trees starting to grow, I weed out the smaller, weaker ones and leave only one tree in that location. You can plant papayas fairly close to each other, but be sure to leave at least 5 feet between plants. Mulch your tree with compost and yellowed papaya leaves when you think of it, but my trees continue to grow and produce lots of fruit with no special care at all. If you're interested in growing papayas commercially, Shunyam Nirav has good directions for "proper" papaya planting and care in his book *Hawaiian Organic Growing Guide*.

  One warning about using papayas in compost that I learned early in my Hawai`i residency is not to put the seeds into your compost pile. Although compost piles heat up, they never get hot enough to kill papaya seeds, and when you use the finished compost, you'll get a "carpet" of keiki trees wherever you spread your compost! If this should happen, wait until the little trees are a few inches tall, then pull them and return them to your compost pile, or simply lay them on the ground around other plants as mulch. My chickens absolutely love the seeds, however, so if you have these animals, that's a good place to dispose of your papaya seeds.

If you care about such things, plant only seeds of papayas that have not been genetically engineered. Varieties such as Solo, Sunrise, and Kapoho are good choices. Avoid the Sun Up and Rainbow varieties, which were developed to combat the very serious ringspot virus disease that threatened the papaya industry here, but which can cross-pollinate with other varieties, causing unknown strains to happen.

- Possible insect pests and diseases: Fruit flies absolutely adore papayas, so pick your fruit when it is just starting to show some orange color. Keep any fruit that might drop from the tree cleaned up from the ground. My papayas sometimes get a white variety of scale as well. You can blast them off the tree with a sharp stream of water from your hose, or spray with insecticidal soap or ultrafine oil. Tanglefoot is a good solution for controlling the ants that bring scale: go back to Chapter 6 for details on how to control these pests.
The papaya ringspot virus (PRV) is a very serious problem in some parts of Hawai`i. Aphids spread it, so if you use Tanglefoot at the base of your young trees, you can control the ants that "farm" aphids and scale insects. Check our directions for using Tanglefoot in Chapter 6 before you apply it. If any of your papayas get round "sores" on the fruit and rot before they turn ripe, you might have ringspot. Cut down your tree, get the roots out as much as possible, destroy it and do not plant another papaya tree in the same spot.

- Medicinal uses, invasiveness potential and other special notes of interest: In addition to being a delicious fruit that gives us lots of vitamins A, C, potassium and calcium, green papayas also contain a valuable enzyme called papain that is excellent for the digestive system. Another ingredient of papayas is an alkaloid that can help to reduce heart rate, blood pressure and respiration, according to *Polynesian Herbal Medicine.*
Medicinal uses of many parts of the papaya tree have been common in Hawai`i. The latex, or sticky, milky juice found especially in green papayas, has been used to treat sores, wounds and bee stings. Papayas have also been used to treat certain stomach problems. In other parts of Polynesia, the seeds are grated and given to people suffering from intestinal worms: it's the papain that does the trick.
As I've said, papayas are definitely a wonderful weed and can pop up where you least expect them--or want them! If too many papaya trees pop up, you can pull them out and add them to your compost. Or simply chop them into shorter pieces and use them as mulch around any nearby plants.

Sweet and Sour Green Papaya Pickles

I adapted a very old recipe from my paternal grandmother one day when a loaded papaya tree fell over in a windstorm. What to do with all those green papayas?

- 1 or 2 green papayas, cut into cubes
- 3 cups sugar
- 1-1/2 cups apple cider vinegar
- 1/2 cup water
- several tsp. of cinnamon
- 1 tsp. ground cloves

Pack your papaya pieces into clean canning jars, along with a cinnamon stick and a slice of lemon. Then fill the jars with the sugar/vinegar syrup, which you have made earlier and allowed to boil for a few minutes.

Cover your jars with a tight-fitting canning lid and boil for 15 minutes in a large kettle.

Makes about 6 pints. If you leave the proper canning lids on them, you don't even need to refrigerate your jars after they cool.

Passionfruit (*Passiflora* spp.)

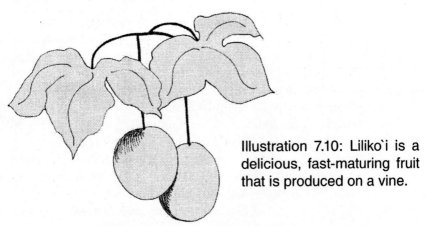

Illustration 7.10: Liliko`i is a delicious, fast-maturing fruit that is produced on a vine.

- Description: Passionfruit, or liliko`i, is a rampant vine that produces beautiful, exotic flowers and delicious fruit, which can be yellow or purple, with hard shells or soft ones. A wild Hawaiian liliko`i exists, but the fruit is not edible. This wild passionfruit creates a

125

weedy mess and is not, in my opinion, a wonderful weed. The first passionfruit were introduced in the Liliko`i Gulch on Maui in the late 1800's.

- Climate zone where it thrives:
  Windward areas: yes
  Leeward areas: yes, but they may need more water than the rain provides.
  Elevation: Near sea level to about 3000 feet, although some varieties are grown in mainland areas and can tolerate temperatures as low as 20 degrees. The purple varieties do best at higher, upcountry locations.

- How to grow it: Most importantly, do not grow the "banana poka" variety of passionfruit (*Passiflora mollisma*), as it is a serious invasive pest in parts of Hawai`i. Refer to Chapter 2 for a complete discussion of this and other invasive plants. Other varieties such as *Passiflora incarnata* are the best ones to grow. *Passiflora edulis* produces delicious purple fruit, but be sure to keep the fruits well picked and prune the vines periodically to control this plant from taking over your yard. Passionfruit is a fast-growing yet short-lived plant, with a lifespan of 5 to 7 years. You can easily start new plants from the seeds you collect from fruit you have enjoyed:
  1. Scoop out the seeds and flesh of a very ripe liliko`i.
  2. Wash the pulp off a little bit: it's sticky so you won't be able to remove it all.
  3. Prepare a pot or flat with some nice, rich potting mix. Add some compost if you have it and then water your pot or flat well.
  4. Scatter your seeds on the surface, and then cover them with just a little soil--perhaps 1/4 inch.
  5. Set your pot in a sunny spot, keep it moist, and watch for germination to occur within a few weeks.
  6. Transplant your keiki vines to a spot in the garden that gets full sun and has somewhere for the vines to climb. Trellises and arbors are great for this, but you can also use liliko`i vines to cover unattractive fences and other areas. Do not allow the vines to climb trees as they can strangle them.

- Possible insect pests and diseases: Nematodes can attack the roots of some passionfruit species and of course fruit flies love them, especially the soft-shelled varieties. But you can beat the fruit flies to your ripening fruit by picking it while it's slightly green and allowing it to ripen in the relative safety of your kitchen. Check Chapter 6 for natural insect controls.

- Medicinal uses, invasiveness potential and other special notes of interest: Again, do NOT grow the banana poka variety of passionfruit. For other species, watch for signs of invasiveness: It's simple to control it by picking the fruit and pruning the vines. Passionflower is a well-known and time-honored medicinal plant. You can brew the fresh leaves into a tea that can help to induce sleep, as they are a mild, natural sedative. This tea can also help to ease anxiety, especially that caused by high blood pressure. It is often mixed with other herbs to create a nice nightcap tea or tincture.

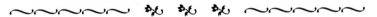

 **CAUTION**: According to Dr. Roger Baldwin, you should always boil passionflower leaf tea for at least 10 minutes to destroy any possible toxicity that some species contain. He says, "The hulls of the fruits are always toxic, with cyanide levels the highest of any plants in Hawai'i. There have been no incidents of human poisoning from eating fruit hulls, (probably because of the unpleasantly bitter taste of the hulls), but there have been numerous cases of poisoning of stock which were fed whole fruits. The leaves, however, vary from non-toxic to extremely so. Eating the leaves is like playing 'Russian roulette' -- most of the time the plants are harmless and contain substances that are medicinally useful. However, depending upon the particular species, the condition of the plant, and other unknown causes, the plants may suddenly produce highly toxic leaves. With proper precautions you should be able to avoid the toxicity of the plant. First, do not eat the leaves or fruit hulls, whether cooked or raw. Any cyanide in the leaves should be destroyed by heat when making tea, but to be certain, you should boil the tea for at least 10 minutes (preferably longer) to destroy any cyanide which may be leached from the leaves."

Hilo Dreams Sleep-Promoting Tincture

I use fresh passionflower leaves and flowers, along with other herbs, to make a nice bedtime helper. The herbs mentioned in this recipe should be available in bulk at natural foods stores in your area. I recommend purchasing passionflower leaves to be certain you're using the correct, nontoxic species.

Place the following herbs in a clean 1-quart glass jar with tight-fitting lid, such as a canning jar:
- 1/4 cup purchased dry passionflower leaf
- 1/4 cup valerian root, cut and sifted if dry or minced if fresh

- 1/4 cup chamomile flowers
- 1/8 cup `awa (kava kava) root, cut and sifted if dry or minced if fresh
  Fill the jar with vodka, brandy or apple cider vinegar.
  Allow your mixture to sit in a shady spot for about 4 weeks. Remember to shake it up every day. Strain it before you use it and store it in a dark, cool place.
  Dosage: 2 droppersful 1/2 hour before bedtime as needed. You can mix this with fruit juice, as the taste is not particularly pleasant!

Poha berries (*Physallis peruviana*)

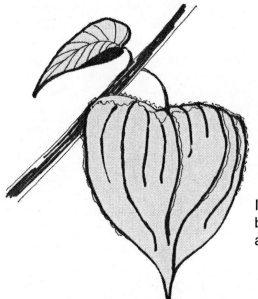

Illustration 7.11: Poha berries resemble tomatillos and make a delicious jam.

- Description: Related to the tomato and tomatillo, poha berries are tasty little fruits, no larger than 1/2 inch in diameter, that are enclosed in a convenient, papery insect-proof wrapper. It was introduced from South America. Bushes are shrubby with light green, downy leaves. They get to be only about 4 feet tall, and can spread to 4 feet wide. If you can beat the birds to these treats, pick them when the "wrapper" is dry and papery-brown. It's sometimes called the "ground cherry" because when the fruit it at its perfect stage of ripeness, it drops to the ground. Today, people in Hawai`i make a delicious jam from poha berries. Look for it at your supermarket, and if you get a lot of fruit, you might try making a batch yourself.

- Climate zone where it thrives:
    Windward areas: yes
    Leeward areas: yes
    Elevation: Near sea level to 4000 feet.
- How to grow it: You should be able to find a plant at your neighborhood nursery or farmer's market. Plant it in well-drained soil and give it room to roam. After it starts producing fruit, poha can sprout anywhere in your garden, so you can transplant a keiki plant to either a pot or a more appropriate location when you find one. They transplant very successfully. My three poha berry plants are in a shallow bed with cinder and macadamia nut compost and I have never watered or fertilized them. They continue producing berries in the summer months, but I've found that the cardinals in my area tend to eat them all before I can get to them.
- Possible insect pests and diseases: none, unless you consider cardinals or other birds to be pests.
- Medicinal uses, invasiveness potential and other special notes of interest: Because poha seeds can be spread by birds, volunteers of this plant can appear in unwanted places in your yard. But since it's a wonderful weed, you can choose to let them grow into more plants or dig them up and give them away. No medicinal or other uses have been reported for the poha berry.

Sweet potato (*Ipomoea batatas*)

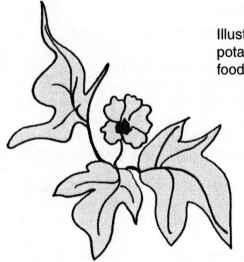

Illustration 7.12: The sweet potato is one of the staple foods of the Pacific.

- Description: The familiar `uala is a canoe plant, brought to Hawai`i by the first settlers. It is a member of the morning glory family and has similar, heart-shaped leaves on trailing vines. The fruit, or potato, is formed underground and can be yellow or purple.
- Climate zone where it thrives:
    Windward areas: yes
    Leeward areas: yes, they can survive in areas with little rainfall.
    Elevation: Sea level to 1500 feet is the range reported where `uala have been grown commercially.
- How to grow it: Jill Wagner of Future Forests Nursery on the Big Island says that "`uala requires little care and can be grown in marginal places. Where there is low rainfall, it was traditionally planted after soaking rains. The cuttings were planted in mounds where weeds were mulched to create good soil. The tubers mature in four to eight months. Sweet potatoes make a good ground cover, as they can cover an area very quickly. But if you want to grow them for the tubers, you can plant them in mounds of soil. You can also plant them inside wooden box borders filled with soil. This way the tubers can get fat and the vines can be contained. It is hard to go wrong with a plant this easy."
If you can find a plant in someone's yard, the *Hawaiian Organic Growing Guide* tells how to take a stem cutting if you want to start a sweet potato vine of your own:
1. Cut a piece of stem about 6 to 9 inches long.
2. Prepare an area for them that has some deep sandy loam.
3. Plant your cuttings every foot or so around the edges of the garden bed to allow the vines to wander outside of the planting area.
4. Keep the bed moist until you see growth happening, then cut back on water.
5. Fertilize with phosphorus and potash if you feel they need it. Compost is also good for them. Too much nitrogen encourages growth of the leaves and vines, at the expense of the delicious potatoes developing underground, so don't use a fertilizer like "Triple 16."
- Possible insect pests and diseases: Nematodes and hornworms can affect sweet potatoes. Check Chapter 6 for ideas on how to control these pests.
- Medicinal uses, invasiveness potential and other special notes of interest: Of course, sweet potatoes are a delicious starchy food that is widely grown throughout the Pacific islands. The leafy portions of the plant are edible and you can steam them, stir-fry them, or use them in soups and stews. I don't believe they have the potential of becoming invasive.

Medicinal Plants

This section includes a few medicinal plants that are extremely easy to grow and which often become naturalized in a garden. I'll tell you what each plant is used for and make some suggestions about how you can prepare a plant medicine from it. Please remember that herbs are serious medicine and if you want to use any of them for any disease or condition to first check with your doctor or other qualified health care provider. Be sure to follow our preparation and dosage instructions for each plant.

Basic Tincture-Making Directions

Strong tasting herbs might not taste so good in a tea, so you can make a tincture that is more palatable. Tinctures are very simple to make and they are more potent than teas, they're portable, and they last forever.

I prefer using freshly cut herbs, but if you don't have them growing nearby, you can purchase dried herbs from your neighborhood natural foods store. When you use fresh herbs, use a little more than you would use of the dried variety.

1. If using fresh herbs, chop or mince them. Dried herbs are usually sold as a powder or "cut and sifted."
2. Put your herbs in a clean jar, about 1/3 full.
3. Cover the herbs with vodka or brandy. I use inexpensive vodka for most tinctures. You can also use vegetable glycerin and/or apple cider vinegar.
4. Close the jar tightly.
5. Keep your jar in a place where it won't get direct sun.
6. Shake your brewing tincture every day for 4 weeks.
7. Then strain it and bottle it, preferably in dark glass.
8. Store in a cool, dark place at room temperature. Don't forget to label what's inside!

DOSAGE: Normally, tinctures come in a small brown bottle with a dropper. For many herbs, take a fairly large amount 2 to 3 times each day in juice until your symptoms are gone. For example, take 2 to 4 FULL droppers 2 to 3 times each day. Taking a couple of drops comes from homeopathy and is not correct for this type of medicine.

Herbal Teas: 101 Nourishing Blends for Daily Health and Vitality, by Kathleen Brown and Jeanine Pollak

Gotu kola (*Centella asiatica*)

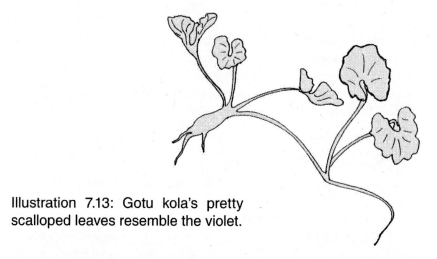

Illustration 7.13: Gotu kola's pretty scalloped leaves resemble the violet.

- Description: The Hawaiians call this small ground-hugging viney little plant pohe kula. It came to us from tropical Asia and is now a common weed in many environments, from dry and sunny areas to damp, shady places. The leaves are light green and round with scallops. You'll probably never see a flower, as they are tiny and inconspicuous.
- Climate zone where it thrives:
    Windward areas: yes
    Leeward areas: yes, but keep it watered.
    Elevation: near sea level to less than 350 feet
- How to grow it: If you find a patch of gotu kola growing, dig up a clump with roots and transplant it to your garden. It makes a nice ground cover and helps to block out other weeds. During dry spells, my gotu kola shrivels a little and has sometimes looked like it's dead, but it always comes back after the rains return.
- Possible insect pests and diseases: I have seen none.
- Medicinal uses, invasiveness potential and other special notes of interest: Gotu kola has not been widely used in Hawai`i for medicinal purposes, but today we know that it is a potent memory-enhancing herb, available for purchase in capsules, as a tincture, and in bulk for making tea. It's also good for the nervous system and for topical use as a remedy for eczema, wounds and other skin problems, according to *Herbal Remedies for Dummies*. It has been reported that this plant provides natural cures for over 90 ailments.

If you want to use gotu kola to improve your memory or for any other purpose, you can make a tea or tincture from the leaves. Simply throwing a few leaves into your salad is nice, but unless you do it regularly, it will not give you a therapeutic dosage. If you make or buy gotu kola tincture, take 2 to 4 full droppers 2 to 3 times every day. If you prefer to make a tea, put about a dozen leaves into a teacup or teapot and pour boiling water over it. Let it steep for 10 minutes, then strain it and drink 3 cups every day. You can make a large teapot full and simply heat each cup of tea before you drink it. Store leftover tea in the refrigerator.

Although gotu kola can spread into your garden beds, it never really becomes an invasive problem because it helps to block out other weeds. It is an attractive groundcover that can help to prevent erosion and will keep the soil moist and cool around your other plants. You might want to keep it cleared away from the base of native Hawaiian plants, however, because they might not be able to compete with such a close neighbor.

Noni (*Morinda citrifolia*)

Illustration 7.14: Although it smells unpleasant, noni has many beneficial medicinal properties.

- Description: The Indian mulberry was so important to early Polynesians that they brought it to Hawai`i aboard their canoes. It is an attractive small tree, up to 20 feet tall, with large shiny leaves and stinky yellow fruit that is highly medicinal. In ancient Hawai`i, humans ate noni only during times of famine.
- Climate zone where it thrives:
  Windward areas: yes, especially near the ocean
  Leeward areas: yes
  Elevation: Noni does best at low elevations on both the windward and leeward sides and not very well higher than 1700 feet.

- How to grow it: I've put noni in this chapter because it truly is a "wonderful weed." It will grow in almost no soil at all: I've seen it thriving in what appears to be solid rock. If you purchase a young tree, prepare the soil as you would for any plant that will grow fairly large. That is, dig a hole about twice the size of the pot, dig in some compost, and then plant your noni tree up to the top of the soil in which it is potted. If the roots are cramped, loosen them a little before you plant your tree. Later, you can apply some mulch around the tree to keep weeds away, but I have never fertilized my trees and they continue to grow and produce plenty of fruit.
- Possible insect pests and diseases: Nothing likes to eat noni!
- Medicinal uses, invasiveness potential and other special notes of interest: Every part of this wonderful tree has been used for medicine, both in Hawai`i and around the world. Its bark, leaves, flowers, fruit and seeds all provide healing for certain ailments. Noni's properties include, but are certainly not limited to these: it's antibacterial, antimicrobial, alterative, antiparasitic, stomachic, anticancer, anti-inflammatory, antiarthritic, antioxidant, analgesic and antihypertensive. I like to say that it's "pro" everything good and "anti" everything bad. You can't go wrong with noni! It's used for chronic respiratory conditions such as tuberculosis, influenza, asthma, coughs, colds, sinusitis and sore throats. It's good for digestive disorders such as diarrhea, constipation and indigestion. The roots and bark were used as a red or yellow dye. Entire books have been written about this miraculous fruit, so if you're interested in the whole story, a trip to your library or bookstore will be an educational adventure.

Noni is not classified as a problematic invader. If you grow noni, try to keep the fruit picked before it turns translucent white, drops to the ground and makes a big, smelly mess. Noni keikis occasionally pop up from the root system of established trees. I suspect that birds or other critters spread noni seeds in places that are far from my other noni trees. If you should get too many volunteer noni trees, be grateful! It's simple to recognize a young noni tree when it is just a few inches tall because it has the same shiny leaves as the parent tree. If you don't want it, simply pull it out and toss it into the compost pile. But it's a shame for a noni tree to go to waste. Why not pot up your keikis and give them to friends and family?

Even Noni Leaf Is Good For You

If you have a bee sting or other insect bite, a boil or any kind of skin problem, here's a simple and effective treatment.

1. Pick one young, medium-sized noni leaf.
2. Using tongs, pass both sides of the leaf over a flame momentarily.
3. When the leaf cools, fold it up into a little package.
4. Place the "package" directly onto your wound and use adhesive tape or a bandage to secure it in place.
5. Leave the noni bandage on your wound for one day or overnight.
6. Replace it the following day if you need to.

In my case, I have seen dramatic improvement of boils on two occasions with just a one-day noni leaf treatment. It has not worked as well for certain other skin problems, but don't be afraid to experiment.

Noni vinegar is super simple to make and so good for you

1. Take ripe noni, chop them up and fill a jar about half full with the fruit.
2. Fill your jar with apple cider vinegar.
3. Let it sit in the sun for a few days, then strain it and use the vinegar in salad dressings and in any recipe that calls for vinegar. It's also great as a gargle when you have a sore throat.

It keeps forever in a cool, dark cupboard.

Noni Oriental Wasabi Salad Dressing

For about 1 pint of dressing, combine the following in a glass jar:

1 cup sesame oil
1/4 cup noni vinegar, made with rice wine vinegar
2 TB lime juice
1 TB chopped garlic
1 tsp. wasabi paste (or more, according to taste)
1/2 cup shoyu (soy sauce)

Cover tightly, then shake your dressing and let the flavors blend in the refrigerator for a few hours before using.

This goes great with "Sushi Salad":

1/2 pound fresh ahi, either raw or quickly sautéed, cut into Julienne strips
1 Japanese cucumber, cut into Julienne strips about 1" long

4 scallions, sliced
1 avocado, cut into slices
2 cups cooked white rice, cooled and mixed with 1 TB each of rice
vinegar and sugar
4 - 6 cups mixed salad greens
Furikake or roasted nori sprinkled over the top

Prepare each plate individually: Lay down salad greens first, and then
place a scoop of rice (about 1/2 cup) in the center of each plate. Arrange
the ahi, cucumber, scallions and avocado in a wagon wheel pattern
on the rice and around the plate. Sprinkle liberally with furikake or
roasted nori and dress. Serves 4.

Plantain (*Plantago* spp.)

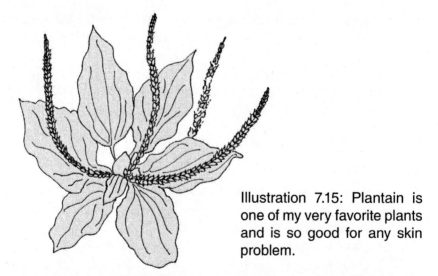

Illustration 7.15: Plantain is
one of my very favorite plants
and is so good for any skin
problem.

- Description: This is not the cooking banana you might know as a
  plantain, but rather a small herb that's often considered a lawn weed.
  The Hawaiians call the native species lau kahi. It's a low-growing
  pretty little plant with leaves in a rosette pattern. When it blooms, it
  sends up a flower spike that's from 3 to 12 inches tall. Some variety
  of plantain grows on every continent on Earth, and all of the native
  peoples have used it for the same basic purposes of skin healing and
  liver and kidney health.

- Climate zone where it thrives:
  Windward areas: yes
  Leeward areas: yes
  Elevation: near sea level to 3300 feet.
- How to grow it: You might already have plantain growing in your yard, whether you want it or not. If you don't have any, it should be fairly simple to find some: it grows under adverse conditions, like between the cracks of sidewalks. When you find some, you can dig it up and transplant it to your yard. It does like some moisture and tends to droop on hot sunny days, but mine always recovers. I do water it during very dry spells. You can also collect some seeds and scatter them where you'd like to have it grow.
- Possible insect pests and diseases: Slugs and snails sometimes eat my plantain leaves, but have not killed any plants. Check in Chapter 6 for ideas on how to control these creatures without poison.
- Medicinal uses, invasiveness potential and other special notes of interest: Over 30 years ago, plantain was the first plant that I learned could be used as medicine, and I continue to rely on it today for skin healing. I make a poultice from it and apply it to my wound, often combining it with comfrey or other plants that are good for the skin. See below for directions for making a poultice from plantain. Hawaiian people of the past used plantain to treat boils, abscesses, and wounds from such things as sea urchin spikes. For this use, they often combined the lau kahi with salt in a mortar and pestle and mashed it to a paste. This works well because this plant contains tannins and sodium salts, which give it astringent properties.
  One species of plantain (*Plantago ovata*) has slippery little seeds called psyllium, which are a well-known remedy for constipation. You can buy psyllium seed in capsule form or in bulk at your natural foods store. These seeds are a common ingredient in bowel-cleansing and laxative formulas.

Plantain Poultice for Skin Healing

1. Gather 10-12 large plantain leaves and some flower spikes if available.
2. Chop up the plant material into 1-inch lengths.
3. Boil 1 quart of filtered water in a non-metallic pan, such as Pyrex.
4. Add your plantain and reduce the heat to a simmer.
5. Allow it to simmer for 20 minutes, then remove the pot from the heat and let it cool.
6. When it's cool enough to work with, scoop out the mushy plant material, squeeze the excess water from it and hold it on your wound for as long as you can. You can use tape to hold the plantain in place for longer periods of time.

Purslane (*Portulaca oleracea*)

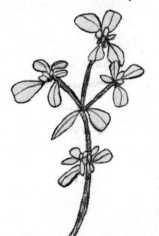

Illustration 7.16: Purslane is delicious and nutritious. Drawn by B. Fahs.

*   Description: This weedy-looking little succulent is called ʻakulikuli-kula in Hawaiʻi. Try saying that--it's fun! It's also sometimes called pigweed. A low-growing plant with small, fleshy leaves and tiny yellow flowers, it can look ugly in garden beds--it spreads widely and quickly after it takes root. But it's not only medicinal; it's a great culinary plant, so read on.
*   Climate zone where it thrives:
    Windward areas: yes
    Leeward areas: yes
    Elevation: I've seen it growing right next to the ocean and my sources report it to exist to about 3000 feet.

- How to grow it: I'm not sure I recommend that you introduce purslane to your property if you don't already have it, because it can get to be rather weedy looking and once it's on your property it's there to stay. However, if you have an area where nothing else will grow and you want something that's healthy for you and totally low maintenance to grow, or you just want a plant to cover some rocks or an unattractive area, you could transplant some purslane from someone else's yard.
- Possible insect pests and diseases: none
- Medicinal uses, invasiveness potential and other special notes of interest: Purslane is a delicious, nutritious food. It's cultivated in France as a lemon-flavored salad delicacy and enjoyed in fancy New York restaurants. It's a rich source of vitamin C and alpha linolenic acid, one of the Omega-3 fatty acids. Why buy fish oil in capsules when this little plant grows wild? It's a powerful antioxidant, which is one of the characteristics of plants that help to fight cancer, according to Michael Tierra in *The Way of Herbs*. The U.S. Department of Agriculture is looking into purslane as a possible crop for cultivation as they try to introduce healthy changes into the American diet.

Purslane does have the ability to spread where you don't want it and it can be hard to get rid of. But every time I see it in my garden, I remember that it's good for me, and that makes me feel better about this "wonderful weed."

Vervain (*Stachytarpheta urticifolia*)

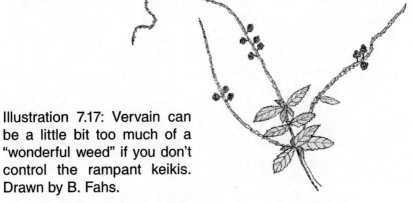

Illustration 7.17: Vervain can be a little bit too much of a "wonderful weed" if you don't control the rampant keikis. Drawn by B. Fahs.

- Description: Vervain is a member of the large mint family and is called ha'uoi, owi, or oi in Hawai'i. Sometimes called "cayenne" vervain, it's shrubby, up to 5 or 6 feet tall, with woody stems and funny-looking flower spikes that contain a few small lavender to purple flowers that taste slightly of mushrooms. Go ahead--it's safe to eat them and they'll make an attractive and exotic addition to your next salad.

- Climate zone where it thrives:
    Windward areas: yes
    Leeward areas: yes
    Elevation: Sea level to about 2500 feet
- How to grow it: This is another plant that I don't recommend introducing to your property if you don't already have it. It grows out of solid rock in areas of my property and we allow a few to grow in the garden as specimen plants, but often weed out the prolific keikis. It is a valuable nectar plant and the bees certainly love it; as a nectar plant it might also attract and encourage beneficial insects. If it grows in lawn areas or areas that you weed-whack, you can control it by mowing and whacking. When I pull non-blooming keikis out by the roots, I always deposit them at the base of our valuable plants to provide those plants with nourishing mulch.
- Possible insect pests and diseases: none that I have seen.
- Medicinal uses, invasiveness potential and other special notes of interest: As with many of the species of herbs found in Hawai`i, formal laboratory studies have not been conducted to analyze this vervain's medicinal properties. However, the "official" vervain (*Verbena officinalis*) is used for liver congestion and related disorders such as painful or irregular menstrual periods, according to Michael Tierra in his important book *The Way of Herbs*. He goes on to say that vervain is also good for hepatitis, jaundice, cirrhosis of the liver, colds, flu and fever, nervousness that is caused by liver congestion, anger, shock and other ailments. Folklore uses in Hawai`i indicate that this plant has antiseptic and antibiotic properties: it has been used as both a tea and a poultice for infections such as staphylococcus.

The wild Hawaiian vervain is very invasive and because we don't know all of its chemical constituents as we do for other members of the vervain family, I keep the prolific keikis weeded out and don't often use this plant for medicine.

Chapter 8
Carefree Hawaiian Plants to Grow (including Polynesian Introductions)

What? Grow endangered native plants in my home garden? What a concept, but many of our natives are very easy to grow because they belong here! They don't require a lot of fussing, fertilizing and care and are therefore not only desirable landscape plants, they're simple to grow and maintain as well.

Be sure to read this chapter to learn about 21 easy to grow native Hawaiian plants or canoe plants, which the ancient Polynesian settlers brought with them to their new home in Hawai`i. In all cases, these plants have been here long enough to have acquired a Hawaiian name and have been used for building houses, temples, canoes, for medicine, and so forth. To refresh your memory of the definitions of the terms endemic, indigenous, native and alien, check Chapter 2.

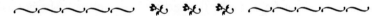

☞ **NOTE:** Do not remove any plants from the wild. Our native plants are often endangered and it is important for us all to be custodians of our precious plant heritage. Conversely, it's also important that none of us plant native plants in the wild, as their introduction can confuse the ecosystem into which they are planted by introducing insect pests or diseases and altering the natural diversity that is found in the wild.

Let the Plants Tell You What They Like

When I try to force something to grow, I find it often fails. For example, my valerian and lemon balm, normally hardy and even invasive in other environments, are struggling members of my plant family. They might not survive here forever. When I find myself digging up a plant, repotting it and babying it in my nursery area while I re-build its bed with more soil, compost, mulch and other good stuff, I begin to think, "why am I doing this?" Why not make gardening easy on myself by growing only the plants that can withstand life on a lava flow, in a place where it can rain buckets for a month or more and on the other hand, not rain at all for similar periods of time? One of my central philosophies about gardening in paradise is that if a plant can adapt to the whims of the weather and can live through times of drought as well as constant, drenching rains, that plant is happy in my garden. If it cannot endure such dramatic climate fluctuations, it will not succeed here. I tell people that if a plant survives, I'm glad. If it doesn't, "too bad, so sad." But many of the native Hawaiian plants are extremely hardy and carefree. Their numbers continue to increase in my garden, while I learn and accept that many plants from other parts of the world are simply less well adapted to the periodic parching droughts and torrential rains.

A Garden in the Midst of Urban Honolulu is a Haven for Indigenous Plants

Native Hawaiian plants are important to our heritage, and they are disappearing because of urban development and agricultural needs. Most are attractive and very simple to grow.

"Native plants are plants that got here by themselves," according to Betsy Gagne of the Hawai`i Natural Area Reserves System. "They were dropped by birds or floated over the ocean. The point is, nobody brought them here."

The next closest to native plants are the so-called "canoe plants," brought here from the South Pacific by the first settlers. They include bananas, taro, sweet potatoes, sugar cane, and many others that are familiar to us in Hawai`i today.

"After that, came the exotic plants," Betsy said. "I don't like that name because it makes the plants sound like something special. Exotic, when applied to horticulture, simply means a non-native, introduced plant. And too many of them have escaped cultivation and have gone wild. Now we spend a large portion of our time trying to kill them off. Examples are the Australian tree fern and strawberry guava. You see people actually landscaping with these noxious weeds."

Once they mature, the natives need very little water or fertilizer. Most native plants are sensitive to fertilizers, and balanced plant foods should be used at half the recommended strength. Over-watering, over-fertilizing and over-pruning are the worst threats to backyard cultivation.

Honolulu Star-Bulletin, Ever Green column by Lois Taylor, 11/28/97

This chapter includes instructions for growing 21 easy to care for Hawaiian plants. For each plant I describe, you will find this information about it:

- Illustration
- Description of the plant: The descriptions are general and non-technical! That is, I won't be using words like "pinnate" or "savoyed" to describe the shape and characteristics of the leaves.
- Climate zone where it thrives: Here, I'll include information for windward and leeward gardens and mention the elevation at which each plant is likely to succeed. But the information about many of our native plants can be a little spotty, and we just don't know whether some plants might grow in cultivation at elevations that are different from their typical range. So you can be a pioneer or an inventor by experimenting with some of the plants in this chapter in your microclimate.
- How to grow it: Generally, I'll be assuming that you, the home gardener, will be purchasing young plants and planting them into garden beds that you have created and nourished with compost and mulch. If it's appropriate, I'll mention how to start some of the plants from seed or cuttings, but the specific directions for doing this and also for transplanting young plants are in Chapter 4. Be sure to check the Resources Appendix for ideas on where you might find starter plants or seeds on all the islands. And when you visit your favorite nursery or garden center, encourage the owner to consider carrying more of our interesting and important native plants.
- Possible insect pests and diseases: We don't know everything there is to know about our Hawaiian natives, so you might discover that a different insect just loves to nibble on one of your new native plants. By following the general directions for natural insect control in Chapter 6, you'll be able to apply your new knowledge to the insect pests that you encounter in your own yard. But I've found that most of the native plants in my garden are amazingly insect-resistant, and I hope this is your experience as well.
- Medicinal uses, invasiveness potential and other special notes of interest: Basically, all of the Hawaiian native plants have practical uses, and so do the canoe plants that the first Polynesian settlers introduced. I'll mention whether a plant was used for medicine, for building, or for uses such as fishhooks or spears -- if that information and knowledge is still available.

General Planting Directions for Natives

Just like the title of this book, planting native plants is "super simple."

I prefer to do all of my transplanting in the late afternoon to give my new plants a chance to adjust to their surroundings in the cooler hours of the day and overnight, rather than stressing them out by planting them in the burning sun. Do not plant native plants in ground that is denser than potting soil. Well-drained soil is important for most native plants.

☞ **Here's how to plant your Hawaiian natives:**

1. Find an appropriate location for the plant in your garden, based on information in this chapter and your own space availability and requirements. For example, if your plant is a tree that will grow as tall as your house, keep that in mind and allow plenty of space around it. Consider also how much shade it will cast when it's mature and what other plants will occupy spaces in the same environment.

2. Dig a hole about twice as wide as the pot your plant is in, but not much deeper.

3. Dig in some compost, peat moss or other good stuff. Using your shovel or a spading fork, mix the amendment into the bottom of the hole like you're tossing a salad.

4. Add a bit of compost or the soil that you have just dug out to ensure that your plant will sit nicely in the hole without crowding the roots or causing the top of the soil in the pot to sit above the top of the hole. You can set the plant, still in its pot, directly into the hole to get an idea of how much soil to add.

5. Native plants have sensitive root systems, so gently remove your plant from its pot. If it's stuck in a large pot, you might need to use a screwdriver or an old kitchen knife to loosen it: slide the blade down the sides of the pot and gently squeeze the sides of the pot. You'll soon be able to slide your plant out. If it's really stuck, you might need to cut the pot open with your pruning shears. Be careful not to disturb the plant's root system any more than is absolutely necessary. But if any large roots are circling around the pot and confining other smaller roots, do loosen them gently.

6. When your plant is out of the pot, loosen the root ball a little by gently squeezing the clump of soil that holds the roots. If you skip this step, which a lot of people do, your plant might continue to keep its roots bound into the pot-shaped clump and might have its growth

stunted. Freeing the roots in this way helps to give the plant a head start in its new home.

7. Place your plant into the hole you have just dug. Be sure to center it and check to see that the top of the soil from the pot is level with the top of the hole, or perhaps a little lower.

8. Backfill should consist of at least 50% compost and black cinder if the soil is clay, less cinder if the soil is sandy. Hold your plant in place while you gently shovel or scoop the dirt you have just dug out back into the hole. Do not use redwood compost, as it is too acidic for the natives. Put a little soil in the hole then gently pat it down, and then repeat this process until the hole is full. One mistake that some people make is to leave a pit around the plant, thinking that will help water from running off. But this practice is only appropriate for plants such as tomatoes that need an infrequent deep soaking. With the amount of rain we get in parts of Hawai`i, you'll want to be careful not to create a sinkhole around your precious plants -- this might cause them to get root rot and die from too much water.

9. Water your new plant thoroughly and check it regularly to make sure it stays damp but not soggy until you see new growth appearing. Don't let it dry out completely until it's at least six months old. After that, most native plants do not need you to give them more water than the rain naturally provides.

10. A last optional step is to pound a stake into the ground a few inches from your plant and tie it loosely with a piece of cloth or plastic nursery tape. You might also want to build a small fence around your plant to protect it from pets and other critters. You can easily make a simple 6-foot cage from steel mesh fencing, sometimes called "hog wire," hooked together to form a circle. If your plant is something that might be attacked by snails or slugs, take appropriate measures to protect it by using Sluggo, a copper barrier, or diatomaceous earth. Take a look at Chapter 6 for more hints and tips about natural insect and pest control.

☞ Sometimes I like to put shade cloth over or around new plantings to protect them from the burning sun until they get a little bigger and stronger. It's simple:

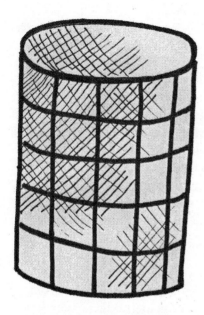

Illustration 8.1: A shadecloth frame is inexpensive and simple to make.

1. Cut a piece of shadecloth the same size as the hog wire "cage" you'll be putting around the plant to protect it. I usually cut hog wire six feet long and hook the sides together.
2. Tie the shadecloth onto the hogwire frame with plastic nursery tape in several places.
3. Place your shade frame over the plant and secure it with stakes. If you have strawberry guava growing on your property, you might use stakes made from its branches. The directions are in Chapter 2.

If you're planting a number of small plants in the same bed near each other, you can make a simple shaded "hoop" covering:

1. Cut a piece of hog wire about 6 or 8 feet long (or the length of your garden bed).
2. Bend the wire to form a slightly arching, but low, hoop.
3. Tie your shade cloth onto the wire frame and place it over your new plants.

`A`ali`i (Dodonaea viscosa)

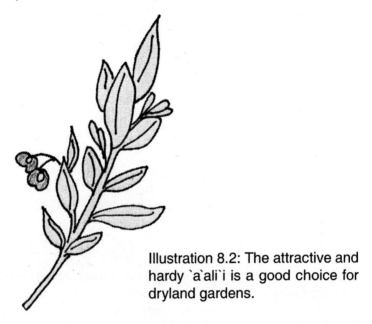

Illustration 8.2: The attractive and hardy `a`ali`i is a good choice for dryland gardens.

- Description: Once considered an invader of open pastures and meadows, the indigenous `a`ali`i is an attractive shrub to small tree that can grow to almost 30 feet tall. It is very easy to grow. The attractive seedpods, which are used in haku leis and dried flower arrangements, are red to brown, yellow, green, or even pink, and are dry and papery looking. It's common in dry places and in areas that have suffered fires or fairly recent lava flows.
- Climate zone where it thrives:
  Windward areas: yes. In wet forests it grows into a small tree.
  Leeward areas: yes. It does well in windy areas.
  Elevation: Does well at low elevations on the windward and leeward side and up to 8000 feet, even in dry locations.
- How to grow it: `A`ali`i is often available at nurseries and plant sales as a starter plant. Jill Wagner of Future Forests Nursery on the Big Island says that `a`ali`i "supports the growth of new trees around it by protecting them from harsh conditions." She likes to plant it "near new tree plantings for a bit of shade. For planting projects it is one of those essential companions that make up a Hawaiian ecosystem."

147

☞ It's simple to start `a`ali`i from seed:

1. Collect the small black seeds from the papery seedpods.
2. Boil some water and pour it over the seeds in a coffee cup.
3. Allow the seeds to soak for 24 hours.
4. Plant the seeds in potting mix (our recipe is in Chapter 4). Make sure not to bury the seeds deeper than 1/4 inch.
5. Water daily and watch for germination in two to four weeks.
6. Transplant the keikis to individual pots when they have two sets of leaves.
7. When your young plants are 6 inches to 2 feet tall, you can transplant them into your garden.

- Possible insect pests: `A`ali`i is very pest-free, but can be affected by certain aphids, scale insects and mealy bugs. And some caterpillars have been found to feed on the flowers and buds. Check Chapter 6 for natural controls of these insects.
- Medicinal uses, invasiveness potential and other special notes of interest: Large branches of the `a`ali`i were used for building timbers and weapons. Its leaves were used medicinally for rashes and itches. Like hops, the flowers were used to impart a bitter flavor and were used as a tonic. A red dye has been made from the seedpods. `A`ali`i is sacred to the hula goddess Laka.

`Awa (Piper methysticum)

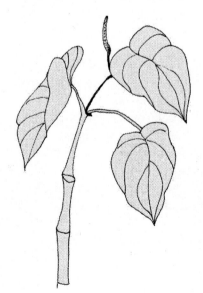

Illustration 8.3: `Awa adds interest to any landscape and if you dig up the roots, you can make a relaxing beverage.

- Description: Also called kava kava, this member of the pepper family is a native Pacific island plant, brought to Hawai'i by the early settlers. It's a woody shrub that grows up to 12 feet tall. It has leathery, heart-shaped leaves that can grow to 8 or 10 inches long and almost as large across the center. Kava forms solitary male flowers that are up to 2-1/2 inches long. Female flowers and fruits are unknown, which makes it impossible for kava to reproduce itself. When it is found in the wild, this usually indicates that someone planted it.
- Climate zone where it thrives:
    Windward areas: yes
    Leeward areas: yes, but it prefers some shade and additional water.
    Elevation: Does fine at lower elevations on the windward side, especially if you give it some partial shade. It grows even larger above 300 feet, but don't expect it to thrive at very high elevations.
- How to grow it: When you first plant an 'awa plant, try to find a place that has fairly deep soil, because the roots are the valuable part of this plant and need "room to roam." Commercial 'awa growers prefer a soil mix consisting of 1/3 topsoil, 1/3 black cinder and 1/3 macadamia nut compost. Dig a hole large enough for your plant and fill it with the soil mix, patting it down gently as you backfill the hole. Keep it well watered until it starts sending out new growth, and if it doesn't rain for several days, keep an eye on your plant and give it a nice long soak if it starts to wilt. When it's mature, 'awa continues to like a fair amount of water, so watch it when the rainfall is absent and if it looks droopy, give it a good long soak, especially if it's in a sunny area.

To propagate 'awa, you must start it from stem cuttings or root divisions because it does not form seeds.

Stem cuttings are very simple:

1. Cut several 6-inch lengths of healthy stem that include at least 2 "nodes," or joints.
2. Prepare a shallow pot or flat with potting mix and water it thoroughly.
3. Lay your cuttings flat on top of the soil and lightly press them into it.
4. Keep the soil moist and watch for new shoots within a couple of weeks.

5. When new plants are 4 to 6 inches tall and have a couple sets of leaves, you can pot them into gallon nursery pots. I prefer to wait until my new plants are about 1 foot tall before I transplant them into the garden.

If you want to try root divisions, you'll need to dig up an existing plant, then cut the root mass into several pieces. Plant each piece in a pot of the appropriate size, keep it well watered, and watch for new growth to appear before you transplant it into the garden.

At the Waimea Valley Audubon Center and Arboretum on Oʻahu, they propagate ʻawa by using a sharp-bladed spade and shaving off a piece of the trunk that includes both roots and leaves. With this method, you then plant that piece in a pot or directly into the ground. The scar that you make on the parent plant will heal in time.

- Possible insect pests and diseases: Slugs and snails can sometimes get onto an ʻawa plant and cause some damage, but I have not seen aphids, scale or other insect pests.

Phoma shot hole is a fungal disease that affects the ʻawa plant above the soil surface. It can cause most of the leaves of affected plants to drop. You'll know if your plant gets shot hole because the leaves will look like they have been shot by a shotgun, with small holes about 1/16 to 1/8 inch in diameter. The lower leaves can be more affected than new growth.

When my ʻawa plants came down with shot hole fungus, I cut them almost to the ground and sprayed them with a sulfur spray once a week for six weeks. Eventually, the new growth started coming out, hole-free. Every once in a while I spray with sulfur to control the organisms that cause shot hole and my plants continue to stay healthy.

- Medicinal uses, invasiveness potential and other special notes of interest: Kava has long been prepared in Polynesia as a tranquilizing beverage. It is the best-researched herb for reducing feelings of anxiety and promoting relaxation and restful sleep. It helps to relieve insomnia, fatigue, and nervousness. It also cleanses and flushes the urinary tract, relaxes tense muscles and helps relieve chronic pain, such as arthritis, with its analgesic and diuretic effects. It's also been said that ʻawa is an aphrodisiac.

The grated, crushed, or chewed roots, which contain several active lactones, are mixed with water to produce the traditional Polynesian drink, which looks like weak coffee and has a peppery taste that numbs your mouth and tongue. In large quantities, it is mildly

150

paralyzing and creates a euphoric but clear-minded state in which the drinker cannot be annoyed.

`Awa received some bad press a couple of years ago because of a flawed European study that made people think that this plant can cause liver damage. Thanks to the American Botanical Council's research efforts (www.herbalgram.org), we now know that this plant is not directly responsible for liver toxicity. As with many other pleasurable parts of life, we should take kava and other herbs in moderation. Always follow label instructions if you're taking it from a pill bottle or in tincture form. If you enjoy a cup or two of kava juice at your farmer's market or kava bar, continue to do so. However, herb-drug interactions can occur, so if you're taking any prescription tranquilizers (brand names such as Alprazolam and Diazepam or Valium), other sedatives such as sleeping pills, anesthetics or analgesics, you should not take kava. Combining drugs of this type with kava might interfere with your mental or motor functions because the herb can magnify the drugs' effects. You should always check with your doctor or other qualified health care provider if you have any questions about taking herbal medicines or remedies of any kind. And people who have known liver disease should not take alcohol-based tinctures.

Tasty `Awa Elixir

Kava's taste is not particularly pleasant and many people claim that it tastes like dirt. However, there are other, more pleasing ways to benefit from this important healing plant. You can make a tincture or tasty elixir by following these steps:

1. Use fresh root, if available. If you are using dried root, try to find root pieces instead of powder. Wash it thoroughly, then grind or chop it and put the pieces in a clean glass jar, about 1/3 full.
2. Cover the root with vodka or brandy. You can also use vegetable glycerin and/or apple cider vinegar. If you wish, you can add other ingredients to improve the taste, such as cinnamon sticks, cloves, other fruit such as mango, dried apricots, etc.
3. Close the jar tightly.
4. Shake your tincture every day for 2 to 4 weeks. Then strain it and add a little molasses, honey or maple syrup.
5. Last, bottle it, preferably in dark glass, and store it in a cool, dark place at room temperature. Don't forget to label what's inside!

DOSAGE: Normally, tinctures come in a small brown bottle with a dropper. For many herbs, take a fairly large amount 2 to 3 times each day until symptoms are gone. For example, take 2 to 4 FULL droppers 2 to 3 times each day.

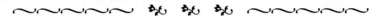

`Ekaha (Asplenium nidus)`

Illustration 8.4: Prized as a houseplant, the bird's nest fern thrives when you grow it in a tree.

- Description: `Ekaha is the attractive bird nest fern that is prized as a houseplant, but which grows wild in Hawai`i. The fronds are light green, long and strap-shaped with a "rib" in the center. The center of the plant is fuzzy looking and resembles a bird's nest.
- Climate zone where it thrives:
    Windward areas: yes
    Leeward areas: At higher elevations
    Elevation: Does fine at lower elevations on the windward side in shady areas and at higher elevations on both sides.
- How to grow it: `Ekaha is readily available at nurseries. As its name implies, the `ekaha likes to live in trees. This makes it very easy to plant: just tie your plant to the crotch of a tree with nursery tape. After a year or two, its roots will hold it to the tree and you can remove the tape. You can also grow `ekaha in the ground in a shady place or in a pot as a houseplant or on your lanai.

- Possible insect pests and diseases: I have not noticed any significant insect pests or diseases among the plants at Hi`iaka's Garden or in the wild.
- Medicinal uses, invasiveness potential and other special notes of interest: Young shoots of this indigenous plant were used for general weakness, ulcers and sores. It is not invasive and you'll be very lucky if your `ekaha creates any keikis from its spores.

Hapu`u (Cibotium splendens)

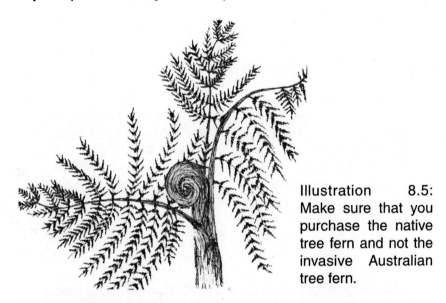

Illustration 8.5: Make sure that you purchase the native tree fern and not the invasive Australian tree fern.

- Description: The hapu`u is the Hawaiian tree fern, which you will see in abundance at higher elevations, especially on the Big Island near Volcanoes National Park. This slow-growing native can get quite large in the wild: up to 25 feet tall. The fronds can grow huge and can spread 10 feet or more from tip to tip. Although the hapu`u looks similar to the Australian tree fern, be careful not to accidentally buy this non-native invader. Two distinguishing characteristics of the Australian invader are the light colored scales on the frond bases and the frond scars on the trunk. Also, the new growth that appears on these ferns is white and hairy looking, which helps to differentiate it from the native hapu`u, whose new growth is typically red. If you look closely, the Australian tree fern's spores (on the underside of the leaves) are rectangular shaped rather than round, like the hapu`u. If you need a refresher course in invasive

153

species in general, or the Australian tree fern in particular, go back to Chapter 2.

- Climate zone where it thrives:

    Windward areas: Yes. The hapu`u is native to cool, wet windward forests at the higher elevations.

    Leeward areas: No, unless you're at a high elevation where it's cooler and gets a fair amount of rain.

    Elevation: Hapu`u does much better above 500 feet elevation, such as around Volcanoes National Park, which is 4000 feet at Kilauea caldera. It does not like to exist close to the ocean because it's generally too warm for this fern. It doesn't do well in very windy areas and prefers protected forest settings, especially in and around native `ohi`a trees.

- How to grow it: Although hapu`u are not endangered, it is important not to dig them from the wild. They are available at most nurseries or you can try your hand at starting them from spores that you collect from a friend's fern. Plant your hapu`u in partial shade and give it plenty of water. When you water the hapu`u, it's best to water from the top, so the newly forming fronds get some moisture.

- Possible insect pests and diseases: I have not found evidence of any significant insect pests or diseases in my research or personal experience. However, feral pigs and goats can be a problem if they uproot young hapu`u plants, so if you are planting them in an area where these hairy invaders live, be sure to protect your hapu`u with fencing.

- Medicinal uses, invasiveness potential and other special notes of interest: The brown silky "pulu" on hapu`u stems was used as an absorbent surgical dressing, for embalming, and as pillow and mattress stuffing. The starchy "flesh" inside the trunk was eaten during times of famine and was also used as medicine for blood purification and for stimulating the appetite.

Ilie`e (Plumbago zeylanica)

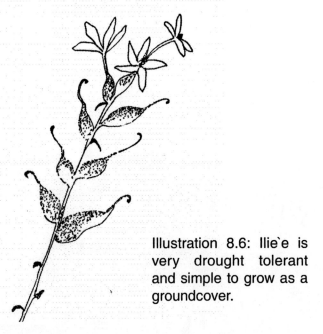

Illustration 8.6: Ilie`e is very drought tolerant and simple to grow as a groundcover.

- Description: This member of the plumbago family is a spreading groundcover with small, sticky white flowers.
- Climate zone where it thrives:
    Windward areas: yes
    Leeward areas: yes
    Elevation: Ilie`e thrives at low elevations on the windward side.
- How to grow it: You can purchase a plant or start one from a cutting or seed. Keep your young plant well watered until it begins to crawl along the ground and shows good signs of robust growth; then you need not provide it with additional water. I have one growing wild at the top of a lava mound in full sun and it is very happy in this environment.
- Possible insect pests and diseases: None
- Medicinal uses, invasiveness potential and other special notes of interest: Ilie`e bark was used in tattooing dye and the leaves and stems were used medicinally for swelling and sores. I keep my ilie`e pruned back from the paths that it sometimes starts to cover.

`Ilima (Sida fallax)

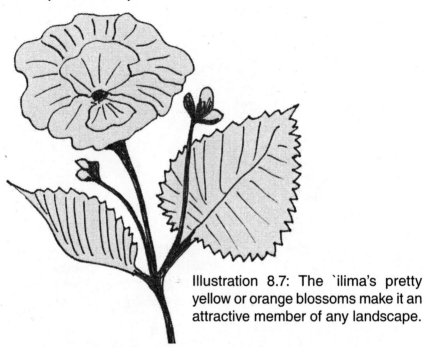

Illustration 8.7: The `ilima's pretty yellow or orange blossoms make it an attractive member of any landscape.

- Description: A native member of the hibiscus family, `ilima has toothed, slightly heart-shaped leaves that are a light gray-green color. Several varieties of `ilima grow in Hawai`i, from a tall, upright variety to a low, spreading groundcover, called `ilima papa. The plants range in size from 6 inches to 10 feet tall. All varieties have similar small yellow or orange flowers, about one inch in diameter. The pretty flowers of this small hibiscus-type plant are used in leis. In ancient times, the ali`i wore `ilima leis, which sometimes contained thousands of flowers. `Ilima is the flower of O`ahu.
- Climate zone where it thrives:
    Windward areas: yes, at lower elevations where it is drier.
    Leeward areas: yes, this is its preferred habitat. It is a common roadside plant.
    Elevation: `Ilima lives from sea level on the windward side to higher elevations on the leeward side, to 5000 feet or higher.
- How to grow it: `Ilima prefers full sun. Once it's established, your `ilima will need no additional water or fertilizer, especially if you're near the ocean. Upcountry, varieties of `ilima that are adapted to this climate like more rainfall or irrigation. It's simple to grow `ilima from seed:

1. Soak seed in lukewarm water for 24 hours.
2. Plant in a pot with good potting soil about 1/4 inch deep.
3. Keep your pot or flat moist but not soggy.
4. Transplant into the ground when plants are 6 to 8 inches tall.
Cuttings can be a little trickier and result in a fairly low percentage
of successful rooting.

• Possible insect pests and diseases: As with other hibiscus species, the introduced Chinese rose beetle can munch on `ilima's leaves, but rarely causes death. At higher elevations, nematodes can sometimes attack the roots. Check Chapter 6 for some suggestions on how to control Chinese rose beetles and nematodes without insecticides.

• Medicinal uses, invasiveness potential and other special notes of interest: The flower buds were used as a laxative for children and the flowers were used for uterine problems. The bark was brewed into a tea, which was said to help people who were feeling weak. The root bark, mixed with flowers, was used for asthma. Fibers from the `ilima papa were used for making baskets.

Kalo (Colocasia esculenta)

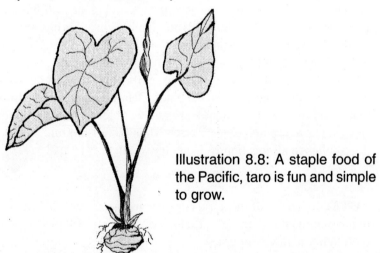

Illustration 8.8: A staple food of the Pacific, taro is fun and simple to grow.

• Description: Taro has large arrow-shaped leaves and a bulbous root or corm. The leaves can range in color from light green to red, purple or nearly black, depending on the variety. Taro was one of the most important staple crops of the ancient Polynesians, who carried corms of this plant on their canoes. Over 300 varieties of taro existed, including dryland and wetland varieties. Today, we still have about 80 different varieties.

- Climate zone where it thrives:
    Windward areas: yes, especially wetland taro.
    Leeward areas: yes, dryland taro does well if given additional water.
    Elevation: Does well at low elevations to middle elevations on the windward sides.
- How to grow it: New plants grow from dormant buds or new tubers or the huli, which are the tops of tubers with about 6 inches of leaf stems.

    If you want to create a taro paddy, or lo`i, for wetland taro, you can do it if you have a pond or want to build an area that can be flooded with water. In former times, taro farmers flooded a pond with water, trampled the soil until it was firm, and then planted the huli, or corms, according to Shunyam Nirav in his book *Hawaiian Organic Growing Guide.* Taro reaches maturity in one year or a little less. It's simple to grow dryland taro, especially if you live upcountry where rainfall is plentiful. Jill Wagner of Future Forests Nursery on the Big Island advises that taro likes a well-drained soil that includes plenty of cinder. Prepare a garden bed or mound with lots of rich organic materials such as compost, and plant your huli about 12 inches apart. Make sure that you give it plenty of water when the rains don't come. In coastal areas of old Hawai`i, the practice was to mulch heavily with leaves and branches of the nearby, plentiful kukui nut trees. At higher elevations, early Hawaiians mulched with fronds and other parts of the hapu`u, the Hawaiian tree fern. Jill says that if you're growing dryland taro at lower elevations on the leeward side, water your patch twice a week when there is no rain. Of course, this applies to all locations during dry weather.

☞ **NOTE:** To get rid of the acrid component of taro, which is irritating to the mouth and throat, be sure to cook all parts of the taro plant thoroughly before eating it.

- Possible insect pests and diseases: No insects have a serious impact on taro in Hawai`i, although the apple snail can eat holes in the leaves of wetland taro. A type of hornworm feeds on taro in Samoa, but hasn't found its way to Hawai`i at this time. A type of leaf blight is common.

- Medicinal uses, invasiveness potential and other special notes of interest: 100 years ago, Hawaiians and others ate this nourishing food at nearly every meal. Today, modern residents continue to pound the bulbous root into poi, which remains a staple food of the islands. The leaves can be steamed and are used to wrap laulau. If you want to experience taro growing in much the same way as it was in traditional times, you can visit the Hanalei Valley on Kaua`i, Waipio Valley on the Big Island and Ke`anae on Maui. Taro is still connected with many cultural and spiritual beliefs. In ancient times, the raw root was grated and mixed with sugar cane juice and other plants for a laxative effect. Do not try this at home!

Ki (Cordyline terminalis)

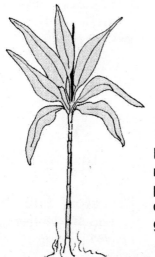

Illustration 8.9: Ti plants are a must in any garden. It is said that planting one at each of the four corners of your property will bring good luck.

- Description: The familiar ti plant was one of the most important of the canoe plants. Ti comes in a rainbow of colors, from green to red to striped, although the more colorful varieties have been introduced in modern times. Ti is a shrubby plant that can reach heights of 12 feet or taller. It has a slender stem with its 1 to 2 foot long narrow leaves encircling it. When it blooms, the flowers are lilac-colored and very pretty. Ti makes a nice potted plant for the lanai and is prized in cooler climates as a houseplant.
- Climate zone where it thrives:
    Windward areas: yes, especially in sunny, moist lowlands.
    Leeward areas: yes
    Elevation: Ti grows nicely from sea level to the higher elevations.

159

- How to grow it: Ti is so easy to grow you probably already have some. To start it, simply cut off a piece about 6 inches long from the top of an existing plant, put it in a pot with soil and keep it well watered. In wet climates, you can often simply poke a cutting directly into the garden and it will soon root and grow into an attractive and useful plant. Ti likes to grow in full sun, although some varieties like partial shade.
- Possible insect pests and diseases: Ti is very resistant to insects and diseases.
- Medicinal uses, invasiveness potential and other special notes of interest: People continue to plant green ti around their homes today for good luck and to drive away evil spirits. It is not invasive. In former times, juice from the flowers was used for the nose; ground flowers and leaves were used for asthma; and leaves were placed on patients' foreheads for headache. The leaves were also wrapped around hot stones and applied to sore backs.

Koki`o and Other Hibiscus (Hibiscus spp.)

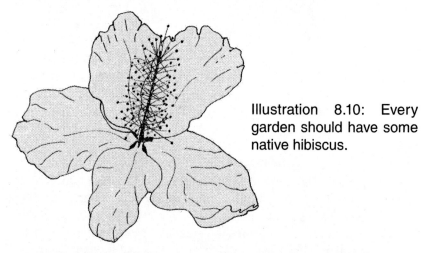

Illustration 8.10: Every garden should have some native hibiscus.

- Description: Hundreds of species of native hibiscus and cultivated varieties exist in the world, and each Hawaiian island has its own native hibiscus. There are five or six true species of Hawaiian hibiscus, four of which have either two or three subspecies, according to David Orr at the Waimea Valley Audubon Center on O`ahu. Hibiscus range from medium-sized shrubs to fairly large trees, and all have very attractive flowers, in shades of white, yellow, pink or red. They are widely used in landscaping and contribute to the tropical look and beauty of shopping malls, airports, hotels and homes. Their flashy flowers last only about one day, either on the plant or as a cut flower and are very tender, so were not used in leis.

- Climate zone where it thrives:
  Windward areas: yes
  Leeward areas: yes
  Elevation: Depending on the variety, the normally hardy hibiscus species do well from sea level to the higher elevations.

- How to grow it: Hibiscus prefers light, well-drained, moderately rich, loamy soil in full sun, although they will tolerate some shade. You can start most hibiscus from seed or cuttings. Here is how to grow them from seed:
  1. Collect seeds when the seedpods have dried out after your plant has finished flowering.
  2. Remove seeds from their seedpods.
  3. Soak seeds in water overnight.
  4. Plant the seeds about 1/2 inch deep in a pot with a good, light potting mix and keep it evenly moist until you see them beginning to sprout. Then cut back on the water and allow the soil to slightly dry out between waterings.
  5. Transplant keiki plants to the garden when they are 8 to 12 inches tall: this can take several months, so be patient.
  6. Protect young plants from harm by staking them or enclosing them in a wire cage, into which you can do "in place composting" to nourish the plant as it grows. Return to Chapter 5 for a reminder of how to do this.

- Possible insect pests and diseases: Chinese rose beetle. Refer to Chapter 6 for suggestions on how to control the Chinese rose beetle without poison. Several species of a mite called Eriophiid might infest the leaves, forming "galls," or knots. Control is difficult, but its existence does not usually threaten the plant: it just makes the leaves look kind of ugly.

- Medicinal uses, invasiveness potential and other special notes of interest: Flower buds of members of the hibiscus family were used as a laxative, for purifying blood and for dry throats. The bark was used for congested chests and for helping to ease childbirth. The bark was also made into ropes and cordage. Hibiscus is not invasive.

Ma`o hau hele (Hibiscus brackenridgei)

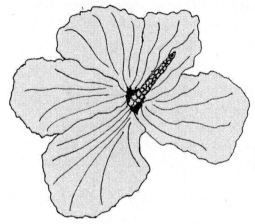

Illustration 8.11: If every government building in Hawai`i had plantings of our state flower, the ma`o hau hele might not remain endangered.

- Description: The beautiful native yellow hibiscus is an easy plant to grow in many landscapes. It can reach a height of up to 8 feet and generally flowers in the spring. I encourage everyone to grow at least one ma`o hau hele. They are available at special nurseries, so check the Resources Appendix for some leads on where to find plants on your island. (Hint: Home Depot often carries them!)
- Climate zone where it thrives:
    Windward areas: yes
    Leeward areas: yes, it's very hardy and can tolerate dry conditions after it's established. Be sure to keep it watered until it's six months to one year old.
    Elevation: Our state flower grows from low elevations on the windward side to approximately 2600 feet, where the folks at the Waimea Valley Audubon Center have collected specimens. My sources at the Amy Greenwell Garden report that wild plants grow from 300 to 1800 feet, but are not certain whether cultivated plants might do well at higher elevations.
- How to grow it: Ma`o hau hele prefers to live in the full sun, but can tolerate some afternoon shade. I have not had good luck growing it in pots. And unfortunately, it is a short-lived perennial, lasting only four to six years. I have started it from both seeds and cuttings, both of which perform very well. You can prune it and shape it to suit your garden space. Follow the planting directions for other hibiscus, above.
- Possible insect pests and diseases: Chinese rose beetle. To refresh your memory on natural control of this insect, return to Chapter 6.

- Medicinal uses, invasiveness potential and other special notes of interest: Medicinal uses are the same as for other hibiscus species, described above. I would love it if my ma`o hau hele would reproduce themselves by dropping viable seeds to the ground, but this has not yet happened with any of my four year-old plants. I've been told by my sources at both the Waimea Valley Audubon Center and the Amy B.H. Greenwell Ethnobotanical Garden that their ma`o hau hele reproduce themselves by seed quite readily, however.

Ko`oko`olau (*Bidens amplectens* and *other species*)

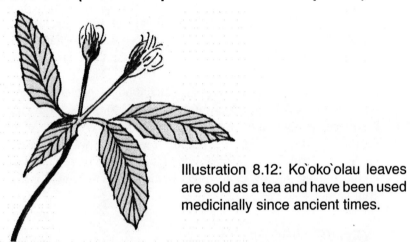

Illustration 8.12: Ko`oko`olau leaves are sold as a tea and have been used medicinally since ancient times.

- Description: There are close to 20 species of this plant in Hawai`i. It belongs to the Compositae family, along with marigolds, which it slightly resembles. A typical ko`oko`olau plant is small, usually less than 3 feet tall, and has small yellow to orange marigold type flowers. A related plant known as Spanish needle (*Bidens pilosa*) has been introduced: you might know this plant as the "hitchhiker" plant because of its barbed seeds that "hitch" a ride on your clothes.
- Climate zone where it thrives:
    Windward areas: yes
    Leeward areas: yes, especially at higher elevations.
    Elevation: Grows near sea level on the windward side and at higher elevations on both sides.
- How to grow it: Because the different species of ko`oko`olau can cross-pollinate and freely hybridize, be careful when growing it in your garden. It's important to grow only one species at a time because we don't want the native ko`oko`olaus to cross with the more weedy introduced varieties.

163

If you collect seeds, it's simple to start new plants:
1. Fill a pot or flat with potting mix that contains a lot of vermiculite or black cinder, then water it well.
2. Scatter the seeds and cover with a small amount of potting mix.
3. After germination occurs in 1 to 2 weeks, the seedlings will grow quickly.
4. When your keikis have four to six leaves, transplant them into their own small pots.
5. When plants are about 6 inches tall, you can put them into the garden in a spot with lots of sun.
6. Keep young plants well watered until they really start to grow robustly, at which time you can cut back on watering.
- Possible insect pests and diseases: Protect your ko`oko`olau from slugs and snails while the plants are small. There appears to be no other insect danger or disease.
- Medicinal uses, invasiveness potential and other special notes of interest: Ko`oko`olau tea continues to be used today as a tonic for weak or ill people. In former times, it was mixed with other plants for throat and stomach ailments and for asthma. It was also used for preventing strokes and purifying the blood. It can reseed itself, so be on the lookout for unwanted keikis if you decide to grow this plant in your garden.

Kou (Cordia subcordata)

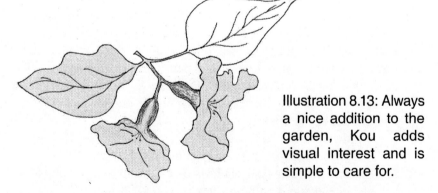

Illustration 8.13: Always a nice addition to the garden, Kou adds visual interest and is simple to care for.

- Description: This attractive plant, which we now know is native, is a medium-sized tree that can reach 15 to 35 feet. It has attractive 1 to 2 inch orange crepe-paper-like flowers. A round fruit will form, which is green or yellow and 1 inch in diameter. Each seedpod contains 1 to 4 seeds. Kou trees add color to small yards in hot, dry areas near the ocean. Kou is related to another species of *Cordia*, the *Cordia sebestena*, which is a favorite landscape plant that has abundant red flowers.

- Climate zone where it thrives:
  Windward areas: yes, at lower elevations in full sun.
  Leeward areas: yes, it's drought tolerant.
  Elevation: Grows well at low elevations on both the leeward and windward sides. It's salt- and wind-tolerant so it provides welcome greenery and shade near the ocean. My sources at the Amy B.H. Greenwell Ethnobotanical Garden in South Kona tell me that it is well adapted to their cooler upcountry elevation of 1500 feet.

- How to grow it: Kou is a fast-growing tree that you can easily start from seeds or cuttings. Here's how to start the seeds:
  1. If you find a kou tree that has fruit, or seedpods, you can easily collect them. Select seeds without insect holes.
  2. Soak seeds for about five days.
  3. Spread a layer of red or black cinders or sand in the bottom of your pot or flat to provide good drainage, then fill it with potting soil.
  4. Scatter seeds on top of your soil and barely cover them with a little potting mix.
  5. Keep your seeds in a sunny location and make sure they stay evenly moist until you see them starting to sprout.
  6. Water seedlings once or twice a week--it's important not to let the soil remain too wet because you can introduce fungal diseases.
  7. Transplant seedlings into larger pots when they are 1 to 2 inches tall.
  8. Transplant keikis into the garden when they are 8 to 12 inches tall and robust.

- Possible insect pests and diseases: None are known.
- Medicinal uses, invasiveness potential and other special notes of interest: The kou's brilliant flowers were strung into leis and the fruit was eaten in old Hawai`i. Leaves were used in other areas of Polynesia for bronchitis, asthma, cirrhosis of the liver, inflammation of the lymph nodes and menstrual disorders. The wood is very useful and was used for bowls and houses. Calabashes called `umeke la`au were made from kou wood because it doesn't make food taste like the tannins common in koa wood. Kou also provided a red dye that was used in making tapa cloth. It should not present an invasiveness problem.

Kulu`i (Nototrichium sandwicense)

Illustration 8.14: Kului is very simple to grow.

- Description: A member of the amaranth family that is native to O`ahu, kulu`i is a dryland forest shrub that reaches 3 to 6 feet in height. It has pale green, silvery leaves that are 2 to 5 inches long. The small flowers are not very noticeable--if you see it bloom at all. It's a common shrub on all of the islands, and is sometimes used for maile-type leis and dried flower arrangements.
- Climate zone where it thrives:
  Windward areas: yes, at lower elevations.
  Leeward areas: yes; it's drought tolerant.
  Elevation: Grows near sea level on the windward sides and on dry slopes on both sides.
- How to grow it: You can easily start kulu`i from cuttings. Just follow these steps:
  1. Cut non-blooming tips from the branches, about 4 to 6 inches long.
  2. Strip the lower leaves from the branch.
  3. Fill a pot with potting soil, Perlite or a mixture of Perlite, vermiculite and cinder.
  4. Water the pot thoroughly and allow it to drain for a few minutes.
  5. Poke holes into the soil for your cuttings.
  6. Insert one cutting into each hole and gently press the soil down around each cutting.

7. Put your pot in a shady area and keep the soil evenly moist until you see new growth appearing.
8. When your new plants are 8 to 12 inches tall, transplant into the garden, keeping them watered for several months until they become established.
- Possible insect pests and diseases: I have not seen any evidence of either insect damage or disease. If anything, it might be too hot and dry at my lowland windward location for kulu`i, as I have lost one that was planted in very shallow soil.
- Medicinal uses, invasiveness potential and other special notes of interest: The pretty, silvery leaves are made into attractive leis, similar to those made from maile. Ancient medicinal uses are not known. I don't believe the kulu`i can become invasive, as my four year old plant has never dropped any seeds that have resulted in keikis.

La`amia (Crescentia cujete)

Illustration 8.15: The large fruit of the la`amia is always a conversation piece in my garden.

- Description: The calabash tree is a low-growing, spreading shrub with small leaves. Everyone who visits my garden asks about the la`amia because of its amazing grapefruit-sized seedpods that look like gourds. It's a native of Central and South America, but has been here long enough to have been given a Hawaiian name.
- Climate zone where it thrives:
  Windward areas: yes, near sea level.
  Leeward areas: yes -- it's very drought tolerant.
  Elevation: Thrives near sea level on the windward side. It also does well at higher elevations on the leeward side, such as at the Amy B.H. Greenwell Ethnobotanical Garden in South Kona (1500 feet).

- How to grow it: I have not figured out how to open one of the hard-shelled seedpod/gourds that the la`amia produces, so haven't begun any new plants from seed. My attempts at starting cuttings have failed, although the folks at the Amy Greenwell Garden report that they have easily started cuttings. They cut pieces of stem that are the diameter of your finger and 6 to 8 inches long. Very little information is available about the la`amia.
- Possible insect pests and diseases: I have never seen any evidence of insect attack. My four year-old plant is very healthy, without fertilizer or additional irrigation.
- Medicinal uses, invasiveness potential and other special notes of interest: The shells of the la`amia's woody seedpods, combined with seeds of the li`ipoe (*Canna indica*), are used for hula rattles. They are also carved and used as receptacles. Marie Neal, in her book *In Gardens of Hawai`i*, reports that in Mexico the seedpod pulp is used medicinally and the seeds are sometimes cooked and eaten. The la`amia has tough wood that is used in Mexico for boats, wheel hubs and fuel. My la`amia has not created any keikis or shown any signs of possible invasiveness.

Loulu (*Pritchardia* spp.)

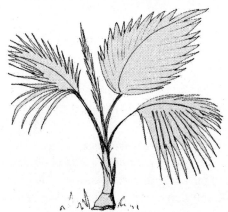

Illustration 8.16: Every home garden needs a loulu!

- Description: The Pritchardia genus includes nearly 20 species, some of which are extinct or endangered. All loulus have fan-shaped leaves, a smooth trunk and no spines. The seeds, or fruit, are dark purple, brown or black, and are the size of large grapes. Some loulus, such as the endangered *P. schattaueri*, which is native to the Big Island, can reach heights of 100 feet. Smaller species, such as the endangered *P. affinis*, grow to about 30 feet and make an attractive landscape palm that you can plant in the ground or in large pots on your lanai.

- Climate zone where it thrives:
    Windward areas: yes, loulus are found in both moist and dry forests.
    Leeward areas: yes, some of the species do well in dry lowland areas, especially *Pritchardia affinis*, which is native to the Kona area of the Big Island.
    Elevation: Loulu prefers dry forests at sea level but they have been reported to occur at almost 4000 feet, mainly from 2000-3000 feet.
- How to grow it: Loulu palms are very low maintenance and look great in landscaping. Make sure you have plenty of space for one, as they grow into large trees. Keep your newly planted trees watered until they show signs of good growth, but remember that palms do not do well in soggy soil. Mulch it with fronds that have yellowed and periodically add a shovel full of compost at the base to keep the roots well covered. If you do a little research and learn which species is native to your area, or close to it, you'll have better success at getting a loulu to become established on your property. Several of my sources report that cross-pollination is possible, so if you decide to grow some loulu, try to stick to just one species. If you grow more than one species, plant them far away from each other.

If you can find seeds, here's how to start them:
1. Soak seeds in water for 5 days, making sure you change the water every day.
2. Remove the outer husk, or exocarp, the fibrous middle layer, or mesocarp, and most of the hard inner endocarp. You might need pliers to gently crack the endocarp: be careful that you don't damage the seed inside.
3. Using a gallon-sized pot with a light potting mix such as vermiculite, Perlite and peat moss, plant your seeds one to a pot and bury them about 1 inch deep.
4. Water frequently to keep the soil moist, but not soggy: be patient--palm seeds can take months to sprout, but with this method, you often see germination within a few weeks.
5. Grow your keiki loulu in its pot until it's about 1 foot tall. At this time, it's a good idea to transplant it into your garden or into a larger pot. After a few years, it's best to plant your potted loulu into the ground. They are rather slow growing, according to the authors of *A Native Hawaiian Garden*.

- Possible insect pests and diseases: Rats, goats, and wild pigs love to eat the loulu's small fruit. A type of sugar cane borer that comes from Papua New Guinea can attack loulus. Mealybugs, scale or whiteflies sometimes infest the fronds, so use some insecticidal soap to control them if any of these insects become a problem on your plant. If you decide to apply a product such as Tanglefoot to the loulu's trunk to prevent ants from bringing these damaging insects into the tree, be sure to heed our caution for using this product in Chapter 6.
- Medicinal uses, invasiveness potential and other special notes of interest: Hawaiians made hats (papale) from the young leaves and used the mature leaves for thatching and fans. They also made spears from the hard wood of some loulu species. Loulu trunks were also used to make fences. The small, immature soft seeds, called hawane, are edible and taste like coconut. Unfortunately, introduced pests such as rats, pigs and certain insects also like the taste of these seeds and have contributed to the demise of loulus in the wild.

Mamaki (Pipturis albidus)

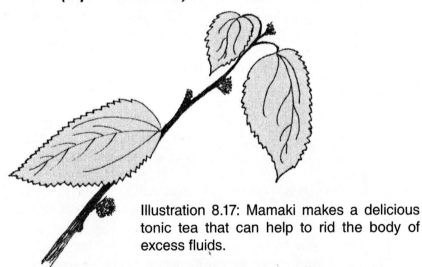

Illustration 8.17: Mamaki makes a delicious tonic tea that can help to rid the body of excess fluids.

- Description: I call mamaki the Hawaiian nettle, because it is a close relative of this plant in the *Urticaceae* family. Unlike "stinging" nettles, however, mamaki has no stinging hairs because during its evolution there were no predators that threatened its survival. Mamaki is a small tree or shrub that can reach 15 feet in height. It's attractive, with large leaves that normally have red veins. The

170

"fruit," or seedpod, is a white fuzzy ball with little black dots that are the actual seeds. Mamaki tea is a popular beverage today that's gaining in popularity: I've seen dried mamaki for tea making at such stores as Long's Drugs! As with other herbs that you can use for tea, I always say that "fresh is best," so if you grow mamaki, you can reap the benefits of fresh, healthful tea when you want a cup. But read on for more information about mamaki's medicinal properties.

- Climate zone where it thrives:

  Windward areas: yes, but give it some shade if you're growing it near sea level. And water it during dry periods.

  Leeward areas: yes, it will grow in drier conditions, but provide some shade while your plants are young and definitely keep it watered during dry spells.

  Elevation: Does well at low elevations if you give it a little shade and some additional irrigation during dry periods. It generally does better at higher elevations.

- How to grow it: I once collected 18 very robust 6-inch tip cuttings and all of them died, despite my best efforts at rooting them. Seeds, however, are easy to collect and start. Here's how:

  1. Soak the white, gooey "fruit" in water for an hour or so. Or easier yet, wait for the fruit to dry on the plant, which you can then scatter on top of your potting mix.
  2. Separate the tiny seeds from the pulp.
  3. Prepare a pot or flat with a fine potting mix that you have watered thoroughly and patted down to compact.
  4. Scatter your seeds on top of the potting mix and lightly press them into the soil: no need to cover them with additional soil.
  5. Keep your pot or flat well watered and transplant the keikis to pots of their own when they're about 2 inches tall. I usually wait until plants are about 1 foot tall before I plant them in the garden. Then I surround each plant with a wire cage, around which I tie some shadecloth (but my garden is in a hot lowland elevation, so you might skip this step if you live in a cooler climate). I mulch generously with raked leaves from nearby trees, and when I see my plants starting to droop on a hot afternoon, I give them a good soaking drink of water.

- Possible insect pests and diseases: I haven't seen a single thing attack my mamaki, but the leaves are a favorite food for the Kamehameha butterfly's larvae (*Vanessa tameamea*).

- Medicinal uses, invasiveness potential and other special notes of interest: Mamaki tea is still used as a tonic and cleansing agent (it's a diuretic). It's also used for general run-down conditions. The meat of the seed was used for general debility and for expectant mothers. The white fruit or sap was used as a mild laxative. The leaves are edible, and good, either raw in salads or cooked like spinach. Properties of other members of the nettle family are: blood purifier (alterative), diuretic, expectorant and astringent. The bark was pounded and used in tapa making. Although I have had keikis sprout in nursery pots near a blooming mamaki, I do not believe it will present any invasiveness problems.

☞ **NOTE:** Do not drink large quantities (more than three or four cups) of mamaki tea on a daily basis unless your doctor indicates that a diuretic is appropriate for a specific illness.

Nanu or Nau (Gardenia brighamii)

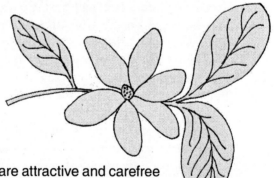

Illustration 8.18: Nanu are attractive and carefree to grow, but keep an eye open for ants, which bring scale insects to your plant.

- Description: This beautiful native gardenia is endangered but thrives in home gardens with very little care. It is the smallest of the three native gardenias and has dark green shiny leaves and small white fragrant flowers.
- Climate zone where it thrives:
    Windward areas: yes
    Leeward areas: yes
    Elevation: Does well at low elevations and up to 1600 feet in the wild.

- How to grow it: I haven't tried this yet because my nanu plant hasn't produced any seed, but I've read that this is the recipe for starting new nanu plants in the book *A Native Hawaiian Garden*:
  1. The seedpod, or fruit, is ripe when it's the size of a golf ball, is soft and stains your fingers when you gently squeeze it.
  2. Remove the seeds and clean the pulp from them.
  3. Place the seeds in water for one hour--the viable, or good, seeds will sink.
  4. Fish out the good seeds at the bottom of the water.
  5. Plant the seeds in vermiculite 3/16 inch deep and keep the pot moist until sprouting occurs.
  6. Wait until your keikis are about 1 foot tall before you plant them in your garden. This can take a year or so.
- Possible insect pests and diseases: Fire ants have been reported to build nests at the base of nanu plants. You can blast them away with a hose, use Tanglefoot on the plant's stem, or spray with natural sprays such as soap, garlic and hot peppers. I've been told that scale insects and sooty mold are common on the plants at the Amy Greenwell Garden in South Kona. Check back to Chapter 6 for reminders of natural insect controls.
- Medicinal uses, invasiveness potential and other special notes of interest: In making tapa cloth, ancient Hawaiians beat wauke bark, also known as paper mulberry, on an anvil made from nanu wood. The nanu fruit, or seedpods, were also used in tapa making to provide a yellow dye. And of course this lovely flower has been used in leis. In Chinese medicine, the fruit is used as an antibacterial against strep throat infections, staphylococcus and dysentery, but any Hawaiian medicinal use is unknown.

Niu (Cocos nucifera)

Illustration 8.19: The coco palm is an essential plant in any tropical garden. Watch for falling coconuts, however!

- Description: The familiar coco palm is among the 10 most useful tree species to mankind in the world. Coco palms were so important to sustaining life in the South Pacific islands where Hawai`i's original settlers came from that they brought them on their canoes. Coco palms grow fairly quickly and begin to bear the familiar coconut when they're about six years old. The nuts mature in 9 or 10 months. Dwarf varieties are recommended for ornamental planting around homes, as falling coconuts and fronds can be dangerous.
- Climate zone where it thrives:
    Windward areas: yes, especially near sea level.
    Leeward areas: yes, especially near sea level.
    Elevation: Coco palms do best near the ocean, but they thrive at 1500 feet and higher on the leeward sides of the islands.
- How to grow them:
    1. Bury a coconut half way in any type of soil. You don't even need to remove the outer shell.
    2. Prune off the long fronds when they start getting yellowish and ragged looking: they make excellent mulch for the coco palm itself

and other plants in the garden. You can chop them into shorter lengths if that's the solution for keeping things looking tidy. I have never given my coco palms any fertilizer, and after seven years, they're as tall as my house and doing beautifully in my lowland setting.

- Possible insect pests and diseases: Coconut scale is an armored scale that affects coco palms. Go back to Chapter 6 for ideas on how to control scale insects.

- Medicinal uses, invasiveness potential and other special notes of interest: Coconuts provided food and drink in ancient times and continue to be popularly used for many culinary purposes. The white meat and coconut milk were used as medicine. All parts of the coconut tree are used for thatching, baskets, brooms, string, sandals, cordage used in fishing, house construction and many other uses. Coconut oil was used for light, ointment and hair oil. Shells were made into utensils and implements. The hard outer part of the trunk served as wood for posts, furniture, construction and spears. The sweet sap of the flowering buds was tapped as a source of sugar, wine and vinegar. In an odd sense, coco palms can become invasive because when their nuts drop to the ground literally all of them will sprout if you don't collect them, creating a charming "oasis" of palm trees that is so typical of tropical settings. But you might not want so many coco palms in your back yard: just keep the nuts pruned off the trees or pick them up off the ground when they drop. Coconut husks make good mulch for your coco palms and other plants, but be sure to place them curved side down so they don't collect water in which mosquitoes will breed.

`Ohi`a lehua (Metrosideros polymorpha)

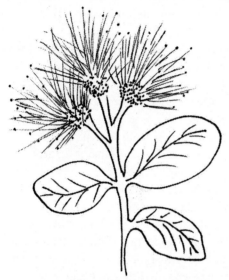

Illustration 8.20: Please do not remove any `ohi`a trees, as they are sacred to the Hawaiian gods and goddesses.

- Description: A member of the Myrtle family, `ohi`a trees live on all of the main islands and can reach heights of 100 feet or more, although they are so adaptable to different environments that they can also take the form of a shrub. The flowers are like little pompoms and range in color from yellow, salmon, pink, or orange to red, with red being the most common color. You'll see a lot of large `ohi`a trees at higher elevations near Volcanoes National Park on the Big Island. It can be drought tolerant when it grows in warm lowland areas, but will not reach the height it achieves at higher, cooler elevations.
- Climate zone where it thrives:
    Windward areas: yes, primarily.
    Leeward areas: yes, they are very common.
    Elevation: `Ohi`a grows at lower elevations, although trees tend to be smaller. At cooler, moist higher elevations you will see very large `ohi`a trees. It is a very adaptable tree and is one of the first "pioneers" that sprouts after a fresh lava flow has cooled.
- How to grow it: Keep invasive plants such as autograph trees and schefflera cleared from the base of `ohi`as because they are epiphytes that can suck the life right out of your `ohi`as. Starting `ohi`a trees from seed is the simplest way to start new trees. Here's how to do it:

1. Collect the tiny seeds from their ripe seed capsules.
2. Prepare a pot or flat with a light potting mix with plenty of peat moss and Perlite and water it well.
3. Sprinkle your seeds onto the soil surface and gently press them into the soil. Do not cover them with more potting soil.
4. Keep the soil evenly moist for up to one year. You might need to water your pot or flat every day.
5. When the keikis have two sets of leaves, you can transplant them into larger pots.
6. This is a fairly slow-growing tree, so it might take one year for your seeds to grow into a 2-foot plant that is ready to transplant into the garden. Be sure to plant it in an area that gets good drainage and keep your young `ohi`a well watered. If you live in a windy area, provide some protection against strong winds by planting your keiki behind another tree or a windbreak.

- Possible insect pests and diseases: Chinese rose beetles can chew on `ohi`a leaves. Nematodes can sometimes also present a problem. You can keep fungal diseases at bay if you provide your `ohi`a tree with good drainage. Take a look back at Chapter 6 for suggestions on controlling rose beetles and nematodes if they should become a serious problem.

- Medicinal uses, invasiveness potential and other special notes of interest: The `ohi`a lehua flowers are very beautiful and are still used in leis. These same flowers were used to help women during childbirth in ancient times: hau sap and water were mixed with rubbed lehua flowers, then strained and given to the woman in labor to drink with each painful contraction. Bark or young leaves were also used as a gargle for sore throats. The dense, hard wood was used for canoes, houses, poi boards, bowls and temple statues, but it can crack. In Hawaiian mythology, the goddess Hi`iaka tended her favorite grove of `ohi`a trees in the Puna district of the Big Island. The flowers are also sacred to Hi`iaka's friend Laka, the goddess of hula. Although `ohi`a readily forms forests by dispersing its seeds in the wild, it isn't considered invasive. If a volunteer `ohi`a pops up where you don't want it, just pot it up and give it to a friend.

`Olena (Curcuma longa)

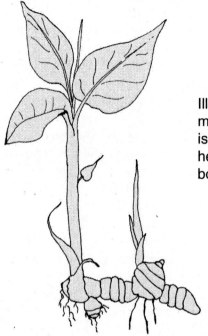

Illustration 8.21: An easy to grow member of the ginger family, `olena is a great addition to tea and will help with any inflammation in your body (such as arthritis).

- Description: `Olena is the familiar spice turmeric and is one of the herbs used to make curry powder. It's a valuable medicinal canoe plant, and a member of the ginger family, so it has the long green strap-like leaves common to other gingers. `Olena gets distinctive white flowers in the center of its foliage toward the end of its annual growing season before it goes into a period of underground dormancy. Harvest the root after the leaves turn yellow and the dormant period begins, usually in late summer or fall.
- Climate zone where it thrives:
    Windward areas: yes
    Leeward areas: yes, if you give it some additional water and protect it from too much sun.
    Elevation: I grow `olena near the ocean on the windward side and it does well, but remember to give it some water during dry spells. At higher elevations, the root can rot in soil that stays too soggy.
- How to grow it: It's easy to find `olena root at farmer's markets and natural food stores. Simply bury a good-sized piece of root, about 1 inch deep. It takes quite a while to sprout, but once it does it grows

178

with abandon and needs very little help from you. No matter how hard you try to dig up all of the delicious, healing root after the fronds have yellowed, chances are you will see more ʻolena sprouting in the same location the following year. What a wonderful weed!
- Possible insect pests and diseases: none.
- Medicinal uses, invasiveness potential and other special notes of interest: Turmeric is a widely used anti-inflammatory herb. You can easily make tea by slicing a few rounds and adding them to your teacup along with your favorite teabag. In ancient Hawaiʻi, the root was used for growths in the nostrils, for cleansing blood, and as a gargle. It is also widely used in Ayurvedic medicine, the medicinal system of India. It provides a yellow or orange dye that was used in making tapa cloth, and is still used today as a traditional dye for hula costumes. ʻOlena is not invasive.

Bibliography

NOTE: Because Internet addresses can change over time, we do not guarantee that the URLs we provide here will continue to be viable.

Arvigo, Rosita and Epstein, Nadine. *Rainforest Home Remedies: the Maya Way to Heal Your Body and Replenish Your Soul*. New York: HarperCollins, 2001.

Ausubel, Kenny. *Seeds of Change*. New York: HarperCollins, 1994.

Big Island Invasive Species Committee. *Target Species List*. Hawai`i State Department of Agriculture.

Bornhorst, Heidi. *Growing Native Hawaiian Plants*. Honolulu: Bess Press, 1996.

Bornhorst, Heidi and Rauch, Fred. *Native Hawaiian Plants for Landscaping, Conservation and Reforestation*. Honolulu: University of Hawai`i College of Tropical Agriculture and Human Resources, Research Extension Series 142, 1994.

Bradley, David. "Ask Contractors The Right Questions." Associated Press. www.yourcastlebuilders.com/askthequestion.html

Brown, Kathleen and Pollak, Jeanine. *Herbal Teas: 101 Nourishing Blends for Daily Health and Vitality. Pownal, VT: Storey Books, 1999.*

Cech, Richo. Finding Your Niche — Making a Living With Medicinal Plants. Williams, OR: Horizon Herbs, 1995.

College of Tropical Agriculture, University of Hawai`i. Woody Plant Control for the Home, Pasture and Forest. www.ctahr.hawaii. edu/freepubs.

College of Tropical Agriculture, University of Hawai`i. *Selecting a Tree Care Professional.* www.ctahr.hawaii.edu/freepubs, CTAHR Fact Sheet, Landscape no. 1, April 1997.

Creasy, Rosalind. *Blue Potatoes, Orange Tomatoes*. Washington, DC: Sierra Club Books, 1997.

Culliney, John L. and Koebele, Bruce P. *A Native Hawaiian Garden: How to Grow and Care for Island Plants*. Honolulu: University of Hawai`i Press, 1999.

Daniels, Catherine H., Fults, Janet. Oregon Department of Agriculture *Fact Sheet for Vinegar/Acetic Acid Recommendations*. Fact sheet PIC-01002, 2002.

de la Tour, Shatoiya and Richard. *The Herbalist's Garden: A Guided Tour of 10 Exceptional Herb Gardens*. Pownal, Vermont: Storey Books, 2001.

Glover, Nancy. *Pacific Islands Farm Manual*, Cover Crop Leaflet no. 2: "Perennial Peanut." Honolulu, University of Hawai`i, ADAP-Integrated Farm Development Project, 1994.

Hawai`i Department of Land and Natural Resources. "Wanted: Miconia Dead or Alive" flyer, 2000.

Hobbs, Christopher. *Herbal Remedies for Dummies*. New York: Hungry Minds, 1998.

Jeavons, John. *How to Grow More Vegetables Than You Ever Thought Possible On Less Land Than You Can Imagine*. Berkeley, CA: Ten Speed Press, 1995.

Kepler, Angela Kay. *Hawaiian Heritage Plants*. Honolulu: University of Hawai`i Press, 1998.

Krauss, Beatrice. *Native Plants Used as Medicine in Hawai`i*. Honolulu: Harold L. Lyon Arboretum, 1981.

Lanza, Patricia. *Lasagna Gardening*. Emmaus, PA: Rodale Press, Inc., 1998.

Little, Elbert L. and Skolmen, Roger G. *Common Forest Trees of Hawai`i*. Washington, DC: United States Department of Agriculture Forest Service, Agriculture Handbook no. 679, 1989.

McBride, L. R. *Practical Folk Medicine of Hawai`i*. Hilo: Petroglyph Press, 1975.

Medeiros, A. C. et al. "Notes on the Status of an Invasive Australian Tree Fern (*Cyathea cooperi*) in Hawaiian Rain Forests." *American Fern Journal*: 82(1): 27-33 (1992).

Merlin, Mark. *Hawaiian Forest Plants: An Illustrated Field Guide*. Honolulu: Pacific Guide Books, 1999.

Merlin, Mark. *Hawaiian Coastal Plants: An Illustrated Field Guide*. Honolulu: Pacific Guide Books, 1999.

Mollison, Bill and Slay, Reny Mia. *Introduction to Permaculture*. Tyalgum, Australia: Tagari Publications, 1999.

Motooka, Castro, Nelson, Nagai and Ching. *Weeds of Hawai`i's Pastures and Natural Areas: An Identification and Management Guide*. Honolulu: College of Tropical Agriculture Publications and Information Office, 2003.

National Gardening Association Editors. *Gardening All-in-One For Dummies*. New York: Wiley Publishing, Inc., 2003. www.garden.org.

National Tropical Botanical Garden. *Ten Native Hawaiian Trees for Urban Landscapes.* Lawai, HI: 1996. Pamphlet.

Neal, Marie C. *In Gardens of Hawai`i.* Bernice P. Bishop Museum special publication 50. Honolulu: Bishop Museum Press, 1965.

Nirav, Shunyam. *Hawaiian Organic Growing Guide.* Kahului, Maui: New Dawn Environmental Services, 1996.

Oregon Dept. of Agriculture Fact Sheet for Vinegar/Acetic Acid Recommendations, Fact sheet PIC-01002. http://oregonstate. edu/dept/nursery-weeds/weedspeciespage/acetic_acid_ factsheet.pdf

Pratt, H. Douglas. *A Pocket Guide to Hawai`i's Trees and Shrubs.* Honolulu: Mutual Publishing, 1998.

Raindrip, Inc. *Drip Watering Made Easy.* Simi Valley, CA, 1992.

Rodale Organic Gardening Books. *Good Bug, Bad Bug: Your Take-Along Insect Identification Guide.* Emmaus, PA: Rodale Inc., 1999.

Staples, George W. and Cowie, Robert H., editors. *Hawai`i's Invasive Species.* Honolulu: Mutual Publishing, 2001.

Sturdivant, Lee and Blakley, Tim. *Medicinal Herbs in the Garden, Field, and Marketplace.* Friday Harbor, WA: San Juan Naturals, 1999.

Sunset Books and Magazine Editors. *Sunset Western Garden Book.* Menlo Park, CA: Sunset Publishing Corp., 1995.

Taylor, Lois. "Gone Native: A Garden in the Midst of Urban Honolulu is a Haven for Indigenous Plants." Ever Green Garden column, *Honolulu Star-Bulletin,* 11/28/97.

Third Age Health Newsletter. www.thirdage.com, 2004.

United States Department of Agriculture Institute of Pacific Islands Forestry. *Albizia: The Tree That Ate Puna.* August, 2003.

University of Hawai`i Cooperative Extension Service. *Insect Pest Series.* Honolulu, HI: University of Hawai`i, various titles and dates.

War on the Purple Plague: A Control Strategy. Hilo: Hawai`i Field Operations, Department of Agriculture, Plant Quarantine Building, date unknown.

Whistler, Dr. W. Arthur. *Polynesian Herbal Medicine.* Lawai, HI: National Tropical Botanical Garden, 1992.

Whistler, Dr. W. Arthur. *Wayside Plants of the Islands.* Honolulu, HI: Isle Botanica, 1995.

Zee, Francis, et al. *Small Scale Tea Growing and Processing in Hawai`i.* Honolulu: University of Hawai`i College of Tropical Agriculture Publications and Information Office, 2002.

Appendix: Resources

☞ **NOTE**: Because telephone numbers, Internet addresses, and other information can change over time, we do not guarantee that any of the contact information we provide here will continue to be viable.

Agencies and Organizations

The University of Hawai`i's College of Tropical Agriculture and Human Resources is a wealth of good information. They have a great website, through which lots of free information is available in PDF format: www.ctahr.hawaii.edu/Freepubs.

For other CTAHR publications that are for sale, The University of Hawai`i's College of Tropical Agriculture Publications and Information Office can be reached at:

3050 Maile Way, Gilmore 119
Honolulu, HI, 96822
(808) 956-7036
e-mail: pio@ctahr.hawaii.edu.
To order publications, e-mail ctahrpubs@hawaii.edu.

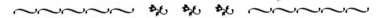

Hawai`i State Department of Agriculture telephone numbers:
Oahu: (808) 973-9560
Maui: (808) 873-3555
Big Island: (808) 974-6500
Kauai: (808) 274-3069

HAW-FLYPM (Hawai`i Area Wide Fruit Fly Integrated Pest Management Program):
University of Hawai`i at Manoa
Cooperative Extension Service -- HAW-FLYPM
Department of Plant and Environmental Protection Sciences
3050 Maile Way, Gilmore 310
Honolulu, HI 96822
(808) 453-6050

Miconia Hotline: (all in area code 808)
Oahu: 973-9541
Maui: 984-8100
Big Island: 961-3299
Kauai: 274-3069
Molokai and Lanai: 1 (800) 468-4644, ext. 48100

Invasive and Alien Species Information and Contacts

University of Hawai`i Weed Risk Assessment Table is located at http://
www.botany.hawaii.edu/faculty/daehler/wra/full_table.asp

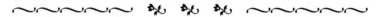

HEAR (Hawaiian Ecosystems at Risk) web site for invasive plants on
Maui: http://www.hear.org/misc/malamaikaaina/mika_dont_plant_
these_on_maui.pdf
(808) 572-4418

PIER (Pacific Islands Ecosystems at Risk): www.hear.org

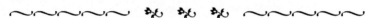

Resources to learn What To/Not to Plant in Hawai`i: http://www.hear.
org/misc/pdfs/misc_whatnottoplant_resources.pdf

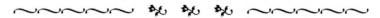

Hawai`i State Alien Species Coordinator, Department of Land
and Natural Resources (DLNR), Division of Forestry and Wildlife
(DOFAW). Worst Invasive Plant List for Hawai`i:
Internet: http://www.state.hi.us/dlnr/dofaw/hortweeds/specieslist.
htm.
1151 Punchbowl St., Room 325
Honolulu, HI, 96813
Telephone: (808) 587-0164.

Coordinating Group on Alien Pest Species (CGAPS)
P.O. Box 61441
Honolulu, HI, 96839
(808) 722-0995

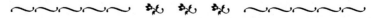

Oahu Invasive Species Committee (OISC):
c/o DLNR/DOFAW
2135 Makiki Heights Dr.
Honolulu, HI, 96816
Telephone: (808) 286-4616
Internet: www.hear.org/oisc/
email: oisc@hawaii.edu

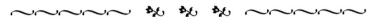

Maui Invasive Species Committee (MISC):
P.O. Box 983
Makawao, HI, 96768
Telephone: (808) 573-6472
Internet: www.hear.org/misc/
email: misc@hawaii.edu

Molokai Subcommittee of the Maui Invasive Species Committee
(MoMISC):
P.O. Box 983
Makawao, HI, 96768
Telephone: (808) 553-5236
Internet: www.hear.org/momisc/
email: tlau@tnc.org

Kauai Invasive Species Committee (KISC):
P.O. Box 1998
Lihue, HI, 96766
Telephone: (808) 246-0684
Internet: www.hear.org/kisc/
email: kisc@lava.net

Big Island Invasive Species Committee (BIISC)/Operation Miconia:
16 E. Lanikaula St.
Hilo, HI, 96720
Telephone: (808) 974-4140
Internet: www.hear.org/biisc/
email: biiscord@aloha.net

Seed and Plant Sources

Perennial peanut seed:
K M Seed Company
67-1159 Mamalahoa Hwy.
Waimea, Big Island, HI 96743
(808) 885-7640

Bamboo and other organically grown landscape plants, including perennial vegetables:
GaiaYoga Nursery: bamboo, coconuts, fruit and nut trees, bananas, perennial vegetables, and other organically grown permaculture plants.
GaiaYoga Goods and Services: books, tools, and practical products for sustainable and holistic living. Based out of the Maku'u Farmer's Market (near Pahoa, Big Island), Sundays from 8am to 2pm.
GaiaYoga Gardens: a permaculture homestead and learning center that offers work-exchange, classes and consulting in nonviolent communication, hatha yoga, and sustainable homesteading. They are also looking for people who share their values and who want to help create a long-term residential intentional community.
(808) 965-5664
RR 2, Box 3334
Pahoa, HI 96778
www.gaiayoga.org (for the community)
www.gaiayoga.org/nursery (for the nursery)
aloha@gaiayoga.org

Organic medicinal plants and seeds from around the world:
Horizon Herbs, LLC
P.O. Box 69
Williams, OR 97544
www.horizonherbs.com
(541) 846-6704

Richter's Herbs (www.richters.com)
Goodwood, Ontario
LOC 1AO
Canada
(905) 640-6677

Seeds of Change (www.seedsofchange.com)
P.O. Box 15700
Santa Fe, NM 87592
1-888-762-7333

The Thyme Garden (www.thymegarden.com)
20546 Alsea Highway
Alsea, OR 97324
(541) 487-8671

Public Gardens in Hawai`i With Native Plants

O`ahu:

Bishop Museum, 1525 Bernice Street, Honolulu, HI, 96817. Phone: 848-4129

Foster Botanical Garden, 180 North Vineyard Street, Honolulu, HI, 96817. Phone: 522-7065

Halawa Xeriscape Garden, 99-1268 Iwaena Street, Halawa Industrial Park, Aiea, 10:00 a.m.-2:00 p.m., Wednesday and Saturday; special tours of Halawa Shaft and garden on Thursdays by request. Phone: 527-6113

Harold L. Lyon Arboretum, 3860 Manoa Road, Honolulu, HI, 96822. Phone: 988-0456

Harold St. John Plant Science Laboratory courtyard garden, corner of Maile Way and East-West road, University of Hawai`i at Manoa

Honolulu Zoo, 151 Kapahulu Avenue, Honolulu, HI, 96815. Phone: 971-7171

Ho`omaluhia Botanical Garden, 45-680 Luluku Road, P. O. Box 1116, Kane`ohe, HI, 96744. Phone: 235-6636

`Iolani Palace, 364 South King Street, Honolulu, HI, 96813

Ka Papa Lo`i o Kanewai, makai side of Dole Street, Diamond Head of Manoa Stream

Koko Crater Botanical Garden, off Kealahou Street, Kalama Valley. Call Foster Botanical Garden for information

Moanalua Gardens, entrance and parking lot along Pu`uloa Road off-ramp from west bound Moanalua Freeway. Phone: 833-1944

Sea Life Park, Makapu`u Point. Phone: 259-7933

Wahiawa Botanical Garden, 1396 California Avenue, Wahiawa, HI, 96786. Phone: 621-7321

Waikiki Aquarium, 2777 Kalakaua Avenue, Honolulu, HI, 96815. Phone: 923-9741

Waimea Valley Audubon Center (Arboretum and Botanical Garden), 59-864 Kamehameha Highway, Haleiwa, HI, 96712. Phone: 638-9199

Kaua`i:

Keahua Forestry Arboretum, Wailua Loop Road at the end of Highway 580, call the Kaua`i District Forester for information. Phone: 241-3433, Forestry and Wildlife Division, Department of Land and Natural Resources.

Koke`e State Park: from Waimea, take Waimea Canyon Drive (route 550); from Kekaha, take Koke`e Road (route 252). Koke`e Lodge phone: (808) 335-6051.

Limahuli Garden, satellite garden of the National Tropical Botanical Garden, located near the end of the road just before Haena Beach.

National Tropical Botanical Garden, end of Ha`ilima Road, P. O. Box 340, Lawai, 96765. Phone: 332-7324

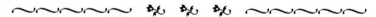

Maui:

Haleakala National Park

Kahanu Gardens, National Tropical Botanical Garden, Alau Place, Hana, Hawai`i 96713. Phone: 248-8912

Kula Forest Reserve, access road at the end of Waipouli Road. Call the Maui District Forester for information. Phone: 243-5352, Forestry and Wildlife Division, Department of Land and Natural Resources

Maui Nui Botanical Gardens, 150 Kanaloa Ave., Kahului, Hawai'i 96732. Phone: 249-2798. Across from the War Memorial Stadium, a non-profit garden committed to conserving Hawaiian plants and cultural heritage. www.mnbg.org

Wailea Point, private condominium residence at 4000 Wailea Alanui. Phone: 879-6106. Visit the coastal garden by walking along the beach through public access points at Four Seasons Resort or Polo Beach.

Big Island:

Amy B. H. Greenwell Ethnobotanical Garden, Bishop Museum, Captain Cook; 100 yards north of Manago Hotel. Phone: 323-3318

Hi`iaka's Healing Herb Garden, HCR 2, Box 9620, Kea`au, HI, 96749. Open by appointment for tours and gift shop. Also offers residency internships and mini-classes and landscape consultations. www.hiiakas.com; goddess@hiiakas.com; 966-6126.

Manuka State Park, 19.3 miles west of Na'alehu Village, off Highway 11.Call 243-5354 for information.

Pu`uhonua o Honaunau, City of Refuge, National Historic Park, Highway 160. Phone: 328-2288

Sadie Seymour Botanical Garden, Kona Outdoor Circle Center, 76-6280 Kuakini Highway, Kailua-Kona, HI, 96740. Phone: 329-7286

Waiakea Arboretum, 1643 Kilauea Avenue, Hilo, HI, 96720. Call the Hawai`i District Forester for information. Phone: 933-4221, Forestry and Wildlife Division, Department of Land and Natural Resources

Plant Nurseries That Sell Natives

The following sources have propagated native plants from seeds and cuttings without endangering wild populations. Please contact these sources if you are interested in acquiring any native plants. If these sources do not have a particular plant, ask for a referral. Sources also can accept requests to propagate plants or explain why a species is not offered for sale.

O`ahu:

Charles Nii Nursery, 908 Kamilonui Place, Honolulu, 96825. Phone: 395-9959

Greg Boyer - Hawaiian Landscapes, 47-410 Pulama Road, Kane`ohe, 96744. Phone: 239-8264

O`ahu District Forester. Phone: 587-0166, Forestry and Wildlife Division (DOFAW), Department of Land and Natural Resources (DLNR)

Plantland, 59-361 Alapi`o Road, Hale`iwa, HI, 96712. Phone: 638-7331

R. & S. Nii Nursery, 938 Kamilonui Place, Honolulu, HI, 96825. Phone: 395-9811

SMI Nursery, 99-074 Ka`amilo Street, `Aiea, HI, 96701. Phone: 488-6315

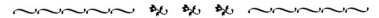

Kaua`i:

Kaua`i District Forester. Phone: 241-3433, DOFAW/DLNR

Kaua`i Nursery and Landscaping Inc., P. O. Box 3013, Lihu`e, HI, 96766. Phone: 245-7747

The Native Landscape, 4560 J Kuawa Road, Kilauea, 96754. Phone: 828-1454

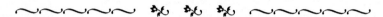

Maui:

Ho'olawa Farms, P. O. Box 731, Ha`iku, HI, 96708. Phone: 575-5099

Kula Botanical Gardens, RR 2, Box 288, Kula, HI, 96790. Phone: 878-1715

Maui District Forester. Phone: 984-8100, DOFAW/DLNR

Maui Nui Botanical Gardens, 150 Kanaloa Ave., Kahului, Hawai'i 96732. Phone: 249-2798. Across from the War Memorial Stadium, a non-profit garden committed to conserving Hawaiian plants and cultural heritage. MNBG has periodic sales. Call or check website: www.mnbg.org

The Hawaiian Collection, 1127 Manu Street, Kula, HI, 96790. Phone: 878-1701

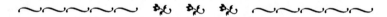

Big Island:

Aikane Nursery; P. O. Box 981, Kapa`au, 96755. Phone: 889-5906

Amy B. H. Greenwell Ethnobotanical Garden; P.O. Box 1053, Captain Cook, HI 96704 (just mauka and north of Manago Hotel). Phone: 323-3318.

Future Forests Nursery; Jill Wagner, P.O. Box 847, Kailua-Kona, HI, 96745. Phone: 325-2377

Grow Native; Box 753, Mt. View, HI, 96771. Phone: 968-8350; Fax: (808) 968-6853; E-mail: endflorahi@aol.com

Hawai`i District Forester. Phone: 933-4221, DOFAW/DLNR

Kapoho Kai Nursery; RR 2 Box 4024, Pahoa, HI, 96778. Phone: 965-8839

Hawaiian Gardens; P. O. Box 1779, Kailua-Kona, HI, 96745. Phone: 329-5702

Lehua Lena Nursery; Box 1479, Kea`au, HI, 96749. Phone: 966-7975

Moeauoa Nursery; 75-0114 Mamalahoa Highway, Holualoa, HI. Phone: 329-5777

Individual Growers

O`ahu:

Heidi Bornhorst, Honolulu, c/o The Nature Conservancy. Phone: 537-4508

Godfrey Ching, P. O. Box 944, Mountain View, HI, 96771. Phone: 968-8437

Burt Lum, P. O. Box 152, Honolulu, HI, 96810. Phone: 546-4919

Randy Mew, Honolulu. Phone: 373-2480

Laura Spiegel; Box 1709, Honoka`a, HI, 96727. Phone: 775-0806

Dianne Zink; 73-4445 Old Government Road, Kailua-Kona, HI, 96740. Phone: 325-1003

Plant Sales

O`ahu:

Foster Botanic Garden tri-annual plant sale, 180 North Vineyard Boulevard, Honolulu, HI 96817. Phone: 537-1708.

Friends of Halawa Xeriscape Garden Unthirsty plant sale, 99-1268 Iwaena Street, Halawa Industrial Park, `Aiea, HI 96701

Harold L. Lyon Arboretum tri-annual plant sale, 3860 Manoa Road, Honolulu, HI 96822. Phone: 988-0456.

Hawaiian Botanical Society semi-annual plant sale, c/o Department of Botany, University of Hawai`i, 3190 Maile Way, Honolulu, HI, 96822. Phone: 956-8369.

Wahiawa Botanic Garden annual plant sale, 1396 California Avenue, Wahiawa, HI, 96786. Phone: 621-7321.

Waimea Valley Audubon Center and Botanical Garden plant sale, 59-864 Kamehameha Highway, Hale`iwa, HI, 96712. Phone: 638-9199.

Big Island:

Amy B. H. Greenwell Ethnobotanical Garden, Captain Cook, HI, 96704. Phone: 323-3318; June and December semi-annual plant sales, "open house" on 2nd Saturday of every month, and Monday-Friday, 7 a.m. - 2:30 p.m.

Composting Classes

Big Island:

Piper Selden is a Master Composter/Recycler and self-proclaimed "worm wrestler" who teaches composting classes on the Big Island. Her company, Hawai`i Rainbow Worms, sells native compost worms and affordable worm bins and supplies to residents of Hawai`i. Class schedules and information are listed on her web site: www.HawaiiRainbowWorms.com

Some classes are also listed on Recycle Hawai`i's web site under "Events": www.RecycleHawaii.org.

(808) 959-7257

piper@HawaiiRainbowWorms.com.

O`ahu:

Waikiki Worm Company
Mindy Jaffe
234 Ohua Ave. #118
Honolulu HI 96815
(808) 382-0432
www.waikikiworm.com
waikikiworm@hawaii.rr.com

Compost Worms

Hawai`i Rainbow Worms
Piper Selden
(808) 959-7257
www.HawaiiRainbowWorms.com.
piper@HawaiiRainbowWorms.com.

Waikiki Worm Company
Mindy Jaffe
234 Ohua Ave. #118
Honolulu HI 96815
(808) 382-0432
www.waikikiworm.com
waikikiworm@hawaii.rr.com
Worms, worm bins, vermicomposting education and project consultation

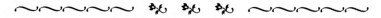

Permaculture/Sustainability Farms

Many of the following farms offer work/study internships. Lodging and some meals are often included in exchange for an agreed-upon number of hours of working in their gardens and fields. Contact each one individually for details and availability. All of them are on the Big Island.

GaiaYoga Gardens
Permaculture homestead and learning center that offers work-exchange, classes and consulting in nonviolent communication, hatha yoga, and sustainable homesteading. They are also looking for people who share their values and who want to help create a long-term residential intentional community.
Ano Tarletz and Mercedes Kirkel
RR 2, Box 3334
Pahoa, HI 96778
(808) 965-5664
aloha@gaiayoga.org
www.gaiayoga.org (for the community)
www.gaiayoga.org/nursery (for the nursery)

Hedonisia Hawaii
Hostel accommodations and work/trade.
Mojo and Leah
(808) 965-6153
hawaii@hedonisia.com
www.hedonisia.com

Hi`iaka's Healing Herb Garden
Offers residency internships for students interested in herbalism, Hawaiian native plants and healing. Also offers landscaping consultations.
Barbara Fahs
HCR 2, Box 9620
Kea`au, HI 96749
(808) 966-6126
goddess@hiiakas.com
www.hiiakas.com

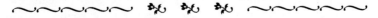

Josanna's Garden

A gorgeous organic garden on six acres south of Hilo, Big Island. Hosts Willing Workers on Organic Farms (WWOOF) volunteers. Fruit stand sells the bounty of their gourmet fruits and vegetables.
Janelle Honer, Steve Shaffer and Doug Shockley
Papaya Farms Road, Pahoa 96778
(808) 640-2157
Josannasgarden@yahoo.com

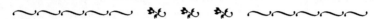

Laughing Waters

P.O. Box 1323
Keaau, HI 96749
A 3-acre vegetarian's delight garden not far from Kilauea volcano.
tutugadfly@yahoo.com
No phone. Vegetarian non-smokers only; encourages families with children to apply.

Pangaia

Raw food community that offers lodging, classes and work/study.
Papaya Farms Road
Pahoa, HI 96778
(808) 965-9988

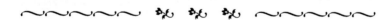

Puna Health Garden

Three acres in the rainforest with lots of medicinal and edible plants, located 14 miles from Hilo on the Big Island. Offers a camping cabin that houses 6 people, plus camping. Host location for Willing Workers on Organic Farms.
Marlene Gilbert
(808) 968-1515
punahealthgarden@hotmail.com

Yoga Oasis

Holds daily yoga classes and has rooms for rent. Also, as a bed and breakfast inn, they offer week-long yoga intensives with local teachers. If an intensive is more yoga than you want, you can participate in a yoga class for an hour each morning, enjoy an organic, vegan breakfast, and spend the rest of the day hiking, exploring the island, or indulging

in whatever other vacation pleasures you discover. Also hosts work/exchange.
Star Townshend and Hayward Coleman
P.O. Box 1935
Pahoa, HI 96778
(800) 274-4446
(808) 965-8460
info@yogaoasis.org
www.yogaoasis.org

Miscellaneous Information and Contacts

Starplate connector kits:

Strombergs' Chicks
P.O. Box 400
Pine River, MN 56474
Phone orders: 1-800-270-1134 (8 a.m.-5 p.m., Monday-Friday, Central time)
Kits currently cost $55.00 plus shipping. Instructions are included.
Website: www.strombergschickens.com/starplate_building_system/starplate_index.htm

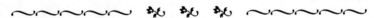

Horticultural vinegar:
Greenergy's Blackberry and Brush Block product can be ordered through their web site, www.greenergyinc.com. It costs $25 for a 128 oz. jug. Shipping, of course, is extra and will put your total up a bit.

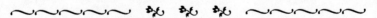

Gardener's Supply Catalog, for a wealth of gardening supplies such as earth staples. www.gardeners.com. To order a catalog or to order by phone, call toll-free: 1-888-833-1412.

For processing of kukui and kamani nuts into oil:
Oils of Aloha
P.O. Box 685
Waialua, HI, 96791
(800) 367-6010; (808) 637-5620

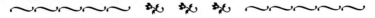

Fact Sheets. In addition to its publications, the Hawaiian Plant Conservation Center (HPCC) of the National Tropical Botanical Garden provides information on the propagation and cultivation of Hawaiian native plants. Write to HPCC for their fact sheets on how to grow and use native Hawaiian plants in cultivation.

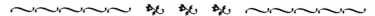

Directory of Sources. The HPCC has also published a Directory of Sources for Native Hawaiian Plants. It lists by island the mailing address, phone number, specific natives available, and shipping policy. To order, send $4 per copy with your name, mailing address, and also phone number to: Hawaiian Plant Conservation Center, NTBG, P. O. Box 340, Lawai, Kaua`i, Hawai`i, 96765.

Appendix:
Top 10 Medicinal Plants That Can and Should be Grown in Hawai`i

If you own some appropriate acreage, you can make money growing carefree medicinal plants for the herbal supplement industry, which continues to grow as more people turn to alternative medicine. Because of this, the companies that make herbal teas and sell bulk dried herbs need growers for the many plants in their catalogs. The beauty of the medicinals that I'm suggesting Hawaiian farmers consider growing is that they're easy to grow and often thrive in poor soil and neglectful conditions. Why spend a lot of time and money creating an environment that is conducive for a particular plant (like a greenhouse) when there are plenty of plants that need no special care? Here are the traits that I believe medicinal cash crops should have:

✓ They require very little fertilization and irrigation.
✓ They will not escape cultivation and become yet another invasive species in our already-fragile environment.
✓ They have no significant insect pests.
✓ They have a short harvest so you can realize a quick return on your investment.
✓ They have a good market in the herbal supplement industry.

Which Medicinal Plants Should Be Grown in Hawai`i?

What if you could grow a crop that required very little fertilizer, irrigation and insect controls? And what if that crop matured and gave you a harvest within the first year of planting? Here's my 2005 Top 10 list of the plants I've had success growing that fit these criteria:

10. The mints (*Mentha* spp.; peppermint, spearmint, etc.)
    Used by companies such as Celestial Seasonings in many of their tea blends.

9. Siberian motherwort (*Leonurus Sibericus*)
   This is used in Chinese medicine. It's an excellent heart tonic and is helpful for women's health concerns such as pre-menstrual syndrome and menopausal symptoms. It's also used in the practice of moxibustion.

8. Psyllium (*Plantago psyllium*)

Psyllium is in the plantain genus (not the cooking banana, the lawn weed plantain). The seeds are a powerful intestinal cleanser that gets rid of toxins and improves regularity. Psyllium seed currently sells for about $10 a pound.

7. Lemon Balm (*Melissa officinalis*)

Delicious lemony herb used in tea blends. It's mildly sedative, good for stomachaches, and helpful when you have a cold.

6. Stevia (*Stevia rebaudiana*)

A natural sweetener, this plant makes a product that is increasing in popularity as health-conscious consumers discover this delicious substitute for sugar and calorie-laden honey.

5. Mugwort (*Artemesia vulgaris*)

This is the exact species used in Chinese medicine for nervous conditions and the lungs.

4. Kamani (*Calophyllum inophyllum*)

Although it takes longer than one year to get a crop from a young tree, the oil from kamani nuts (called Tamanu in Tahiti) is said to be a miraculous skin healer.

3. Fo-ti (*Polygonum multiflorum*)

Known as He-shou-wu in Chinese medicine, the root of this attractive, spreading plant is a "rejuvenating tonic that will restore energy, increase fertility and maintain strength and vigor," according to Michael Tierra in his book, *The Way of Herbs.*

2. Red Zinger Hibiscus (*Hibiscus sabdariffa*)

This delicious, nutritious edible hibiscus is used in many commercial tea blends such as Red Zinger and Lemon Zinger, both made by Celestial Seasonings.

1. Green tea (*Camellia sinensis*)

Sales continue to increase, partly due to studies that have demonstrated that it's effective against the formation of certain types of cancerous cells. It's delicious and refreshing and is a staple of life in Asian countries. It should become a staple of life in the United States as well.

More About Green Tea

Green tea belongs to the camellia family. According to *The Way of Herbs,* green tea is a stimulant (it has caffeine), diuretic (increases urination), and an astringent (constricts or binds, meaning that it's useful for stopping hemorrhages and secretions). It also halts diarrhea. Green tea mouthwash also helps to prevent cavities. Most importantly, several clinical studies have proven that green tea helps to prevent certain types of cancer, especially cancers of the pancreas, colon, small intestine, stomach, breast and lung. (*Physician's Desk Reference for Herbal Medicines*) Recent research shows that green tea may also be useful in preventing osteoarthritis by blocking the body's enzyme that destroys cartilage. (American Botanical Council, www.herbalgram.org)

It's a shrub that thrives in very little soil on my pahoehoe. I sometimes toss a shovel full of compost at the base of my plant, but have only fertilized it with worm castings. Chinese rose beetles like to munch on the leaves, but the new growth is unaffected, which is fine because the medicinal part is the young leaves. When it doesn't rain for two weeks or more, I water it if I remember. I consider it to be a hardy survivor and a good candidate for commercial production. It grows even better at higher elevations and I know a number of Big Island growers who are experimenting with it.

Where to Buy Seeds

I get most of my medicinal herb seeds from two companies in Oregon, both organic:
- Horizon Herbs: www.horizonherbs.com; 541-846-6704.
- The Thyme Garden: www.thymegarden.com; 541-487-8671.

Idea for Selling Medicinal Crops

Frontier Natural Products Co-op, located in Iowa, contracts with growers and buys bulk herbs for their large catalog. Call them at 1-800-669-3275 or visit their web site: www.frontiercoop.com.

Appendix:
Okay Plants to Grow

The plants listed in this Appendix are species that have been evaluated by the Hawai`i Weed Risk Assessment (WRA), which has determined that they pose no threat to native or managed ecosystems in Hawai`i or any other of the high islands of the Pacific. This information is current as of January 30, 2004.

If you have any concerns, you can report them to hpwra@hear.org.

Common name	Genus/species name	Family
African fern pine	*Podocarpus gracilior*	*Podocarpaceae*
agati	*Sesbania grandiflora*	*Fabaceae*
Aglaonema	*Aglaonema commutatum*	*Araceae*
Aglaonema	*Aglaonema nitidum*	*Araceae*
angel's trumpet	*Brugmansia x candida*	*Solanaceae*
Ashoka tree	*Saraca indica*	*Fabaceae*
Australian tallowwood	*Eucalyptus microcorys*	*Myrtaceae*
avocado	*Persea americana*	*Lauraceae*
baby rubberplant	*Peperomia obtusifolia*	*Piperaceae*
bamboo, common	*Bambusa vulgaris*	*Poaceae*
banana shrub	*Michelia figo*	*Magnoliaceae*
baobab tree	*Adansonia digitata*	*Bombacaceae*
Barbados lily	*Hippeastrum puniceum*	*Liliaceae*
beefsteak plant	*Acalypha wilkesiana*	*Euphorbiaceae*
betel nut palm	*Areca catechu*	*Palmae*
black olive and spiny black olive	*Bucida buceras and B. molinetii*	*Combretaceae*
bloodwood	*Eucalyptus intermedia*	*Myrtaceae*
blue daze	*Evolvulus glomeratus*	*Convolvulaceae*
blue Latan palm	*Latania loddigesii*	*Arecaceae*
blue mahoe	*Talipariti elatum*	*Malvaceae*
bluestem yucca	*Yucca guatemalensis*	*Agavaceae*
bodhi tree	*Ficus religiosa*	*Moraceae*
bottle gourd	*Lagenaria siceraria*	*Cucurbitaceae*

Common name	Genus/species name	Family
breadfruit (ulu)	*Artocarpus altilis*	*Moraceae*
Brexia	*Brexia madagascariensis*	*Grossulariaceae*
Brisbane box	*Lophostemon confertus*	*Myrtaceae*
bush thunbergia	*Thunbergia erecta*	*Bignoniacaeae*
busy Lizzy	*Impatiens wallerana*	*Balsaminaceae*
buttercup tree	*Cochlospermum vitifolium*	*Bixaceae*
button mangrove	*Conocarpus erectus*	*Combretaceae*
cabbage tree	*Andira inermis*	*Fabaceae*
cabbage tree	*Cussonia spicata*	*Araliaceae*
calabash tree	*Crescentia cujete*	*Bignoniaceae*
calamondin	*Citrus×Citrofortunella mitis*	*Rutaceae*
calapo	*Calopogonium mucunoides*	*Fabaceae*
cape jasmine	*Gardenia jasminoides*	*Rubiaceae*
cape leadwort	*Plumbago auriculata*	*Plumbaginaceae*
cardboard plant	*Zamia furfuracea*	*Zamiaceae*
caricature-plant	*Graptophyllum pictum*	*Acanthaceae*
carob tree	*Ceratonia siliqua*	*Fabaceae*
Carolina wild petunia	*Ruellia caroliniensis*	*Acanthaceae*
Caroline ivory nut palm	*Metroxylon amicarum*	*Arecaceae*
cashew tree	*Anacardium occidentale*	*Anacardiaceae*
cast iron plant	*Aspidistra elatior*	*Liliaceae*
Cavendish banana	*Musa acuminata*	*Musaceae*
chenille plant	*Acalypha hispida*	*Euphorbiaceae*
cherimoya	*Annona cherimola*	*Annonaceae*
chinese cinnamon	*Cinnamomum aromaticum*	*Lauraceae*
Chinese hatplant	*Holmskioldia sanguinea*	*Verbenaceae*
Chinese hibiscus	*Hibiscus rosa-sinensis*	*Malvaceae*
Chinese juniper	*Juniperus chinensis*	*Cupressaceae*
Chinese perfume plant	*Aglaia odorata*	*Meliaceae*
climbing ylang-ylang	*Artabotrys hexapetalus*	*Annonaceae*
cockspur coral tree	*Erythrina crista-galli*	*Fabaceae*
cocoa	*Theobroma cacao*	*Sterculiaceae*
Colville's glory	*Colvillea racemosa*	*Fabaceae*
common bamboo	*Bambusa vulgaris*	*Poaceae*

Common name	Genus/species name	Family
common fig	*Ficus carica cv. brownturkey*	*Moraceae*
Cook's pine	*Araucaria columnaris*	*Araucariaceae*
coral tree	*Erythrina variegata*	*Fabaceae*
crape myrtle	*Lagerstroemia indica*	*Lythraceae*
creeping mirrorplant	*Coprosma repens*	*Rubiaceae*
crimson bottlebush and weeping bottlebrush	*Callistemon citrinus and C. viminalis*	*Myrtaceae*
Crinum lily	*Crinum asiaticum*	*Liliaceae*
croton	*Codiaeum variegatum*	*Euphorbiaceae*
dragon tree	*Dracaena draco*	*Agavaceae*
drooping she oak	*Allocasuarina verticillata*	*Casuarinaceae*
dry zone mahogany	*Khaya senegalensis*	*Meliaceae*
dwarf poinciana	*Caesalpinia pulcherrima*	*Fabaceae*
ear tree	*Enterolobium cyclocarpum*	*Fabaceae*
elephant hedge bean tree	*Schotia brachypetala*	*Fabaceae*
empress diamond	*Paulownia fortunei*	*Scrophulariaceae*
evergreen frangipani	*Plumeria obtusa*	*Apocynaceae*
false aralia	*Schefflera elegantissima*	*Araliaceae*
false heather	*Cuphea hyssopifolia*	*Lythraceae*
false olive	*Elaeodendron orientale*	*Celastraceae*
fern tree	*Filicium decipiens*	*Sapindaceae*
fiddleleaf fig	*Ficus lyrata*	*Moraceae*
Fiji fan palm	*Pritchardia pacifica*	*Palmae*
fire cracker plant	*Russelia equisetiformis*	*Scrophulariaceae*
firespike	*Odontonema cuspidatum*	*Acanthaceae*
Flemingia	*Flemingia macrophylla*	*Fabaceae*
Florida royal palm	*Roystonea regia*	*Arecaceae*
floss-silk tree	*Chorisia speciosa*	*Bombacaceae*
footstool palm	*Livistona rotundifolia*	*Arecaceae*
forest red gum	*Eucalyptus tereticornis*	*Myrtaceae*
frangipani	*Plumeria rubra*	*Apocynaceae*
geiger tree	*Cordia sebestena*	*Boraginaceae*
Geraldton wax	*Chamelaucium uncinatum*	*Asteraceae*

Common name	Genus/species name	Family
geranium aralia	*Polyscias filicifolia*	*Araliaceae*
gold tree	*Tabebuia donnell-smithii*	*Bignoniaceae*
golden shower tree	*Cassia fistula*	*Fabaceae*
golden trumpet tree	*Tabebuia ochracea*	*Bignoniaceae*
guachipelín	*Diphysa americana*	*Fabaceae*
Hawaiian bamboo	*Schizostachyum glaucifolium*	*Poaceae*
hearts and flowers	*Aptenia cordifolia*	*Aizoaceae*
Hong Kong orchid tree	*Bauhinia x blakeana*	*Fabaceae*
horse bush	*Desmodium umbellatum*	*Fabaceae*
horse-raddish tree	*Moringa oleifera*	*Moraceae*
hurricane palm	*Dictyosperma album*	*Arecaceae*
Illawarra flame tree	*Brachychiton acerifolius*	*Sterculiaceae*
Indian banyan	*Ficus benghalensis*	*Moraceae*
Indian beech	*Pongamia pinnata*	*Fabaceae*
Indian hawthorn	*Rhaphiolepis indica*	*Rosaceae*
Indian rubberplant	*Ficus elastica*	*Moraceae*
Indonesian gum	*Eucalyptus deglupta*	*Myrtaceae*
ironbark	*Eucalyptus crebra*	*Myrtaceae*
ivyleaf geranium	*Pelargonium peltatum*	*Geraniaceae*
jacaranda	*Jacaranda mimosifolia*	*Bignoniaceae*
jack in the box tree	*Hernandia ovigera*	*Hernandiaceae*
jackfruit	*Artocarpus heterophyllus*	*Moraceae*
Jamaica oak	*Catalpa longissima*	*Bignoniaceae*
Japanese cedar	*Cryptomeria japonica*	*Taxodiaceae*
Japanese yew	*Podocarpus macrophyllus*	*Podocarpaceae*
Joannis palm	*Veitchia joannis*	*Arecaceae*
king palm	*Archontophoenix cunninghamiana*	*Arecaceae*
kolomona	*Senna surattensis*	*Fabaceae*
Korean lawngrass	*Zoysia japonica*	*Poaceae*
kou	*Cordia subcordata*	*Boraginaceae*
kwila	*Intsia bijuga*	*Fabaceae*
lady palm	*Rhaphis excelsa*	*Palmae*
large-leaf mahogany	*Swietenia macrophylla*	*Meliaceae*

203

Common name	Genus/species name	Family
lecheso	*Stemmadenia litoralis*	*Apocynaceae*
lemon	*Citrus limon*	*Rutaceae*
lemonyellow rosemallow	*Hibiscus calyphyllus*	*Malvaceae*
lignum vitae	*Guaiacum officinale*	*Zygophyllaceae*
lilyturf	*Liriope muscari*	*Liliaceae*
lipsticktree	*Bixa orellana*	*Bixaceae*
lobster claw	*Heliconia caribaea*	*Heliconiaceae*
logwood	*Haematoxylum campechianum*	*Fabaceae*
looking-glass tree	*Heritiera littoralis*	*Sterculiaceae*
Madagascar periwinkle	*Catharanthus roseus*	*Apocynaceae*
maga	*Montezuma speciosissima*	*Malvaceae*
Malabar chestnut	*Pachira aquatica*	*Bombacaceae*
Manila palm	*Veitchia merrillii*	*Arecaceae*
marang	*Artocarpus odoratissimus*	*Moraceae*
metallic plant	*Hemigraphis alternata*	*Acanthaceae*
Ming Aralia	*Polyscias fruticosa*	*Arailiaceae*
mondo grass	*Ophiopogon japonicus*	*Liliaceae*
money tree	*Dracaena marginata*	*Agavaceae*
monkey apple	*Posoqueria latifolia*	*Rubiaceae*
monkeypod tree	*Samanea saman*	*Fabaceae*
Monterey pine	*Pinus radiata*	*Pinaceae*
Montgomery palm	*Veitchia montgomeryana*	*Arecaceae*
mother of cocoa	*Gliricidia sepium*	*Fabaceae*
mountain cabbage tree	*Cussonia paniculata*	*Araliaceae*
natal plum	*Carissa grandiflora*	*Apocynaceae*
neel	*Indigofera teysmannii*	*Fabaceae*
Nepalese alder	*Alnus nepalensis*	*Betulaceae*
Nicaragua rosewood	*Dalbergia retusa*	*Fabaceae*
Norfolk Island pine	*Araucaria heterophylla*	*Araucariaceae*
orange champaca	*Michelia champaca*	*Magnoliaceae*
oriental arborvitae	*Platycladus orientalis*	*Cupressaceae*
panax	*Polyscias guilfoylei*	*Araliaceae*
papaya	*Carica papaya*	*Caricaceae*

Common name	Genus/species name	Family
paperflower	*Bougainvillea glabra*	*Nyctaginaceae*
passion fruit	*Passiflora edulis*	*Passifloraceae*
peace lily	*Spathiphyllum wallisii*	*Araceae*
peregrina	*Jatropha integerrima*	*Euphorbiaceae*
perennial peanut	*Arachis glabrata*	*Fabaceae*
perennial peanut	*Arachis pintoi*	*Fabaceae*
perfume tree	*Cananga odorata*	*Annonaceae*
photina	*Photinia davidiana*	*Rosaceae*
pigeon pea	*Cajanus cajan*	*Fabaceae*
pink ivory	*Berchemia zeyheri*	*Rhamnaceae*
pink shower tree	*Cassia bakeriana*	*Fabaceae*
pink shower tree	*Cassia grandis*	*Fabaceae*
pink shower tree	*Cassia javanica*	*Fabaceae*
pink trumpet-tree	*Tabebuia heterophylla*	*Bignoniaceae*
pink-eyed Cerbera	*Cerbera manghas*	*Apocynaceae*
plum pine	*Podocarpus elatus*	*Podocarpaceae*
poinsettia	*Euphorbia pulcherrima*	*Euphorbiaceae*
Polynesian arrowroot	*Tacca leontopetaloides*	*Taccaceae*
Polynesian chestnut	*Inocarpus fagifer*	*Fabaceae*
pomegranate	*Punica granatum*	*Punicaceae*
ponytail palm	*Nolina recurvata*	*Agavaceae*
primrose jasmine	*Jasminum mesnyi*	*Oleaceae*
pua keni keni	*Fagraea berteroana*	*Loganiaceae*
pygmy date palm	*Phoenix roebelenii*	*Arecaceae*
queen palm	*Syagrus romanzoffiana*	*Arecaceae*
queen's crape myrtle	*Lagerstroemia speciosa*	*Lythraceae*
Queensland kauri	*Agathis robusta*	*Araucariaceae*
Queensland Maple	*Flindersia brayleyana*	*Rutaceae*
rainbow shower tree	*Cassia xnealiae*	*Fabaceae*
red spurge	*Euphorbia cotinifolia*	*Euphorbiaceae*
royal poinciana	*Delonix regia*	*Fabaceae*
sandpaper vine	*Petrea volubilis*	*Verbenaceae*
sausage tree	*Kigelia africana*	*Bignoniaceae*
sea grape	*Coccoloba uvifera*	*Polygonaceae*

Common name	Genus/species name	Family
sea putat	*Barringtonia asiatica*	*Lecythidaceae*
shampoo ginger (`awapuhi)	*Zingiber zerumbet*	*Zingiberaceae*
shavingbrush tree	*Pseudobombax ellipticum*	*Bombacaceae*
shrimp plant	*Justicia brandegeeana*	*Acanthaceae*
shrubby desmodium	*Desmodium nicaraguense*	*Fabaceae*
shrubby stylo	*Stylosanthes scabra*	*Fabaceae*
Siamese cassia	*Cassia siamea*	*Fabaceae*
silk oak	*Grevillea robusta*	*Proteaceae*
slender goldshower	*Galphimia gracilis*	*Malphigiaceae*
snow bush	*Breynia disticha*	*Euphorbiaceae*
soursop	*Annona muricata*	*Annonaceae*
southern magnolia	*Magnolia grandiflora*	*Magnoliaceae*
spathe flower	*Spathiphyllum cannifolium*	*Araceae*
spiny black olive	*Bucida molinetii*	*Combretaceae*
spring cinquefoil	*Potentilla verna*	*Rosaceae*
star jasmine	*Jasminum multiflorum*	*Oleaceae*
starfruit	*Averrhoa carambola*	*Oxalidaceae*
stiff bottlebrush	*Callistemon rigidus*	*Myrtaceae*
strawberry saxifrage	*Saxifraga sarmentosa*	*Saxifragaceae*
sugar apple	*Annona squamosa*	*Annonaceae*
swamp mahogany	*Eucalyptus robusta*	*Myrtaceae*
swiss-cheese plant	*Monstera deliciosa*	*Araceae*
Tahitian gardenia	*Gardenia taitensis*	*Rubiaceae*
tamarind	*Tamarindus indica*	*Fabaceae*
teak	*Tectona grandis*	*Verbenaceae*
templegrass	*Zoysia tenuifolia*	*Poaceae*
thatch palm	*Thrinax parviflora*	*Arecaceae*
tipu tree	*Tipuana tipu*	*Fabaceae*
toi	*Alphitonia zizyphoides*	*Rhamnaceae*
toporite	*Hernandia sonora*	*Hernandiaceae*
trailing African daisy	*Osteospermum fruticosum*	*Asteraceae*
tree heliotrope	*Tournefortia argentea*	*Boraginaceae*
tropical almond	*Terminalia catappa*	*Combretaceae*
tropical ash	*Fraxinus uhdei*	*Oleaceae*

Common name	Genus/species name	Family
tulipwood	*Harpullia pendula*	*Sapindaceae*
Turk's cap	*Malvaviscus penduliflorus*	*Malvaceae*
turmeric	*Curcuma longa*	*Zingiberaceae*
waipahu fig	*Ficus tikoua*	*Moraceae*
weeping bottlebrush	*Callistemon viminalis*	*Myrtaceae*
West Indian mahogany	*Swietenia mahagoni*	*Meliaceae*
white champaca	*Michelia x alba*	*Magnoliaceae*
wi apple	*Spondias dulcis*	*Anacardiaceae*
wild pepper	*Capsicum frutescens*	*Solanaceae*
Winin palm	*Veitchia winin*	*Arecaceae*
wisteria tree	*Bolusanthus speciosus*	*Fabaceae*
yellow flame	*Peltophorum pterocarpum*	*Fabaceae*
yellow necklacepod	*Sophora tomentosa*	*Fabaceae*
yellow tree bauhinia	*Bauhinia tomentosa*	*Fabaceae*

Appendix:
Weed Risk Assessments (WRA)

The Hawai`i-Pacific Weed Risk Assessment [HP-WRA] is a research project that has been supported by funding from the USDA Forest Service and from the Hawai`i Division of Forestry and Wildlife Urban and Community Forestry program. The intent of the HP-WRA research project is to identify plants that pose a high weed risk in Hawai`i and other Pacific Islands.

The HP-WRA score does not measure actual invasiveness, economic or ecological harm in the field. Rather, a designation of H(HPWRA) is a prediction that a species will become invasive. The HP-WRA ratings have no regulatory authority and the HP-WRA "list" is not an official State list of invasive plants. To determine which species are prohibited in Hawai`i, please consult the official State of Hawai`i List of Plant Species Designated as Noxious Weeds. The list we provide here is accessible on the Internet at the following URL: www.botany.hawaii.edu/faculty/daehler/WRA/full_table.asp. The official listing on this site lists plants by their genus names. However, for ease of use, we have organized the list by common name. If you want to search for a specific plant, the Internet listing is the place to go. Our list is current as of June 2005. The WRA list is a dynamic tool that is frequently updated, so for the latest information and ratings, we recommend that you check the Internet list.

WRA Designation	Meaning
L	LOW: Not currently recognized as invasive in Hawai`i, and having a low likelihood of becoming major ecological or economic impacts on other Pacific Islands based on the HP-WRA screening process.
L (Hawai'i)	LOW in Hawai`i: Not currently recognized as invasive in Hawai`i based on a low track record of not becoming naturalized despite being widely planted in Hawai`i for at least 40 years.
H (HPWRA)	HIGH likelihood of becoming invasive in Hawai`i and on other Pacific Islands as determined by the HP- WRA screening process, which is based on published sources describing species biology and behavior in Hawai`i and/or other parts of the world.

H (Hawai'i) HIGH in Hawai`i: Documented to cause significant ("high")
ecological or economic harm in Hawai`i, as determined
from published information on the species' current impacts
in Hawai`i. H (Hawai'i) -- Actual ecological or economic
impacts by this species in Hawai'i have been documented
from published information. Information sources are
provided in the HP-WRA spreadsheet. Minimally, a species
given the H(Hawai'i) designation has met one of the
following criteria:

- Published statements by at least two experts having field
  experience in Hawai'i indicated that the species has
  caused major ecological or economic harm in Hawai'i.
- A published statement by one expert having field
  experience in Hawai'i indicated that the species has
  caused major ecological or economic harm AND
  published information indicates that this species has
  been the target of active control efforts in Hawai'i.
- An expert with field experience in Hawai`i has published
  a description of specific harm caused by the plant
  in Hawai'i (including location(s) where the problem
  was observed), AND the description appears to meet
  minimal criteria for significant harm, as defined by the
  Hawai`i Exotic Plant Evaluation Protocol (HEPEP).

EVALUATE The species has been assessed using the HP-WRA system;
however, no assessment of risk can be provided at this
time because 1) important information is missing from the
assessment or 2) the species possesses a combination of traits
and characteristics that make its likely behavior difficult to
assess using the WRA system.

Completed Assessments Sorted by Common Name

Common Name	Genus and Species	WRA Designation
Abelia, glossy	*Abelia x grandiflora*	L
Acalypha	*Acalypha godseffiana*	L
African fern pine	*Podocarpus gracilior*	L
African tulip tree	*Spathodea campanulata*	**H (HPWRA)**
Agati	*Sesbania grandiflora*	L
Aglaonema	*Aglaonema commutatum*	L
Aglaonema	*Aglaonema nitidum*	L

Common Name	Genus and Species	WRA Designation
Alexander palm	*Ptychosperma elegans*	EVALUATE
Alexandra palm	*Archontophoenix alexandrae*	EVALUATE
Allspice tree	*Pimenta dioica*	H (HPWRA)
Amer buffalo grass	*Buchloe dactyloides*	L
American joint vetch	*Aeschynomene americana*	H (HPWRA)
Andaman redwood	*Pterocarpus dalbergioides*	L
Angel's trumpet	*Brugmansia x candida*	L
Annual lion's ear	*Leonotis nepetifolia*	H (HPWRA)
Annual ryegrass	*Lolium multiflorum*	H (HPWRA)
Areca palm	*Dypsis lutescens*	L (Hawai'i)
Arrowhead plant	*Syngonium podophyllum*	H (HPWRA)
Ashla tree	*Saraca indica*	L
Asparagus fern	*Asparagus densiflorus*	H (HPWRA)
Athel tamarisk	*Tamarix aphylla*	H (HPWRA)
Australian acacia	*Acacia mearnsii*	H (Hawai'i)
Australian blackwood	*Acacia melanoxylon*	H (HPWRA)
Australian cheesewood	*Pittosporum undulatum*	H (HPWRA)
Australian red cedar	*Toona ciliata*	EVALUATE
Australian tallowwood	*Eucalyptus microcorys*	L
Australian tree fern	*Cyathea cooperi*	H (Hawai'i)
Autograph tree	*Clusia rosea*	EVALUATE
Autumn olive	*Elaeagnus umbellata*	H (HPWRA)
Avocado	*Persea americana*	L
Baby rubberplant	*Peperomia obtusifolia*	L
Babylon weeping willow	*Salix babylonica*	H (HPWRA)
Bahia grass	*Paspalum notatum*	H (HPWRA)
Balloon vine	*Cardiospermum halicacabum*	H (HPWRA)
Balsam impatens	*Impatiens balsamina*	EVALUATE
Banana shrub	*Michelia figo*	L
Baobab tree	*Adansonia digitata*	L

Common Name	Genus and Species	WRA Designation
Barbados lily	*Hippeastrum puniceum*	L
Bay rum tree	*Pimenta racemosa*	**EVALUATE**
Beefsteak plant	*Acalypha wilkesiana*	L
Belly-ache bush	*Jatropha gossypiifolia*	**H (HPWRA)**
Be-still tree	*Thevetia peruviana*	**H (HPWRA)**
Betel nut palm	*Areca catechu*	L
Bird of paradise	*Strelitzia reginae*	L
Birds nest Anthurium	*Anthurium hoLeri*	L
Bishopwood	*Bischofia javanica*	**H (HPWRA)**
Bismarck palm	*Bismarckia nobilis*	L
Black olive	*Bucida buceras*	L
Blood leaf	*Iresine herbstii*	L
Bloodwood	*Eucalyptus intermedia*	L
Blue daze	*Evolvulus glomeratus*	L
Blue ginger	*Dichorisandra thyrsiflora*	L
Blue hesper palm	*Brahea armata*	L
Blue Latan palm	*Latania loddigesii*	L
Blue mahoe	*Talipariti elatum*	L
Blue mallet	*Eucalyptus gardneri*	L
Blue marble tree	*Elaeocarpus angustifolius*	**EVALUATE**
Blue sage	*Eranthemum pulchellum*	L
Blue trumpet vine	*Thunbergia grandiflora*	**H (HPWRA)**
Bluestem yucca	*Yucca guatemalensis*	L
Bodhi tree	*Ficus religiosa*	L
Bottle gourd	*Lagenaria siceraria*	L
Bottle palm	*Hyophorbe lagenicaulis*	L
Brazilian guava	*Psidium guineense*	**H (HPWRA)**
Brazilian jasmine	*Jasminum fluminense*	**H (HPWRA)**
Brazilian nightshade	*Solanum seaforthianum*	**H (HPWRA)**
Brazilian snapdragon	*Otacanthus caeruleus*	L
Breadfruit	*Artocarpus altilis*	L
Brexia	*Brexia madagascariensis*	L
Brisbane box	*Lophostemon confertus*	L
Broadleaf carpet grass	*Axonopus compressus*	**H (HPWRA)**

Common Name	Genus and Species	WRA Designation
Bronze leaved clerodendrum	*Clerodendrum quadriloculare*	**H (HPWRA)**
Broom teatree	*Leptospermum scoparium*	**H (HPWRA)**
Burmese rosewood	*Pterocarpus indicus*	**L (Hawai‘i)**
Bush thunbergia	*Thunbergia erecta*	**L**
Busy Lizzy	*Impatiens wallerana*	**L**
Buttercup tree	*Cochlospermum vitifolium*	**L**
Butterfly pea	*Clitoria ternatea*	**H (HPWRA)**
Button mangrove	*Conocarpus erectus*	**L**
Cabbage tree	*Andira inermis*	**L**
Cabbage tree	*Cussonia spicata*	**L**
Calabash tree	*Crescentia cujete*	**L**
Calamondin	*Citrus×Citrofortunella mitis*	**L**
Calapo	*Calopogonium mucunoides*	**L**
California fan palm	*Washingtonia filifera*	**H (HPWRA)**
Calliandra	*Calliandra calothyrsus*	**L**
Camphor tree	*Cinnamomum camphora*	**H (HPWRA)**
Canary island st. Johnswort	*Hypericum canariense*	**H (HPWRA)**
Candle bush	*Senna alata*	**H (HPWRA)**
Cape cheesewood	*Pittosporum viridiflorum*	**EVALUATE**
Cape honeysuckle	*Tecoma capensis*	**L (Hawai‘i)**
Cape jasmine	*Gardenia jasminoides*	**L**
Cape leadwort	*Plumbago auriculata*	**L**
Cardboard plant	*Zamia furfuracea*	**L**
Caricature-plant	*Graptophyllum pictum*	**L**
Carob tree	*Ceratonia siliqua*	**L**
Carolina wild petunia	*Ruellia caroliniensis*	**L**
Caroline ivory nut palm	*Metroxylon amicarum*	**L**
Carrotwood	*Cupaniopsis anacardioides*	**EVALUATE**
Cashew tree	*Anacardium occidentale*	**L**
Cassava	*Manihot esculenta*	**L**

Common Name	Genus and Species	WRA Designation
Cast iron plant	*Aspidistra elatior*	L
Catclaw mimosa	*Mimosa pigra*	H (HPWRA)
Cat's claw	*Caesalpinia decapetala*	H (Hawai'i)
Cat's claw vine	*Macfadyena unguis-cati*	H (HPWRA)
Cavendish banana	*Musa acuminata*	L
Centipede grass	*Eremochloa ophiuroides*	L (Hawai'i)
Centro	*Centrosema pubescens*	H (HPWRA)
Chenille plant	*Acalypha hispida*	L
Cherimoya	*Annona cherimola*	L
Chinaberry tree	*Melia azedarach*	H (HPWRA)
Chinese albizia	*Albizia chinensis*	H (HPWRA)
Chinese banyon	*Ficus microcarpa*	H (HPWRA)
Chinese cinnamon	*Cinnamomum aromaticum*	L
Chinese fan palm	*Livistona chinensis*	EVALUATE
Chinese flame tree	*Koelreuteria elegans*	EVALUATE
Chinese hatplant	*Holmskioldia sanguinea*	L
Chinese hibiscus	*Hibiscus rosa-sinensis*	L
Chinese juniper	*Juniperus chinensis*	L
Chinese lespedeza	*Lespedeza cuneata*	H (HPWRA)
Chinese perfume plant	*Aglaia odorata*	L
Chinese privet	*Ligustrum sinense*	H (HPWRA)
Chinese violet	*Asystasia gangetica*	H (HPWRA)
Christmas berry	*Schinus terebinthifolius*	H (Hawai'i)
Cinnamon tree	*Cinnamomum verum*	H (HPWRA)
Climbing ylang-ylang	*Artabotrys hexapetalus*	L
Cockspur coral tree	*Erythrina crista-galli*	L
Cocoa	*Theobroma cacao*	L
Coffee	*Coffea arabica*	H (HPWRA)
Cols pine	*Araucaria columnaris*	L
Colville's glory	*Colvillea racemosa*	L
Common asparagus fern	*Asparagus setaceus*	H (HPWRA)
Common bamboo	*Bambusa vulgaris*	L
Common bugleweed	*Ajuga reptans*	H (HPWRA)

Common Name	Genus and Species	WRA Designation
Common fig	*Ficus carica cv. brownturkey*	L
Common guava	*Psidium guajava*	H (Hawai'i)
Common St. Johnswort	*Hypericum perforatum*	H (HPWRA)
Coral ardisia	*Ardisia crenata*	H (HPWRA)
Coral bean tree	*Erythrina corallodendron*	EVALUATE
Coral gum	*Eucalyptus torquata*	L
Coral hibiscus	*Hibiscus schizopetalus*	L
Coral tree	*Erythrina variegata*	L
Corn plant	*Dracaena fragrans*	L
Cowitch	*Mucuna pruriens*	H (HPWRA)
Crape myrtle	*Lagerstroemia indica*	L
Creeping fig	*Ficus pumila*	L
Creeping mirrorplant	*Coprosma repens*	L
Crimson bottlebush	*Callistemon citrinus*	L
Crimson passion flower	*Passiflora vitifolia*	L
Crinum lily	*Crinum asiaticum*	L
Croton	*Codiaeum variegatum*	L
Crown of thorns	*Euphorbia milii*	L
Cunninghamia beefwood	*Casuarina cunninghamiana*	H (HPWRA)
Cup of gold	*Solandra maxima*	EVALUATE
Dallis grass	*Paspalum dilatatum*	H (HPWRA)
Darwin black wattle	*Acacia auriculiformis*	H (HPWRA)
December tree	*Erythrina subumbrans*	EVALUATE
Desert rose	*Adenium obesum*	L
Dissotis	*Dissotis rotundifolia*	H (HPWRA)
Dragon tree	*Dracaena draco*	L
Drooping she oak	*Allocasuarina verticillata*	L
Dry zone mahogany	*Khaya senegalensis*	L
Dumbcane	*Dieffenbachia seguine (outdoors)*	H (HPWRA)
Dusty miller	*Senecio cineraria*	L

Common Name	Genus and Species	WRA Designation
Dwarf poinciana	*Caesalpinia pulcherrima*	L
Dwarf umbrella-tree	*Schefflera arboricola*	EVALUATE
Dwarf yellow Mussaenda	*Pseudomussaenda flava*	L
Ear tree	*Enterolobium cyclocarpum*	L
East Indian rosewood	*Dalbergia latifolia*	EVALUATE
Elephant ear	*Xanthosoma robustum*	EVALUATE
Elephant grass	*Pennisetum purpureum*	H (HPWRA)
Elephant hedge bean tree	*Schotia brachypetala*	L
Empress diamond	*Paulownia fortunei*	L
Everglades palm	*Acoelorraphe wrightii*	EVALUATE
Evergreen azalea	*Rhododendron indicum*	L (Hawai'i)
Evergreen frangipani	*Plumeria obtusa*	L
False aralia	*Schefflera elegantissima*	L
False heather	*Cuphea hyssopifolia*	L
False olive	*Elaeodendron orientale*	L
Fern tree	*Filicium decipiens*	EVALUATE
Fiddleleaf fig	*Ficus lyrata*	L
Fiddlewood	*Citharexylum spinosum*	H (HPWRA)
Fiji fan palm	*Pritchardia pacifica*	L
Fire cracker plant	*Russelia equisetiformis*	L
Firespike	*Odontonema cuspidatum*	L
Firetree	*Morella faya*	H (Hawai'i)
Fireweed	*Senecio madagascariensis*	H (Hawai'i)
Flag bush	*Mussaenda frondosa*	L
Flame vine	*Pyrostegia venusta*	H (HPWRA)
Flemingia	*Flemingia macrophylla*	L
Florida clover ash	*Tetrazygia bicolor*	EVALUATE
Florida royal palm	*Roystonea regia*	L
Floss-silk tree	*Chorisia speciosa*	L
Footstool palm	*Livistona rotundifolia*	L
Forest red gum	*Eucalyptus tereticornis*	L
Formosan koa	*Acacia confusa*	H (Hawai'i)

Common Name	Genus and Species	WRA Designation
Fountain grass	*Pennisetum setaceum*	**H (Hawai'i)**
Frangipani	*Plumeria rubra*	**L**
Garlic vine	*Mansoa alliaceum*	**L**
Geiger tree	*Cordia sebestena*	**L**
Geraldton wax	*Chamelaucium uncinatum*	**L**
Geranium aralia	*Polyscias filicifolia*	**L**
German ivy	*Delairea odorata*	**H (Hawai'i)**
Giant fern	*Angiopteris evecta*	**H (HPWRA)**
Giant miscanthus	*Miscanthus floridulus*	**H (HPWRA)**
Giant salvinia	*Salvinia molesta*	**H (Hawai'i)**
Giant sensitive plant	*Mimosa diplotricha*	**H (HPWRA)**
Gimlet	*Eucalyptus salubris*	**L**
Glory bush	*Tibouchina urvilleana*	**H (HPWRA)**
Glossy privet	*Ligustrum lucidum*	**EVALUATE**
Gold tree	*Tabebuia donnell-smithii*	**L**
Golden dew drop	*Duranta erecta*	**H (HPWRA)**
Golden shower tree	*Cassia fistula*	**L**
Golden trumpet tree	*Tabebuia ochracea*	**L**
Goldflame honeysuckle	*Lonicera xheckrottii*	**L**
Gorse	*Ulex europaeus*	**H (Hawai'i)**
Grapefruit	*Citrus x paradisi*	**L**
Guachipelín	*Diphysa americana*	**L**
Guinea grass	*Panicum maximum*	**H (Hawai'i)**
Gum arabic tree	*Acacia nilotica*	**H (HPWRA)**
Hawaiian baby woodrose	*Argyreia nervosa*	**L**
Hawaiian bamboo	*Schizostachyum glaucifolium*	**L**
Hawaiian holly	*Leea guineensis*	**L**
Heart-leaf philodendron	*Philodendron scandens*	**L**
Hearts and flowers	*Aptenia cordifolia*	**L**
Herald's trumpet	*Beaumontia multiflora*	**L**

Common Name	Genus and Species	WRA Designation
Hilograss	*Paspalum conjugatum*	**H (Hawai'i)**
Hiptage	*Hiptage benghalensis*	**H (HPWRA)**
Hong Kong orchid tree	*Bauhinia x blakeana*	**L**
Horse bush	*Desmodium umbellatum*	**L**
Horse-raddish tree	*Moringa oleifera*	**L**
Hurricane palm	*Dictyosperma album*	**L**
Ice cream bean	*Inga edulis*	**EVALUATE**
Ice plant	*Carpobrotus edulis*	**H (HPWRA)**
Illawarra flame tree	*Brachychiton acerifolius*	**L**
Indian banyon	*Ficus benghalensis*	**L**
Indian beech	*Pongamia pinnata*	**L**
Indian hawthorn	*Rhaphiolepis indica*	**L**
Indian rhododendron	*Melastoma candidum*	**H (Hawai'i)**
Indian rosewood	*Dalbergia sissoo*	**H (HPWRA)**
Indian rubberplant	*Ficus elastica*	**L**
Indonesian gum	*Eucalyptus deglupta*	**L**
Iron wood	*Casuarina equisetifolia*	**H (Hawai'i)**
Ironbark	*Eucalyptus crebra*	**L**
Ivy gourd	*Coccinia grandis*	**H (Hawai'i)**
Ivyleaf geranium	*Pelargonium peltatum*	**L**
Jacaranda	*Jacaranda mimosifolia*	**L**
Jack in the box tree	*Hernandia ovigera*	**L**
Jackfruit	*Artocarpus heterophyllus*	**L**
Jade plant	*Crassula ovata*	**L**
Jamaica cherry	*Muntingia calabura*	**H (HPWRA)**
Jamaica oak	*Catalpa longissima*	**L**
Japanese cedar	*Cryptomeria japonica*	**L**
Japanese honeysuckle	*Lonicera japonica*	**H (HPWRA)**
Japanese pittosporum	*Pittosporum tobira*	**EVALUATE**
Japanese privet	*Ligustrum japonicum*	**EVALUATE**
Japanese yew	*Podocarpus macrophyllus*	**L**
Jerusalum thorn	*Parkinsonia aculeata*	**H (HPWRA)**
Joannis palm	*Veitchia joannis*	**L**
Kahili ginger	*Hedychium gardnerianum*	**H (Hawai'i)**

Common Name	Genus and Species	WRA Designation
Kamani	*Calophyllum inophyllum*	**EVALUATE**
Kikuyu grass	*Pennisetum clandestinum*	**H (HPWRA)**
King palm	*Archontophoenix cunninghamiana*	**L**
King sago	*Cycas revoluta*	**L**
Kolomona	*Senna surattensis*	**EVALUATE (Field reports from Hawai'i indicate it may be a serious pest; HEPEC documentation in progress)**
Korean lawngrass	*Zoysia japonica*	**L**
Kou	*Cordia subcordata*	**L**
Kris plant	*Alocasia sanderiana*	**L**
Kruse's mallee	*Eucalyptus kruseana*	**L**
Kuhio vine	*Ipomoea horsfalliae*	**L**
Kwila	*Intsia bijuga*	**L**
Lady palm	*Rhaphis excelsa*	**L**
Lantana wildtype	*Lantana camara*	**H (Hawai'i)**
Large-leaf mahogany	*Swietenia macrophylla*	**L**
Lavender star flower	*Grewia occidentalis*	**L**
Lecheso	*Stemmadenia litoralis*	**L**
Lemon	*Citrus limon*	**L**
Lemonyellow rosemallow	*Hibiscus calyphyllus*	**L**
Leucaena	*Leucaena leucocephala*	**H (HPWRA)**
Liberian coffee	*Coffea liberica*	**EVALUATE**
Lignum vitae	*Guaiacum officinale*	**L**
Lilyturf	*Liriope muscari*	**L**
Lime	*Citrus aurantifolia*	**L**
Lipsticktree	*Bixa orellana*	**L**
Lobster claw	*Heliconia caribaea*	**L**
Logwood	*Haematoxylum campechianum*	**L**

Common Name	Genus and Species	WRA Designation
Loling-glass tree	*Heritiera littoralis*	**L**
Loquat	*Eriobotrya japonica*	**EVALUATE**
Lychee	*Litchi chinensis*	**L**
Lysiloma	*Lysiloma watsonii*	**L**
Macarthur palm	*Ptychosperma macarthurii*	**H (HPWRA)**
Madagascar olive	*Noronhia emarginata*	**EVALUATE**
Madagascar periwinkle	*Catharanthus roseus*	**L**
Madagascar rubber vine	*Cryptostegia madagascariensis*	**H (HPWRA)**
Madras thorn	*Pithecellobium dulce*	**H (HPWRA)**
Maga	*Montezuma speciosissima*	**L**
Maile pilau	*Paederia foetida*	**H (Hawai'i)**
Malabar chestnut	*Pachira aquatica*	**L**
Malaysian orchid	*Medinilla magnifica*	**EVALUATE**
Mandarin orange	*Citrus reticulata*	**L**
Manila palm	*Veitchia merrillii*	**L**
Marang	*Artocarpus odoratissimus*	**L**
Matchweed	*Phyla nodiflora*	**H (HPWRA)**
Membranous garlic vine	*Mansoa hymenaea*	**L**
Metallic plant	*Hemigraphis alternata*	**L**
Mexican cigar plant	*Cuphea ignea*	**L**
Mexican creeper	*Antigonon leptopus*	**H (HPWRA)**
Mexican daisy	*Erigeron karvinskianus*	**H (Hawai'i)**
Mexican fan palm	*Washingtonia robusta*	**H (HPWRA)**
Miconia	*Miconia calvescens*	**H (Hawai'i)**
Ming aralia	*Polyscias fruticosa*	**L**
Mistletoe fig	*Ficus deltoidea*	**L**
Mock orange	*Murraya paniculata*	**EVALUATE**
Mondo grass	*Ophiopogon japonicus*	**L**
Money tree	*Dracaena marginata*	**L**
Monkey apple	*Posoqueria latifolia*	**L**
Monkeypod tree	*Samanea saman*	**L**

Common Name	Genus and Species	WRA Designation
Monterey pine	*Pinus radiata*	**EVALUATE (Field reports from Hawai'i indicate it may be a serious pest; HEPEC documentation in progress)**
Montgomery palm	*Veitchia montgomeryana*	**L**
Moreton bay fig	*Ficus macrophylla*	**EVALUATE**
Mother of cocoa	*Gliricidia sepium*	**L**
Mother-in-law's tongue	*Sansevieria trifasciata*	**H (HPWRA)**
Mountain cabbage tree	*Cussonia paniculata*	**L**
Mountain ebony	*Bauhinia variegata*	**L (Hawai'i)**
Narrowleaf firethorn	*Pyracantha angustifolia*	**H (HPWRA)**
Natal plum	*Carissa grandiflora*	**L**
Neel	*Indigofera teysmannii*	**L**
Neem	*Azadirachta indica*	**EVALUATE**
Nepalese alder	*Alnus nepalensis*	**L**
New Zealand flax	*Phormium tenax*	**H (Hawai'i)**
Nicaragua rosewood	*Dalbergia retusa*	**L**
Nickerbean	*Caesalpinia bonduc*	**H (HPWRA)**
Norfolk Island pine	*Araucaria heterophylla*	**L**
Northern wattle	*Acacia crassicarpa*	**H (HPWRA)**
Octopus tree	*Schefflera actinophylla*	**H (Hawai'i)**
Oleander	*Nerium oleander*	**L (Hawai'i)**
Olive tree	*Olea europaea*	**EVALUATE**
Orange champaca	*Michelia champaca*	**L**
Orange eye butterflybush	*Buddleja davidii*	**H (HPWRA)**
Oriental arborvitae	*Platycladus orientalis*	**L**
Pagoda flower	*Clerodendrum paniculatum*	**EVALUATE**
Panax	*Polyscias guilfoylei*	**L**
Papaya	*Carica papaya*	**L**

Common Name	Genus and Species	WRA Designation
Paper bark tree	*Melaleuca quinquenervia*	**H (HPWRA)**
Paper mulberry	*Broussonetia papyrifera (Hawaiian seedless)*	**L**
Paperflower	*Bougainvillea glabra*	**L**
Para grass	*Brachiaria mutica*	**H (Hawaiʻi)**
Parrmatta green wattle	*Acacia parramattensis*	**H (HPWRA)**
Parrot's beak	*Lotus berthelotti*	**L**
Partridge pea	*Chamaecrista nictitans*	**L**
Pascuita	*Euphorbia leucocephala*	**L**
Passion fruit	*Passiflora edulis*	**L**
Peace lily	*Spathiphyllum wallisii*	**L**
Peacock tree	*Adenanthera pavonina*	**H (HPWRA)**
Peregrina	*Jatropha integerrima*	**L**
Perenial peanut	*Arachis pintoi*	**L**
Perennial peanut	*Arachis glabrata*	**L**
Perennial soybean	*Neonotonia wightii*	**H (HPWRA)**
Perfume tree	*Cananga odorata*	**L**
Peruvian pepper tree	*Schinus molle*	**H (HPWRA)**
Photina	*Photinia davidiana*	**L**
Pigeon pea	*Cajanus cajan*	**L**
Pila	*Tephrosia purpurea*	**H (HPWRA)**
Pink allamanda hybrid	*Mandevilla × amabilis*	**L**
Pink ivory	*Berchemia zeyheri*	**L**
Pink knotweed	*Polygonum capitatum*	**H (HPWRA)**
Pink orchid tree	*Bauhinia monandra*	**H (HPWRA)**
Pink powderpuff	*Calliandra surinamensis*	**L**
Pink quill	*Tillandsia cyanea*	**L**
Pink shower tree	*Cassia bakeriana*	**L**
Pink shower tree	*Cassia grandis*	**L**
Pink shower tree	*Cassia javanica*	**L**
Pink trumpet-tree	*Tabebuia heterophylla*	**L**
Pink-eyed Cerbera	*Cerbera manghas*	**L**
Plum pine	*Podocarpus elatus*	**L**
Poinsettia	*Euphorbia pulcherrima*	**L**

Common Name	Genus and Species	WRA Designation
Polynesian arrowroot	*Tacca leontopetaloides*	**L**
Polynesian chestnut	*Inocarpus fagifer*	**L**
Pomegranate	*Punica granatum*	**L**
Ponytail palm	*Nolina recurvata*	**L**
Port Jackson fig	*Ficus rubiginosa*	**H (HPWRA)**
Pothos	*Epipremnum pinnatum*	**H (HPWRA)**
Prickly Florida blackberry	*Rubus argutus*	**H (Hawaiʻi)**
Primrose jasmine	*Jasminum mesnyi*	**L**
Princess tree	*Paulownia tomentosa*	**H (HPWRA)**
Pua keni keni	*Fagraea berteroana*	**L**
Pummelo	*Citrus maxima*	**L**
Pygmy date palm	*Phoenix roebelenii*	**L**
Queen palm	*Syagrus romanzoffiana*	**L**
Queen's crape myrtle	*Lagerstroemia speciosa*	**L**
Queensland kauri	*Agathis robusta*	**L**
Queensland maple	*Flindersia brayleyana*	**L**
Rainbow shower tree	*Cassia xnealiae*	**L**
Rattlebox	*Sesbania punicea*	**H (HPWRA)**
Red cinchona	*Cinchona pubescens*	**H (Hawaiʻi)**
Red clerodendrum	*Clerodendrum buchananii*	**H (HPWRA)**
Red ginger	*Alpinia purpurata*	**EVALUATE**
Red mussaenda	*Mussaenda erythrophylla*	**L**
Red passionfruit	*Passiflora rubra*	**H (HPWRA)**
Red powderpuff	*Calliandra haematocephala*	**L**
Red silk oak	*Grevillea banksii*	**H (HPWRA)**
Red spurge	*Euphorbia cotinifolia*	**L**
Red-flowering gum	*Corymbia ficifolia*	**L**
Rex begonia vine	*Cissus discolor*	**EVALUATE**
Rockweed	*Pilea microphylla*	**EVALUATE**
Rondeletia	*Rondeletia odorata*	**L**
Rose myrtle	*Rhodomyrtus tomentosa*	**H (Hawaiʻi)**
Round-leaved moort	*Eucalyptus platypus*	**L**
Royal poinciana	*Delonix regia*	**L**

Common Name	Genus and Species	WRA Designation
Saltcedar	*Tamarix gallica*	**H (HPWRA)**
Sanchezia	*Sanchezia speciosa*	**L**
Sandpaper vine	*Petrea volubilis*	**L**
Satin leaf	*Chrysophyllum oliviforme*	**H (HPWRA)**
Sausage tree	*Kigelia africana*	**L**
Scarlet pear gum	*Eucalyptus stoatei*	**L**
Sea grape	*Coccoloba uvifera*	**L**
Sea putat	*Barringtonia asiatica*	**L**
Seashore paspalum	*Paspalum vaginatum*	**H (HPWRA)**
Serissa	*Serissa japonica*	**L**
Shampoo ginger	*Zingiber zerumbet*	**L**
Shavingbrush tree	*Pseudobombax ellipticum*	**L**
Shoebutton ardisia	*Ardisia elliptica*	**H (Hawai'i)**
Shrimp plant	*Justicia brandegeeana*	**L**
Shrubby desmodium	*Desmodium nicaraguense*	**L**
Shrubby dillenia	*Dillenia suffruticosa*	**EVALUATE**
Shrubby stylo	*Stylosanthes scabra*	**L**
Siamese cassia	*Senna siamea*	**L**
Sickle bush	*Dichrostachys cinerea*	**H (HPWRA)**
Sidney goldern wattle	*Acacia longifolia*	**H (HPWRA)**
Silk oak	*Grevillea robusta*	**EVALUATE (Field reports from Hawai'i indicate it may be a serious H; HEPEC documentation in progress)**
Silver dollar gum	*Eucalyptus cinerea*	**L**
Silver princess	*Eucalyptus caesia*	**L**
Silverleaf cotoneaster	*Cotoneaster pannosus*	**H (HPWRA)**
Siratro	*Macroptilium atropurpureum*	**H (HPWRA)**
Slash pine	*Pinus elliottii*	**EVALUATE**
Slender goldshower	*Galphimia gracilis*	**L**

223

Common Name	Genus and Species	WRA Designation
Slender mimosa	*Desmanthus virgatus*	**H (HPWRA)**
Small lobster claw	*Heliconia stricta*	**L**
Smokebush	*Buddleja madagascariensis*	**H (Hawai'i)**
Snow bush	*Breynia disticha*	**L**
Soursop	*Annona muricata*	**L**
Southern magnolia	*Magnolia grandiflora*	**L**
Spanish broom	*Spartium junceum*	**H (HPWRA)**
Spanish moss	*Tillandsia usneoides*	**H (HPWRA)**
Spathe flower	*Spathiphyllum cannifolium*	**L**
Spiderplant	*Chlorophytum comosum*	**L (Hawai'i)**
Spiked pepper	*Piper aduncum*	**H (HPWRA)**
Spiny black olive	*Bucida molinetii*	**L**
Spring cinquefoil	*Potentilla verna*	**L**
St. Augustine grass	*Stenotaphrum secundatum*	**H (HPWRA)**
Star jasmine	*Jasminum multiflorum*	**L**
Starfruit	*Averrhoa carambola*	**L**
Stiff bottlebrush	*Callistemon rigidus*	**L**
Strawberry guava	*Psidium cattleianum*	**H (Hawai'i)**
Strawberry saxifrage	*Saxifraga sarmentosa*	**L**
Stylo	*Stylosanthes guianensis*	**H (HPWRA)**
Sugar apple	*Annona squamosa*	**L**
Surinam cherry	*Eugenia uniflora*	**H (HPWRA)**
Swamp mahogany	*Eucalyptus robusta*	**L**
Sweet acacia	*Acacia farnesiana*	**H (HPWRA)**
Swiss-cheese plant	*Monstera deliciosa*	**L**
Tahitian gardenia	*Gardenia taitensis*	**L**
Tamarind	*Tamarindus indica*	**L**
Teak	*Tectona grandis*	**L**
Templegrass	*Zoysia tenuifolia*	**L**
Texas ranger	*Leucophyllum frutescens*	**L**
Thatch palm	*Thrinax parviflora*	**L**
Thorny kiawe	*Prosopis juliflora*	**H (HPWRA)**
Tipu tree	*Tipuana tipu*	**L**
Toi	*Alphitonia zizyphoides*	**L**

Common Name	Genus and Species	WRA Designation
Toporite	*Hernandia sonora*	L
Torch ginger	*Etlingera elatior*	L (Hawai'i)
Trailing African daisy	*Osteospermum fruticosum*	L
Trailing lantana	*Lantana montevidensis*	H (HPWRA)
Traveller's palm	*Ravenala madagascariensis*	L (Hawai'i)
Tree heliotrope	*Tournefortia argentea*	L
Treedaisy	*Montanoa hibiscifolia*	H (HPWRA)
Tropical almond	*Terminalia catappa*	L
Tropical ash	*Fraxinus uhdei*	EVALUATE (Field reports from Hawai'i indicate it may be a serious pest; HEPEC documentation in progress)
Tropical kudzu	*Pueraria phaseoloides*	H (HPWRA)
Trumpet tree	*Cecropia peltata*	H (HPWRA)
Tulipwood	*Harpullia pendula*	L
Tumeric	*Curcuma longa*	L
Turk's cap	*Malvaviscus penduliflorus*	L
Umbrella sedge	*Cyperus involucratus*	H (HPWRA)
Umbrella tree	*Maesopsis eminii*	EVALUATE
Velvet leaf	*Kalanchoe beharensis*	EVALUATE
Waipahu fig	*Ficus tikoua*	L
Wedelia	*Sphagneticola trilobata*	H (HPWRA)
Weeping bottlebrush	*Callistemon viminalis*	L
Weeping fig	*Ficus benjamina*	EVALUATE
West Indian mahogany	*Swietenia mahagoni*	L
White champaca	*Michelia x alba*	L
White ginger	*Hedychium coronarium*	H (Hawai'i)
White mussaenda	*Mussaenda philippica*	L
White tephrosia	*Tephrosia candida*	H (HPWRA)
Wi apple	*Spondias dulcis*	L
Wild allamanda	*Pentalinon luteum*	H (HPWRA)

Common Name	Genus and Species	WRA Designation
Wild hops	*Flemingia strobilifera*	**EVALUATE**
Wild indigo	*Indigofera suffruticosa*	**H (HPWRA)**
Wild pepper	*Capsicum frutescens*	**L**
Winin palm	*Veitchia winin*	**L**
Wisteria tree	*Bolusanthus speciosus*	**L**
Woman's-tongue tree	*Albizia lebbeck*	**H (HPWRA)**
Wood rose	*Merremia tuberosa*	**H (HPWRA)**
Yellow alder	*Turnera ulmifolia*	**H (HPWRA)**
Yellow bells	*Tecoma stans*	**H (HPWRA)**
Yellow flame	*Peltophorum pterocarpum*	**L**
Yellow necklacepod	*Sophora tomentosa*	**L**
Yellow nicker	*Caesalpinia major*	**H (HPWRA)**
Yellow tree bauhinia	*Bauhinia tomentosa*	**L**

Appendix:
Quick Reference to Insects and Their Natural Controls

Name	Friend or Foe	Where it Lives	Description	Natural Control(s)/How to encourage
Aphid	Foe	Stems and under leaves.	Small insects; green, pink, yellow, black or gray-- sometimes have wings.	Don't over-fertilize with nitrogen. Spray with insecticidal soap or garlic spray; apply Tanglefoot to base of plant.
Banana root borer	Foe	Corms or pseu- dostems, at ground level.	Weevil with wings, but rarely flies. White sausage- shaped eggs 1/2 inch long. Grubs: 1/2 inch long with reddish-brown heads, no legs.	Clean up plant debris; make split-log traps; remove harvested plants; do not transport planting material from infested fields to uninfested ones. Check young plants for holes at the base and corms. Never move young trees to another island.
Bees: Honeybee Carpenter bee	Friend Carpen- ters can sting and drill holes in wood.	Honeybee: in hives nearby. Carpenter bee: in holes they drill in wood.	Honeybee: Plump, black and yellow, fuzzy; 1/2 to 1 inch long. Carpenter bee: up to 1 in. long. Females black--can sting. Males yellow and stingless.	Honeybee: do not use insecticides. Plant pollen-rich and nectar flowers. Carpenter bee: good pollinators. Control by filling in exterior house crevices with wood putty; paint outdoor wooden surfaces; plug holes with steel wool and caulk.

Name	Friend or Foe	Where it Lives	Description	Natural Control(s)/How to encourage
Centipede and millipede	Friend	In dark places.	Slender and segmented with many legs. Red, brown or blue; up to 5 inches long.	Do not use pesticides. If too many, keep garden beds clean. Deter them with wood ashes, cinders or diatomaceous earth along rows of germinating plants. Stake plants to keep fruit and vegetables off the ground. Don't plant too close to your home. Chickens forage for centipedes.
Chinese rose beetle	Foe	In leaf litter around the plants they eat.	Brown beetle flecked with white; 1/2 inch long.	Provide light at night; use neem chips; hand pick.
Fruit fly	Foe	Orchards, kitchens and anywhere there is fruit.	Small white and yellow flies with clear or marked wings. Larvae: white, wiggly maggots inside fruit.	Keep damaged or rotten fruit cleaned up; spray with soap and garlic; hang sticky traps; harvest fruit slightly green; tie paper bags or floating row cover over ripening fruit.
Horn-worm	Either	On the plants they eat.	Green with diagonal marks along their sides; 4-1/2 - 5 inches long with a single large horn on the tail.	Do not use BT. Take them to a "wild place"; grow nectar or pollen plants.

Name	Friend or Foe	Where it Lives	Description	Natural Control(s)/How to encourage
Ladybird beetle (ladybug)	Friend	On the leaves of plants where other insects like aphids occur.	Shiny, round beetles, red or orange with black spots; 1/16 to 3/8 inch long.	Plant pollen and nectar plants.
Leafminer	Foe	Leaves of vegetables, flowers and weeds.	Larvae: yellow to orange legless maggots. Adults: black or black and yellow flies about 1/10 inch long.	Do not use pesticides. Cover seedlings with floating row covers; attract parasitic wasps by planting nectar and pollen-rich plants; spray with neem extract.
Mealybug	Foe	New growth of flowers, ornamentals and fruit trees.	Tiny insects with soft, oval, pink bodies; 1/10 inch long, covered with white, powdery or waxy fluff.	Rinse plants with a sharp stream of water; spray with insecticidal soap or ultrafine oil; encourage parasitic wasps with nectar plants.
Nematode	Foe	In the soil.	Tiny worm-like creatures: slender, translucent, unsegmented, 1/50 inch long.	Practice crop rotation; grow marigolds; solarize your soil.
Scale	Foe	Plant stems and the underside and top side of leaves.	Adults: oval or round, without legs or wings; they look like 1/4 to 1/2-inch "bumps" or small barnacles. Larvae: small crawlers resembling miniature mealybugs.	Spray plants with a sharp stream of water; hand pick. Wash scales off with a cloth dipped in insecticidal soap. Spray with soap, ultrafine oil or dormant oil on trees. Prune and destroy infested branches. Encourage lady-bugs. Control ants withTanglefoot at base of plants.

Name	Friend or Foe	Where it Lives	Description	Natural Control(s)/How to encourage
Slug and snail	Foe	Cool, moist places.	Snails: crunchy shell. Slugs: no shell. Both: Slimy crawlers with no legs. Gray, tan, green or black, some with darker spots or patterns; 1 - 2 inches long.	Hand-pick, but wear gloves due to possibility of disease; beer traps; Sluggo; copper strips. Spread wide bands of cinders, wood ashes or diatomaceous earth; Chickens forage for slugs and snails.
Spiders	Friend, except "crab" spiders and widow spiders, which bite.	Everywhere, even indoors.	8-legged arachnids.	To attract: mulch with hay or dried grass. To control: sweep webs with a broom; hand pick egg cases; keep things under house stored neatly; dispose of rubbish; inspect crawl spaces under your house and destroy spiders, webs, nests and eggs; vacuum adult spiders and their egg cases; encourage parasitic wasps.
Whitefly	Foe	Undersides of leaves in greenhouses and outdoors.	Small white, powdery-looking flying insects, 1/25 inch long.	Grow nectar and pollen plants to encourage parasitic wasps, lacewings and ladybugs. Hang yellow sticky traps; use a small vacuum cleaner to remove whiteflies from the undersides of leaves; spray with neem extract, insecticidal soap or summer oil.

Index

K

kahili ginger 11, 17, 29–30, 217
kamani 195, 198
Kaua`i Invasive Species Committee
    20, 23, 28
kava kava 128, 149
    elixir recipe 151
    shot hole disease 150
keyhole path 50
ki 159–160
KISC 20, 23, 28
ki paoa 118
ko`oko`olau 163–164
koali 46
koki`o 160
koko-kahiki 45
Koster's curse 11, 17, 32–33
kou 164–165
kowali `awa 46
kuawa (yellow guava) 27–28
kulu`i 166
kupukupu 109

L

la`amia 167
lace fern 110
Lactrodectus 102
ladybug 94
    how to encourage 94
Laka (hula goddess) 148, 177
landscape fabric, as weed control 9,
    34, 35, 66
Lantana camara 30, 218
lasagna gardening 47
laua`e fern 109
lau kahi 136–137
    poultice recipe 138
lawn substitute, perennial peanut used
    for 36–38
leafminer 94–95
lemon balm 88, 141
Leonurus Sibericus 197
li`ipoe 168

liliko`i 125–126
    caution regarding toxicity 127
    recipe for tincture 127–128
Liriomyza 94
living mulch 35
lo`i (wetland taro paddy) 158
loulu 168–170

M

ma`o hau hele 91, 162–163
macadamia nut compost 49, 129, 149
Madosky, William, MD 48
maile-scented fern 109
maile pilau 11, 17, 31, 219
Malama O Puna 19, 21
mamaki 170–171
Manduca blackburni 82, 93
marigold, Mexican 97
Maui Invasive Species Committee 12,
    13, 14, 185
mealybug 81, 96
medicinal plants to grow 197–199
Melastoma candidum 32, 217
Melissa officinalis 198
Mentha species 197
Merlin, Mark, PhD 25
Metrosideros polymorpha 176
Metsulfuron herbicide, for kahili
    ginger 30
Miconia calvescens 18–19, 219
mikana 123
millipede 89, 228
Mimosa pudica 43–44
    making tea from 44
    medicinal uses of 44
mineral oil, as insect control 81
MISC 12, 13, 185. *See also* Maui
    Invasive Species Committee
Mollison, Bill 63
Morinda citrifolia 133. *See also* noni
morning glory 42, 46
    Heavenly Blue 46
    koali 46
    medicinal uses of 46

morning grass 43. *See also Mimosa pudica*

moth, hummingbird (Sphinx) 82, 93–94

muffins, banana 117

mugwort 198

mulberry, Indian 133

mulch 35–37, 74
  definition 35
  different types of 35–37
  importance of 35–38, 74
  living mulch 35
  millionaires, definition 74

Musa 115–118

N

nanu (nau) 172–173

native species 13
  a`ali`i 147–148
  definition 13
  ekaha (bird nest fern) 152–153
  hapu`u (tree fern) 153–154
  hibiscus 160–163
  ilie`e 154–155
  ilima 156–157
  ko`oko`olau 163–164
  koki`o 160–163
  kou 164–165
  kulu`i 166–167
  loulu 168–170
  ma`o hau hele 162–163
  mamaki 170–172
  nanu (nau) 172–173
  ohi`a lehua 176–177

nectar plants, for attracting bees 78, 94, 229

neem 91, 95, 104, 228, 229, 230
  for controlling leafminers 94
  for controlling whiteflies 79, 81, 104

Nematoda (nematode) 96
  introduction in topsoil 5, 49

Nephrolepis 109

nettle, Hawaiian 170
  See also mamaki

next to composting 73

nightshade, black 110, 211

nioi 80, 120–122
  recipe for spicy cooking oil 122

niu 174

non-invasive species 36, 200–207

noni 105, 133–135
  recipe for salad dressing 135
  recipe for vinegar 135

Nototrichium sandwicense 166

O

Ocimum 88, 118
  sanctum 88, 118
  See also basil

ohi`a lehua 78, 178–179
  dangers posed by invasive species 11–33

oil, cooking, recipe for spicy oil 122

oil, dormant 81, 99

olena 178–179
  See also turmeric

Omega-3 fatty acid 139

orchid, bamboo 107–108

Oriental fruit fly 91

Orr, David 160

Oxalis corniculata 42

Oxalis repens 42

P

Pacific Island Ecosystems at Risk 43

Paederia foetida 31, 219

pahoehoe lava 4, 65

pala`a 110

pampas grass 11, 25–26

Pangaia permaculture farm 21, 31, 36
  control of maile pilau with horse 31
  coppicing Albizia 21

papale (loulu hats) 170

papaya 15, 69, 71, 74, 122–125
  genetic engineering 78
  recipe for pickles 125
  ringspot virus (PRV) 124
  seeds as weeds 15, 69

Printed in the United States
48332LVS00004B/109-204

9 781420 886993